THE GREEK ISLANDS

Lawrence Durrell was born in 1912 in India, where his father was an English civil engineer. As a boy he attended the Jesuit College at Darjeeling, and he was later sent to St Edmund's School, Canterbury. His first authentic literary work was *The Black Book*, which appeared in Paris in 1938 under the aegis of Henry Miller and Anaïs Nin. 'In the writing of it I first heard the sound of my own voice . . .' he later wrote. The novel was praised by T. S. Eliot, who published his first collection of poems, *A Private Country*, in 1943. The first of the island books, *Prospero's Cell*, a guide to Corfu, appeared in 1945. It was followed by *Reflections on a Marine Venus*, about Rhodes. *Bitter Lemons*, his account of life in Cyprus, won the Duff Cooper Memorial Prize in 1957. Subsequently he drew on his years in Greece for *The Greek Islands*. Durrell's wartime sojourn in Egypt led to his masterpiece, *The Alexandria Quartet*, which he completed in southern France, where he settled permanently in 1957. Between the *Quartet* and *The Avignon Quintet* he wrote the two-decker *Tunc* and *Nunquam*, now united as *The Revolt of Aphrodite*. His oeuvre includes plays, a book of criticism, translations, travel writings (*Spirit of Place*), *Collected Poems*, a children's adventure, and humorous stories about the diplomatic corps. His correspondence with his lifelong friend Henry Miller has also been published. *Caesar's Vast Ghost*, his reflections on the history and culture of Provence, including a late flowering of poems, appeared a few days before his death at his home in Sommières in 1990.

Books by Lawrence Durrell

NOVELS
The Black Book
The Dark Labyrinth
White Eagles Over Serbia

The Alexandria Quartet
Justine
Balthazar
Mountolive
Clea

The Revolt of Aphrodite
Tunc, Nunquam

The Avignon Quintet
Monsieur, Livia, Constance,
Sebastian, Quinx

TRAVEL
Prospero's Cell
Reflections on a Marine Venus
Bitter Lemons of Cyprus
The Greek Islands
Caesar's Vast Ghost
Spirit of Place

POETRY
Collected Poems 1931–74

HUMOUR
Antrobus Complete

CORRESPONDENCE
The Durrell–Miller Letters 1935–80

BIOGRAPHY
Lawrence Durrell: A Biography
by Ian MacNiven

LAWRENCE DURRELL

The Greek Islands

*

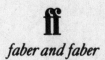

faber and faber

Illustrated edition 1978
designed by George Rainbird Limited
published by Faber and Faber Limited
Bloomsbury House, 74-77 Great Russell Street,
London WC1B 3DA

Faber paperback edition 1980

This reset paperback edition of the text
published 2002
by Faber and Faber Limited

Typeset by RefineCatch Ltd, Bungay, Suffolk
Printed and bound by CPI Group (UK) Ltd, Croydon, CR0 4YY

ISBN 978-0-571-21426-6

8 10 9

Dedicated to Doctor Theodore Stephanides

Contents

CONTENTS

THE HOME GROUP

Preface

The terms of reference accorded me in the making of this book were generous in the extreme; my choice was to be as comprehensive as possible, yet at the same time completely personal. The modern tourist is richly provided with guides and works of reference, particularly about Greece. The idea was not to compete in this field, but simply to endeavour to answer two questions. What would you have been glad to know when you were on the spot? What would you feel sorry to have missed while you were there? A guide, yes, but a very personal one.

I have fulfilled these terms of reference as best I could, but it would not have been possible to do it so well had I not been able to depend on the valuable guidance of friends admirably equipped to vet each section as it was completed, or to provide up-to-date information and suggestions. One of these friends, Kimon Friar, the essayist and translator, was particularly helpful; as a seasoned islomane he claims to have actually resided on forty-six islands – not just gone ashore for a couple of hours – which must be something of a record. More valuable still, he was able to put me in contact with poets, musicians and others at present resident in islands such as Naxos and Paros, which I have not visited for a number of years. With characteristic generosity they have kept me posted about current affairs and brought me up to date.

Meanwhile in London Dr Theodore Stephanides, who is still very actively with us, kindly agreed to examine the text and comment upon it, which he has done with great exactness.

Among standbys from my own small Greek library I was glad to refresh my memory and rekindle my enthusiasm by leafing through Ernle Bradford's *The Companion Guide to the Greek Islands* (1963) as well as a number of other books recalling Crete and Rhodes and other magical places. Notable among such works I should mention my debt to J. C. Lawson's admirable *Modern Greek Folklore and Ancient Greek Religion* (*c.* 1920). I have acknowledged quotations as I proceeded, and do not feel any need to set out an elaborate bibliography for what is more a personal portrait than a detailed guide. There are more than two thousand Greek islands, very many of them mere humps of rock with not more than a field, in which once a year the shepherd pastures his flock having brought them in by water. The inhabited islands vary in size and population, from one tiny village of a hundred souls to a very large place such as Samos which has at least two big towns on it. Some of the tiniest lie in the domain of the small-boat owner; the average tourist will only see them by accident, as it were. Therefore some specially delightful small islands (like Mathraki north of Corfu) are not met with here.

Perhaps someone later on will provide a more complete, and rather different, guide for sailors.

One important question that will raise itself in the reader's mind is why there is no mention of Cyprus, that most Greek of Greek islands; an island where the local peasant speech contains the most ancient Doric forms and where, at Paphos, Aphrodite was born. There is good reason. The present tragic situation has given its contemporary history a provisional nature which at any moment may be resolved or altered by fruitful Greco-Turkish negotiations. In order not to prejudice any such negotiations, or to envenom issues which have done enough harm already to the relationship between these two great countries, it was deemed best to leave the island out.

Lawrence Durrell. Provence 1977

The Ionian Islands

*

Corfu

The traveller, slipping southward along the heel of Italy, as if down a Christmas stocking full of small treasure-towns and unexpected monuments, first feels the intimations of a frontier coming to meet him a good way before he reaches the little terminal town of Brindisi.

Already the wilder southern parts have given place to a collection of charming green counties – a strange and picturesque land of *trulli*, as they call those funny yet quite elaborate conglomerations of clay pots stuck together anyhow which are the native dovecots of the Italian south. Manfredonia and its ominous-looking group of headlands, falls away to the left. And by now evening will be falling too, with its greenish exhausted spring lights. Our traveller is wise to choose the spring for the journey he has in mind, but it is a long pull down the stocking of Italy and night is beginning to overtake him. Whether by train or car it is the same. He empties the last of his wine, eats his last sandwich. Brindisi will replenish both and, if he is a motorist, will also provide him today with a comfortable ferry for the night journey. The little town marks the frontier – this time not a land frontier but a water frontier. Beyond it, will there be a change of element merely? He has no very clear premonition yet of the Greek islands waiting for him out there in the darkness, like hounds of promise. What will they be like?

What is it that gives a frontier its magic? Not the fact that it is a territorial or political boundary, for these are artificial, dictated by history. A sudden change of scenery may be sometimes

3

partly responsible, but often the change from one country to another is not accompanied by any change of flora and fauna (Italy to Greece, for example, France to Spain). Perhaps it is language that gives to the crossing of a frontier its definitive flavour of voyage. Whatever the answer, the magic is there. The traveller's heart will beat to a new rhythm, his ear pick up the tonalities of a new tongue; he will examine the strange new coinage with curiosity. Everything will seem changed, including the air he breathes. In Greece it is . . . But let us not anticipate.

Reaching Brindisi at nightfall he will head for a dinner and a bath, for the old Internazionale where nothing has really changed since the epoch of Mussolini – the menu least of all. The same courteous head waiter who served one in 1938 is still there, still suave and youthful and kind, talking excellent English when necessary. The traveller is leaving a national territory in which Caesar was once the arch-hero, for one where the warrior who most resembled him in his disrespect for frontiers and inflexible thirst for conquest was Alexander the Great. No great difference, would you say?

Frontier-jumpers both, ready to burn their boats at the drop of a Rubicon. Yet they had both been preceded by heroes more ancient. The god-intoxicated young Alexander must have felt suitably chastened when, in the depths of the Scythian hinterland, he came upon an inscription concerning the exploits of one greater than he – the Queen Semiramis. Its poetry commemorates all such secret thirsts:

I ruled the empire of Ninus, which reaches eastward to the River Indus, southward to the land of incense and myrrh, northward to the Saces and Sogdians. Before me no Assyrian had ever seen a sea – I have seen four which none have approached, so far away are they. I compelled the rivers to run where I wished and directed their courses to places where they were needed. I watered the barren lands with my rivers. I built up impregnable fortresses. With iron tools I made roads across impassable rock; I opened them for my chariots in places where even wild beasts had not been able to pass. Yet in the midst of all these occupations I found time for pleasure, I found time for love.

So says Polyaenus.

In the dark, harbour lights wink and there is the whisper and shiver of sea traffic and the light wind which smells of the open sea. You cannot go aboard until midnight, so the traveller passes his time playing solitaire or reading, wondering what lies in store for him once he has crossed over the water and found a dawn landfall in Corfu. If he has any Greek at all he tries to polish it up by glancing through his phrase-book against whatever he might be asked to do or say on the morrow. But the chances are that expectancy and the feeling that he must not doze until he goes aboard will be enough to send him out along the harbour front for a brief walk. And this he will not regret, for hard by the hotel is a little theatrical piazza with a flight of stairs up it and a big block of marble at the top. It bears an inscription. He is reminded that Virgil died here, in Brindisi, one hot September night – returning from Greece; and he ponders that by contrast we do not know where Homer died, nor whether he was really blind. This contrast reminds him once more that he is indeed at a frontier. There is a formidable difference between Rome and Athens, between Italian and Greek; and those with any classical knowledge are astonished to find how constant it is even today. On one side the Italy of finesse and often of finickyness – cherished and tamed by its natives into a formal sweetness. And on the other side Greece, a wild garden with everything running to ruin – violent, vertical and sky-thrusting . . . undomesticated. One thinks of Roman Italy for whom Nature was always wife, nurse and muse; whereas for Greece she was something wilder, something terrible and unbroken – mistress and goddess without mercy all in one. And their heroes have been different from time immemorial. The traveller watches a tanker come in and make fast, while with half of his mind he wonders if in modern Greece he will come upon traces of Odysseus, the ancient hero. (It is nearly time to go.)

A fondness for mythology and folklore is perhaps a handicap when one visits classical sites. It is unwise to spend too much time contrasting the present with the past, since it leads inevitably to dissatisfaction with the present for not being romantic enough. A bell rings and there is a stir in the hall of the hotel where passengers are assembling, some to take possession of their cars, to seize their bags and knapsacks before crossing the dark piers to where the ferry has now made fast – opening its vast hangars like some modern Trojan horse to welcome them into its bowels. By chance it is the Greek ferry too, not the Italian, so that the traveller's first Greeks are there to meet him. He sees already their curly heads and long noses, their bright eyes and flying fingers. They seem alert, vital, mercuric – gesture is copious, but illustratory rather than theatrical like the Italian. The language too is crisp and melodious, full of pebble-like dentals, which give it a lapidary feel. In the clang and clatter of the embarkation he hears words he almost understands. A sailor shouts to another 'Domani, domani. AVRIO!' It is like the Rosetta Stone yielding up its secrets. For 'avrio' must mean 'tomorrow'! A beautiful word! He repeats it once or twice. A maroon sounds on the darkness and with a clang of doors closing the huge creature stirs under him and begins to glide out across the night, out into the new world which is awaiting him. Avrio!

The little lighted piazza is already fast diminishing in size. First it becomes an empty stage set and then, more diminutive still, a room in a dark doll's house. Brindisi – the jumping-off point for all the armies of Imperial Rome – dissolves into the darkness which is now all about the vessel. The ocean breathes calmly and regularly, and the prow echoes the rhythm with its slow *sha sha sha*. The traveller buys himself a drink – perhaps his first *ouzo*, that strong anisette which in Greece does duty for Egyptian *zebib*, Lebanese *arak*, French *pastis*. It is superior to them all in strength though a trifle coarse. Then to sleep, either in the shelter of a bunk, or shrouded in a deck chair in the shelter of the funnel. It is the old complaint – one fears to miss something by going below. But finally the darkness and hushing of water and the drum of the engine send him away into a deep doze which will at least serve to refresh him.

When he awakes it is already dawn, with land ahead of him and one shoulder of an island hunched up to the right of the vessel. It is an easy island to identify – those polished great fruity-looking mountains are Albanian. They are spacious and bare, and warmly painted in by the sun as it struggles up to shine over their shoulders on to the sea. Corfu lies like a sickle beside the flanks of the mainland, forming a great calm bay, which narrows at both ends so that the tides are squeezed and calmed as they pass into it. So much is clear from the map. But for the moment the great ferry simply forges straight ahead, apparently going to crash straight into the screen of golden mountains before them. The northern shoulders of Corfu belie its reputation for luxurious beauty; they are craggy, penurious and empty of villages – dull limestone, covered in scrub and holm oak. The traveller eyes them in some dismay, wondering if the stories he has heard of verdure and beauty were really fables. But gradually the main channel comes into view, and with it the old Venetian sea-mark which warns of shoals. Now the ship turns abruptly, as if on its heel, and heads due south, leaving Albania on her left. To the right is the channel, so narrow that the first few villages are, or seem to be, but a few hundred yards away. In fact, at its narrowest point the northern end of Corfu is only separated from Albania by a stretch of sea two kilometres broad. The general configuration of things becomes clear. The great serene bay is like a punch-bowl. The land mass is dominated by a big domed mountain called Pantocratoras from which, later, he will be able to stare out upon the two seas and upon a number of islands.

The maddening, yet reassuring, thing is that that rosy old satin dawn, sending its warm pencils of light through the ravines of the hills towards the island is really and truly 'rosy-fingered'. 'Damn Homer!' he thinks, determined to stay in the twentieth century. It is at this early point that the traveller begins to recognize the distinctive form and signature of things Greek. As the vessel bowls softly across the smiling bay, as the coast with its dense luscious lagoons unwinds in the fashion of a spool, he sees the famous town coming up at him with its small screen of decorative islands. The journey has not taken as long as he thought – they will dock slightly before seven o'clock, and climb up on to romantic quays lined with as yet empty cafés, where yawning *douaniers* await them with their bills of lading and maddening questions. There is a string of moth-eaten *fiacres* lined up and waiting for him, with their horses wearing characteristic straw hats that are pierced to let the ears of the animals pass through. Hats which give them an arch and rather drunken appearance. But the beauty of the little town! He has been warned that he will not find a prettier in Greece and as time goes on this will become more and more evident. At the moment his only ambition is to step ashore and into one of those carnival *fiacres* which will draw him through the coils and loops of the old Venetian fortress into the town of Corfu – where, doubtless, rosy-fingered waiters will be waiting to ply him with breakfast.

Everything is indeed open, in spite of the early hour. The pavements are being hosed down, and the warm earth releases choice odours of lemon and wet dust. The old town is set down gracefully upon the wide tree-lined esplanade, whose arcades are of French provenance and were intended (they do) to echo the Rue de Rivoli. The best cafés are here and the friendliest waiters in all Christendom. They will even pay for your drink with pleasure if you have no money or have forgotten to change any. This early morning animation is somehow an indication of the tempo at which Greece lives; you rise each morning to a new day, a new world, which has to be created from scratch. Each day is a brilliant improvisation with full orchestra – the light on the sea, the foliage, the stabbing cypresses, the silver spindrift olives . . .

Naturally the traveller, letting the eyes of his mind loose to browse among these bewitching shapes and colours, will find much to remind him of such other momentous places as Orta or Taormina. The tall, spare Venetian houses with their eloquent mouldings have been left unpainted for centuries, so it seems. Ancient coats of paint and whitewash have been blotched and blurred by successive winters, until now the over-all result is a glorious wash-drawing thrown down upon a wet paper – everything running and fusing and exploding. But more precise, though just as eloquent, are the streets between the houses, each a deep gully made brilliant with washing hung out to dry from every balcony – bright as bunting. This great spread of colour moves and sways in the light dawn breeze in a way that reminds one of tropical seaweed. The red dome of the Church of St Spiridion shines aloft with its scarred old clock face; the church which houses the mummy of the island's patron saint. If he knows what is good for him, the traveller will make an indispensable pilgrimage to this dark fane, whose barbaric oriental decoration smoulders among the shadows like the glintings of a fire opal. He will kiss the sacred slipper or a suitable icon and light a candle to place in the tall sconce as he utters a prayer – the subject of which he will confide to nobody.

In this way his journey will be under good auspices and the whole of Byzantine, modern and ancient Greece will be waiting with open arms.

Coming out of the dark church into the market he will be almost blinded by the light, for the sun is up; and it is now that the impact of this extraordinary phenomenon will begin to intrigue him. The nagging question, 'In what way does Greece differ from Italy and Spain?' will answer itself. The light! One hears the word everywhere, 'To Phos', and can recognize its pedigree – among other derivatives is our English word 'phosphorescent', which summons up at once the dancing magnesium-flare quality of the sunlight blazing on a white wall; in the depths of the light there is blackness, but it is a blackness which throbs with violet – a magnetic unwearying ultra-violet throb. This confers a sort of brilliant skin of white light on material objects, linking near and far, and bathing simple objects in a sort of celestial glow-worm hue. It is the naked eyeball of God, so to speak, and it blinds one. Even here in Corfu, whose rich, dense forestation and elegiac greenery contrasts so strangely with the brutal barrenness of the Aegean which he has yet to visit – even here there is no mistake about the light. Italy has no such ray, nor Spain. Flowers and houses and clouds all watch you with a photo-electric eye – at once substantial and somehow immaterial. Each cypress is the only one in existence. Each boat, house, donkey, is *prime* – a Platonic prototype of a sudden invention; maybe an idle god's quite *arbitrary* invention, as if he had exclaimed, 'Let there be donkey.' And in each donkey (by now they are braying all along the Esplanades, waiting for their children) one sees the original, the archetypal donk: the essence, the quiddity of the *idea* of donk.

He is not of course the first visitor to be electrified by Greek light, to be intoxicated by the white dancing candescence of the sun on a sea with blue sky pouring into it. He walks round the little town of Corfu that first morning with the feeling that the island is a sort of burning-glass.

Later, sitting in a tavern built out over the Venetian mole with its sombre lions of St Mark, he thinks of other light-drinkers in the past who have, like himself, suddenly felt that they were moving about in the heart of a dark crystal.

The first impression of the country, from whatever direction one enters it, is austere. It rejects all daydreams, even historical ones. It is dry, barren, dramatic and strange, like a terribly emaciated face; but it lies bathed in a light such as the eye has never yet beheld, and in which it rejoices as though now first awakening to the gift of sight. This light is indescribably keen yet soft. It brings out the smallest details with a clarity, a gentle clarity that makes the heart beat higher and enfolds the nearer view in a transfiguring veil – I can describe it only in these paradoxical terms. One can compare it to nothing except Spirit. Things might lie thus in some wonderful intelligence – so alert and so lulled, so divided and yet so closely linked. Linked by what? Not by mood; nothing could be more remote from that floating sensuous soulful dream-element: no, by the Spirit itself.

Pondering these words of Hugo von Hofmannsthal, the traveller feels within him the first premonitory signs by which the heart recognizes the onset of a great love affair – the light in the eyes of the beloved. He is falling in love.

Enough of our hypothetical traveller; once he was myself, or one of my Victorian ancestors. Today and tomorrow he will be yourself, gentle reader. And how glad you will be to discover that in spite of tales of tourist ravages the island's real beauty and vitality are still there, still palpable. From now on, all day long you will wander about in a delightful daze, drinking in the light. Evening will find you once more seated at your little café – you will already have adopted one – drinking *ouzo*.

Now the sunset-gun booms from the tower of the citadel,

and a faint military music sounds within, recalling the garrison to its duties or to some unspecified recreation. The gun of course is a Crimean echo, though the fortress is Venetian. You sit, as so many before have done and as so many will do after you, quite still and silent over your drink, watching the dusk fall, veil on magical veil, over the blue gulf which itself will soon be turned to lead and then to silver under the visiting moon. You will have heard stories by now of people who came for an afternoon and stayed for a lifetime, or who came for a week and stayed a century and a half; and you will realize the danger of your position. Moreover there is a sacred spring, Kardaki, on the other side of the town which, if drunk from, will clinch things, ordaining a return to the island. 'Yes,' you will find yourself saying, 'I will stay one more day, just one more . . .'

After this first radical experience with the Greek light, you will be surprised at the ease and simplicity with which the island surrenders its charm. Like the great courtesan she is, a real Circe, she leads one first among the sweet inland valleys thickly carpeted with wild flowers and studded with old gnarled but silver-hale olives, or to the dense groves of black brush-strokes, the self-seeded cypresses which seem like something out of prehistory – remember that ancient Greece was densely wooded and watered by broad rivers and rich springs. An exceptional winter rainfall, tropical in intensity, must explain the paradisiacal lushness of everything. You begin, without sophistry, to re-live the arrival of Odysseus here. There is so much to see, but distances are mercifully short and the whole island can be inspected at leisure (as it is today) by motor-scooter or by car: it is some sixty kilometres long, with a tenuous thread of navigable road uniting the choicest places. In the north a stout, blunt mountain and a bare land of limestone hafts and grimly poor villages. Even the peasant dress is magpie-sombre in the north – just black and white; by contrast, in the midriff and south of the island it is rich in its variety and range of plumage.

There may well be a village wedding in progress in some small hamlet near the town of Corfu, and you will marvel at the vivid and sumptuous island costumes from the various villages. The old hieratic circular dances are there too. The dancers look as vivid as a pack of playing cards, circling in the deep dust of some swept threshing floor. You will be assailed by profuse free drinks in honour of the bride, and exhorted to tread a measure – which you will find yourself timidly trying to do, overwhelmed by all the good humour and warmth. Coming from an island with an inexplicable, built-in xenophobia, you will have a pleasant initiatory shock of delight at finding yourself forcefully adopted. And when you see whole oxen or swine turning on their spits in a deep trench full of glowing charcoal, you will recall the Homeric sacrifices of old.

There are astonishingly few harbours on the other side of the island – indeed only one really meriting the name. That is at the famous Paleocastrizza, now half ruined by the tourist-promoter, though the old monastery on its hillock is still a dream-place and the magnificent cliffs upon which Lakones stands offer stupendous views worthy of Taormina. One can imagine what Villefranche must have been like a hundred years ago. But though the whole of the south of France was laid waste by urbanism by about 1930, Paleocastrizza, then largely unknown except to travellers like myself (i.e. not too well off), only had two little taverns in the bay. It rejoiced in an enviable solitude and unapproachability until after the last war; and even now much is left to admire, despite the crowding and the noise. Yes, the sea is left, thank goodness, and if you take a boat ride down the coast a little way you will be rewarded by some of the most dramatic beaches, cliff-bound and majestic with an untamed tide running down on them at express speed from invisible Cape Drasti to the north. But you will have to watch the weather: for once pulled down below Myrtiotissa, there is nothing for it but to continue due south and try to swing round the southern butt of the island and so into the relative calm of the great bay which is crowned by the town.

Odysseus *must* have met Nausicaa at Paleocastrizza; it is not possible to believe otherwise. One of the many talking points among the scholars is that much discussed word, *Polytropos*. It means 'many-sided', 'adaptable', 'resilient', 'up to any eventuality', 'apt for everything' ... and a thousand other things. It is curious to read that Odysseus almost monopolizes the range of epithets beginning with *poly*. He is arch-everything, super-everything. Nor does his physical appearance seem constant. Sometimes he is blond with a black beard; at others he is broad-breasted, a little swart man, slightly bandy-legged and hairy. Yet it is amazing how clearly his total personality swarms out at once from the text: wise, adaptable, cunning, sage – all that, yes; but also with a sense of humour and a common touch. He was no courtier, did not try to charm. Perhaps that is why the grey-eyed Athena was so fond of him. Odysseus was, among other things, an imp.

Another, not less speculative, line of mad reasoning has suggested that Corfu is the site which (perhaps by mere hearsay) Shakespeare chose for his last play *The Tempest*. You may groan as you read this. Is it not enough to have one's brain criss-crossed and fuddled with the attributes of Greece's great ace-personality? Must the British shove their alchemical Prospero into the island? Again you can only look at these green glades, these crystal cliffs and coves, and the whole play enacts itself before your eyes. Is not 'Sycorax' an anagram for Corcyra – the ancient name of Corfu?

What about the history of the island saint? His enormous prestige and influence in the island to this day would justify discussing him here. The relic – and he is a real mummy, a funny little old man like Father Christmas – lies in a chased silver casket in the church of his name which was built in 1589. His original provenance was not local, and for some centuries he belonged to the Bulgaris family. But finally the miracles he wrought proved him to be something more than the *lares et penates* of a single household. He belonged to the island, and the family was only too happy to accede to the request of the authorities to present him to the church. Whoever has seen St Spiridion make a progress round the town is not likely to forget the pomp and magnificence of the strange and baroque procession – the monks and priests like a moving flower-bed with their brilliant gonfalons raised on high. The little figure of the saint lies sideways in his sedan chair, pale and withdrawn, as if in prayer. There are four such processions a year; they take place on Palm Sunday and Easter Saturday, on 11 August and on the first Sunday in November. Naturally the summer appearances benefit from the light – that of August being the most sumptuous and colourful.

Another thing becomes clear as you sit over your afternoon *ouzo* watching the sunlight decline among the green cones and vales of the Ten Saints Mountain. If the scenery has a certain plumpness, a Venetian rotundity (this is what the Athenians will always say about Corfu: but they are jealous because here is limitless shade and water) then the plumpness is corrected and prevented from becoming too sweet by the ravenous white light playing over people and things. It has a queer X-ray impression, as if the sea were really a dark negative of itself against which the swimmers move, burned to the brown of coffee-beans. It has a red-filter photographic effect that one sees sometimes in Alpine photography. But here it is the lens of the eye that drinks it in.

Exactly what are the priorities for a proper appreciation of this captivating place? Obviously perfect Greek would be useful; but you are probably no better placed than Shakespeare, possibly managing a smatter of Latin. If you can learn the Greek alphabet, start by spelling out the shop-signs which are among the most picturesque decorations in the surrounding scene. It is interesting how many words are of ancient provenance (Bibliopoleion, Artopoleion – Bookshop and Breadshop – for example); words which must have been familiar to Plato or Socrates, and which must have been scribbled up everywhere in the ancient *agora* of Athens. But in the spoken tongue, the demotic, bread has become *psomi*. It is curious that if you learn modern Greek with a teacher, he will kick off with the ancient Attic grammar. It is the first memorable lesson in the perenniality of the old Greek tongue. In contrast, you could not teach a Greek English if you started him off with Chaucer. The Attic grammar is that from which Socrates must have learned his letters. Is there, then, something indestructible about Greek?

Among the most venerable words still extant you will come across words like 'man' – *anthropos* means 'he who looks upwards'. In common use also are earth (*gee*), sky (*ouranos*) and sea (*thalassa*). Then, somewhat paradoxically, many of the commonest modern words, though they appear to have no ancient Greek roots, prove on examination to derive from perfectly legitimate ancient Greek sources. Water, for example, (*nero*) has the same root as Nereid – even the freshwater nymph of that name still haunts the springs in remote places. Ask any peasant. Bread also (*psomi*) comes from the ancient Greek word *opson*, anything eaten with bread. Even an apparently modern word like *pallikar* (young blood of the village, or buck, as you'd say in English) comes from two words which mean 'one who tosses a proud head like a horse'. But the most common of all come straight from ancient Greece and remain unchanged today: *ti nea?* (which means 'what's new?') and *chairete* (meaning 'bye-bye' or 'be happy'). And of course both *thanatos* ('death') and even Charon are still on duty.

A glance at the synoptic history of the place will do nothing to decrease the sense of being out of one's depth, submerged by too much data. But as time goes on, as sunny Greek mornings succeed each other, you will find everything sinking to the bottom of your mind's harbour, there to take up shapes and dispositions which are purely Greek and have no frame or reference to history anywhere else.

It is important not to care too much.

One of the magical things in *The Tempest* is the way the atmosphere of the island is experienced and conveyed by ship-wrecked souls when they come ashore. The sleep – the enormous spell of sleep which the land casts upon them. They become dreamers, and somnambulists, a prey to visions and to loves quite outside the ordinary boundaries of their narrow Milanese lives. This sedative quality, its bewitched disengagement from all concern, is something you will not be long in feeling here. The air around you becomes slowly more and more anaesthetic, more blissful, more impregnated with holy sleep. You will realize that this is exactly what happened to the conquerors who landed here – they fell asleep. The French started to build the Rue de Rivoli but fell asleep before it was finished. The British, who had almost a hundred-year lease on the place, decided that it needed a seat of Government and built a most elegant one with imported Malta stone, as well as a Chapter for the Ionian Parliament which they planned to create (for once, memorable and apposite architecture – is there any other British colony with buildings as fine?). But they fell asleep and the island slipped from their nerveless fingers into the freedom it had always desired. Freedom to dream.

Everything absurd, everything tragic, and everything gay seems to have happened here. The place has been a dowry for

kings and queens. Richard Coeur de Lion passed this way.
Napoleon planned to run a frigate aground on the fort and
attack from the rigging. (Lucky he didn't – the plan is madly
impractical.) Byron, Trelawny, and the Greek Liberation Committee brought their squabbles here and were met by arch-
eccentrics like Lord North, dressed in a *chlamys* and crowned
with laurel. Solomos (the first great poet of free Greece), the
author of the national anthem, was received with acclaim by the
British when they ruled Corfu in their graceless and rather
bluff fashion. (They made up for their manners by ennobling
everyone and marrying the prettiest and most talented girls.)

When the French, in their spiteful fashion, burned the Venetian Golden Book in which the names of the great Venetian
families were inscribed, the aristocracy did not die – as it was
intended to; it was in fact reborn phoenix-like in titles stiff and
unreal as old brocade. They live on, these beautiful titles, even
today.

Of the troubles and exactions of Venetian rule we know little,
but the island as a whole prospered under Venice. Why? The
Venetians gave ten gold pieces for every grove of a hundred
olive trees planted. When they in their turn fell asleep and left,
Corfu possessed nearly three million trees. They are still her
pride and her dowry. Not to mention the income derived from
an oil as famous now as that of Delphi. It is indeed due to the
Venetians that Corfu strikes the casual visitor as being one vast
olive forest – it is. Edward Lear, who spent some years in the
island – and wrote some of his funniest letters from here – was
quite haunted by the olive groves, as witness his marvellously
buoyant engravings of the various sites. When the north wind
comes drumming down, this whole Proserine extent of trees
shivers and turns silver. In contrast to most other olives these
have never been pruned, and they climb to unusual heights.
Some are said to be six hundred years old. The Venetians were a

long time here (1386 to 1797) so there was plenty of time to carry out an extensive re-afforestation. The peasantry not only got a bounty for planting but could pay their taxes in oil. In the late 1960s a census of the trees was taken which showed that Corfu alone had 3,100,000 trees.

The ideal subtropical climate is another factor which favours the olive; its rather delicate flowering is seldom disturbed in spring. Despite the abundant winter rainfall, the highest in Greece (1300 mm) a year, there is comparatively little or no snowfall. On the other hand the Albanian mountains which girdle the landward coast are snow-capped all winter, so that the island, despite its Tibetan-looking foreground, enjoys mildness and becomes a veritable sun trap.

In classical times, Corfu and the opposite mainland were famous for their flourishing oak trees (remember that Dodona is only 130 kilometres east); but this is no longer the case. The uplands on both sides of the straits are bare and rocky; they have been stripped. In Corfu itself, what the Venetians gave with one hand they took back with the other – their shipyards in Govino Bay were once extensive; now only a few ruins remain. On the Epirote Hills, the damage was mostly due to the Napoleonic wars. Both British and French Governments bought great quantities of wood from Ali Pacha in order to fit out their fleets. When you think that at least two thousand oaks (not counting other trees) were needed to build one ship of the line . . . Whole forests were swallowed up in this way.

But there is little point in reciting the long bead-roll of visitors and those who called here because they were *en route* for somewhere else and found the island on their way; Nero, heading for the Isthmian Games, at which he was to bestow all the first prizes upon himself, and end by ordering the Isthmus of Corinth to be dug, is a case in point.

It would be fair to consider his case as an early form of

islomania. His concern with the Corinth canal was neither aesthetic nor utilitarian – he simply had a fancy to turn the Peloponnesus into an island. It would be more to the point to speak of Tiberius, that specialist in choice holiday places, who actually made a villa at Cassiopi upon the rocky northern point. Strangely enough, he did the same in Rhodes on a similar point with roughly the same exposure: a headland over the water, situated in a gulf crowned with tall mountains. Cato, Pompey, Caesar, Antony and Cleopatra . . . to the devil with the lot of them! In a later epoch came a visitation which aroused many an echo – The Duse and D'Annunzio chose the island as a place in which to consummate a somewhat stagey love affair. The villa is still pointed out. Noël Coward was devoured there by a flea, or so he told me.

The first sea battle in the history of ancient Greece took place between the Corinthians who had settled Corfu and the Corfiots themselves. The latter won; but it was like the closing bars of an overture which ushers in the long senseless chain of invasions and attacks, plagues and famines which have followed right up to this day. At the outbreak of the last war the Italians used the island for target practice and did the town a great deal of damage; but the saint reacted in characteristic fashion, and it is said that during the greatest raid the citizens of the town (or as many as could) huddled into the church and escaped unscathed, for it was almost the only public building to escape a hit. For a long time Spiridion had not done very much except make routine cures for epilepsy or religious doubts. But this was a return to full form, and it once again reminded the people of Corfu that this same old saint had once dispersed fleets, riding upon the afternoon mistral to do so, and even repulsed the plague more than once – it whisked off with a shriek in the form of a black cat. Perhaps it is really due to him that the merciful sleep of nescience descends on all who come here?

The fact remains that even the Turks when they landed 30,000 troops and ravaged the island in 1537 felt something equivocal in the air which made them nod. They too retired after a while, though they took 15,000 islanders with them as slaves.

The Ionian Islands were, even in modern times, a bone of contention between the great powers. By the Treaty of Tilsit the French were authorized to assume their jurisdiction. They stayed from 1808 to 1814, outfacing the severe British blockade. Indeed they only left after the Treaty of Paris was signed which placed the islands under the jurisdiction of Britain. The British suzerainty was ended only in 1864, when Britain ceded the islands to the newly born Greek kingdom.

The British occupation, which lasted for so long, yielded a rich harvest of memoirs and official dispatches, and a richer gallery of notable eccentrics and famous figures like Gladstone whose infectious Philhellenism was not echoed a century later when the Cyprus issue raised its head. More's the pity. There is no place in the world where the English are more enjoyed and admired than on the island of Prospero.

As for what they left behind, the cricket comes upon one as rather a shock – the noble sweep of the main Esplanade with its tall calm trees is suddenly transformed into an English cricket field, though the pitch is one of coconut-matting. Under the charmed and astonished eye of the visitor a marquee is run up and two teams dressed in white take possession of the ground. It is highly professional and would do justice to Lord's.

What is singular is the deep and pensive appreciation of the game in an audience very largely consisting of Greek peasants who have never had the chance to play it. They have presumably come in to town to shop from some nearby village, and now here they are, apparently deeply engrossed in this foreign game while their fidgeting mules are tied to trees on the Esplanade. The audience for the match, apart from them, consists of young soldiers from the garrison, tourists, waiters, an occasional bank-clerk playing hookey, a dawdling postman. On all their dark, intent faces you see a deep concern, a quiet appraisal and appreciation of the game in progress; its white ritual, and its measured cadences seem to sit well with a Mediterranean rhythm. Moreover, they applaud in the right places, and catch their breaths at any notable stroke with authentic delight. Perhaps, in all their dark intentness, what they really see is something like the white-clad figures racing upon some Minoan vase-painting to soar over a rearing bull. There is a tie between sport and ritual, for one must have grown out of the other.

From almost everywhere in the town one can hear the characteristic click-clock of the ball on the bat, and the rounds of applause. Once upon a time it was mingled with the stately popping of ginger-beer bottles, which as ritual objects, together with drop scones, lingered on in the coloured marquee until about 1937–8. But cricket is not yet just a dead ritual; it is still flourishing among the children of Corfu, for everywhere in town you will find the chalked up practice-wicket on the walls of the houses, for all the world as if one were in the East End of London.

Yet, after your first adventure with the Greek light and your initial rapture at the beauty of the landscape, you may feel slightly restless. The lack of classical remains will probably be the cause of it. The shop front, the foreground of the picture, so to speak, is most vividly filled in with an Offenbach-like array of historical remains – eloquent of France, Britain, Venice, Turkey; but with the advent of Byzance, history seems to lose its outlines. Everything becomes submerged in myth and in poetry. (How did Odysseus find the place?) Somehow the fine tomb of old Menecrates seems rather a slender offering.

At this stage, you should go and visit the Medusa in the Corfu Museum. For she, the mother of the Gorgons, was obviously the warden to the chthonic Greek world just as St Spiridion was the warden of the Byzantine world and the modern. The Medusa, more than life-size, is something which profoundly hushes the mind and heart of the observer who is not insensitive to myth embodied in sculpture. The insane grin, the bulging eyes, the hissing ringlets of snake-like hair, the spatulate tongue stuck out as far as it will go – no wonder she turned men to stone if they dared to gaze on her! She has a strange history, which is not made easier to understand by the fact that several versions of it exist. It is somehow appropriate that in her story we should come upon the name of Perseus, who performed a ritual murder on her, shearing off her head with a scimitar provided by Hermes. It was, in fact, a murder performed with the full complicity of the Olympians; the equipment for such a dangerous task (one glance and he would have been marmorealized) consisted of a helmet of invisibility (courtesy of Hades), winged sandals for speed (the Graiae daughters) and a sack for the severed head. However, it is with Perseus that the confusion of the myths begins and the traveller starts swearing at the unrelieved prolixity of the material, its vagueness, and indeed its incomprehensibility.

Two factors come into play here which are very Greek. The richness and incoherence of Greek myth arise because successive waves of invaders brought new versions, or even different grafts, with them to enrich a composite already extremely old, which had filtered by slow osmosis from places as far away as India, perhaps even China: a vast palimpsest of myths and tales to which real people had become attached, in which real figures had become entangled. Men became kings, and then gods even in their own lifetimes (Caesar, Alexander, for example). When Pausanias came on the scene – already terribly late in the day (the second century AD) – he was shown the tomb of the Medusa's head in Argos and assured that she had been a real queen famous for her beauty. She had opposed Perseus and . . . he cut off her head to show the troops. In Apollodorus's version, however, she upset the touchy Athena, who organized the revengeful killing out of spite – and also because she wanted the powerful, spine-chilling head for her own purposes. Perseus (Athena was almost as affectionate towards him as towards Odysseus) skinned the Medusa as well, and grafted the horrid relic of the insane mask to the shield of Athena. This is a different story.

There are several other episodes among the different biographies of our Gorgon. In Hesiod's poem, she fell in love with the rippling blue hair of Poseidon and gave herself to him in the depths of the sea. The trouble started there. Of the two children born, one was Pegasus, who afterwards flew to Olympus to live on at the side of Zeus – a symbol of aesthetic fancy, creative invention. However, in the Hesiod version too Athena guided the hand that performed the deed; Perseus turned away his face for fear of the eyes, letting Medusa's head mirror itself in the shield he had been given.

The prolixity and apparently basic inconsistency of so much polytheistic material is exasperating, and tends to give travellers in Greece a kind of vertigo. Prolix without precision, self-contradictory more often than not, these gods and goddesses simply confuse one. When monotheism came into being and imposed the rigid rules of its beliefs upon this chaos, much of the old religion went underground, only to re-emerge in new forms. Far from conquering paganism, the new dispensation only succeeded in shoring up the old tattered and patched fabric of the ancient beliefs. Looking at the Corfu Medusa and reflecting on her Greek origins (she is dated 570 BC) one is inclined to think that she would be better interpreted in terms of Indian yogic thought than in any other way. It is not necessary to ask if some new, free interpretation like this is valid – in this domain it is every man for himself. Increasingly one is forced to read one's own fair meanings into all this stratified jumble of myths.

The belt of snakes Medusa wears is significant and would provide the yogic interpretation with a point of departure – for they are bearded, and look like sacred hamadryad king-cobras – a symbol of the ancient yogas of the highest grade, Raja Yoga. This path to the perfected consciousness was known and expounded long before the Medusa came. To the Indian sages, the source of this perfected consciousness lay slumbering, coiled like a spring at the root of the spine in the vestigial and obsolete bone called the *os coccyx*. (Curious that in the Jewish holy books the same bone is described as the bone of prophesy.) Anyway, the art of yoga is to awake this slumbering snake and let it rise, like mercury in a thermometer, to the skull, where it realizes the alchemically perfect consciousness – the highest consciousness of which man is capable. The two snakes of man's basic (even genetic) dichotomy spiral round the central column and pass the holy influence up through a number of stations. (Perhaps the Stations of the Cross in Catholicism descend from here?) Yoga means yoke, and the two primordial forces are yoked and, when perfectly married, reach simultaneously the ultimate experience – the blinding zenith of Nirvana. Our modern medicine still retains the symbol of the caduceus, though the meaning has long since been forgotten. (The pine cone which tops the white wand in Greece once represented the all-seeing pineal eye.) But where the devil is Medusa in all this Jungian rigmarole?

Not far to seek. All the sacred writings emphasize how delicate and how dangerous this procedure is. When it fails, as perhaps it has done very often in the past, because the stress on human nerves is too great, or the techniques perhaps faulty – the result must have been madness. On the distorted face of the

Gorgon we see something like an attack of acute schizophrenia. (She foundered in the ocean of the subconscious as symbolized by her love affair with Poseidon.) The hissing hair symbolizes a short circuit, a discharge of electricity – ideas which have overwhelmed her mind. In fact the mask of Medusa is something to propitiate, to conjure away, a dreadful failure of this yogic process. The scared boy hero, Perseus, head turned away, performs a clumsy act of exorcism; today they try electro-convulsion therapy for such terrifying hypomanias. But the old fear of madness is still there, still rivets us; the glare of a lunatic still turns us to stone. Can we see her then as something like our modern charms against the Evil Eye – the blue beads we find affixed to the dashboards of taxis or the prams of small children? It is suggestive too that in Medusa's case Athena received not only the head and skin, but also two drops of blood – one of which caused instant death, and the other of which was life-giving. The latter found its way into the hands of Aesculapius the healer, and with it he performed wonders, even raising the dead. We see then that certain notes are struck which chime with the ideas of duality, and healing. The old Gorgon reminds us of the ancient methods men chose to perfect themselves, and of the dangers which must be faced in order to achieve full selfhood.

Weighed down with these thoughts and quite unprovable theories, one sits in the little museum and allows the emanations of the Gorgon to sweep over one. The first shock of the insane grin is over. She is there not to cause madness but to avert it. And in the greyness of the approaching evening her smile hangs upon the wall full of tragic resonance. The severed head found its place on the shield of Athena, and was used in battle to shock and dazzle the foe. The skin, like the skin of the snake in all ancient beliefs, was a symbol of renewal after death, a symbol of immortality.

There are other good things in the little museum but nothing which has such a strong vibration; Medusa is indeed the second warden of Corfu, and her existence provides an insight into the nature of the ancient Greek world which one continues to encounter as one journeys on among the islands. In all the various extant versions, her attributes are rather stylized – there are versions of the head in Sicily (from the temple of Selinus) and also among the sculptures of the Acropolis. The little horse, Pegasus, the winged fancy of the creative spirit, was the only creature to escape the general carnage and take refuge among the Olympians; dare we suppose that it represents, as a saving grace, that part of her gift which (all madness purged or refined away) realized itself in high poetry and invention? We cannot be sure, but it seems a likely interpretation.

Yes, it is here, face to face with the Corfu Medusa, that you begin to realize the almost unimaginable antiquity of the Greek land and the Greek tongue. The roots of key words like *anthropos* are lost in the mists of the past, all interpretations remain tentative, halting. Presumably one day it became necessary to define the sort of ape which no longer walked on all fours, no longer sported a tail. The 'man who looked upwards' must have been the 'man who walked upright'. From this sudden shift of the spine came the whole of a new sky-piercing attitude for man – the best and the worst features, but everything vertical, like architecture, astronomy, tomb building and temple building. The birth of a new consciousness, no less. The cave, the burrow, the barrow yielded place to constructions made of clay and stone. The arts followed, with leisure . . .

Modern Greece is only one hundred and fifty years old by today's reckoning; the three hundred years of Turkish rule seem to have had only a superficial effect. But what a very ancient modern little country it is – for one can see the shadow of the ancients shining through the fabric of modern Greek life. The

Romans for all their marvellous engineering could not help feeling that they were hollow copies of something better. They became antiquaries rather than historians, and we are glad of it. How much of our knowledge of Greece do we owe to Pausanias who documented all he saw as late as the second century AD? But by the time he came on the scene, how much had disappeared? We do not know, but what vestiges remain speak eloquently of origins as remote as India (the metaphysics of Pythagoras?). In this earthquake-ridden land the inhabitants seem to reflect all the calamitous instability of the nature around them. Nothing lasted more than a few generations; ruin overtook whole cultures, whole continents, whole towns. In a flash.

These are thoughts to be pondered as you wander about in the soft dusk of the old Venetian town, with its odours of magnolia and sudden draughts of garden scent. The little capital is most bewitching at dusk, and a walk about the battlements will end at some café where you can dine and watch the moon rise over the mainland – as brilliant as it is serene. It will be shining through the toplights of the museum on to the staring face of the Gorgon and her two watchful lions.

Yes, this is Greece!

Moreover, the scale of things is reassuring: within the span of three or four days you have visited all the chief beauty spots in the island and all the principal monuments. Tomorrow your journey will be resumed; but already you will have drunk a glass from the famous fountain.

Paxos · Antipaxos · Lefkas · Ithaca
Cephalonia · Zante

The days dawn fine and cool at this time of the year, and the memory of countless Greek dawns over the land and sea are something which every traveller will value and treasure long after he has returned to the mists of the north. Their crisp, dry felicity is almost shameful. Wilde would have said something nasty about nature imitating art; but in truth the Greek dawn puts words to flight, and throws painters out of business. I am not the first writer to ask whether it is the vertigo caused by this light which bequeathed a sort of colour-blindness, or at least a loss of plastic sense, upon the ancient Greeks. Could a nation which painted its statues really have a sense of plastic values such as we understand them in our modern world? For us the lust of the eye comes from the able manipulation of matter; to paint statues seems supererogatory, almost an insult. But perhaps the old Greeks were content with the sense of anecdote? These are questions to ponder as the old steamer wobbles and dawdles across the green crescent of the bay towards the southern opening, where the marshy end of Lefkimi points out the channel, to the open sea beyond.

One moral injunction must be made, however, for the benefit of future travellers. Do not take a camera nowadays – the photos you can buy are better than any you can take. Instead take a keen pair of binoculars; they are really worthwhile. Even now, standing at the rail, you can turn your eyes on the far lagoons where the Battle of Actium was fought, and see herons flapping about, or the white star of a rising pelican, or the shape of a family of golden eagles moving in slow gyres on the blue. On the other side of you there are two islands of little note – Paxos and Antipaxos. Corfu is falling away to the right, and the thud and swing of the open sea begins to make itself felt. It is here, though, in mid-channel, that a momentous historical event took place.

We owe the anecdote to Plutarch in *The Moralia*, which is an essay on oracles and gods and their habits – ideal holiday reading, by the way. Our Elizabethans must have known the name of Paxos from this text. A ship carrying both freight and many passengers found itself becalmed off Paxos, with night falling. Everyone was awake, and many were lingering over their dinner. Suddenly they all heard a voice coming vaguely from the direction of Paxos, which called upon the ship's pilot, one Thamus, an Egyptian. He was called twice, but he did not answer, presumably disbelieving his ears; the third time he was told in a louder voice: 'When the ship comes opposite Palodes you must announce the death of the Great God Pan.' At first Thamus thought he would not do it; he would sail right past Palodes. But there they lay, becalmed, and finally at the indicated spot he shouted out the news, at which a great wail of lamentation arose out of the sea.

'Momentous' is the *mot juste* – for the heart of the ancient world had stopped beating. Later the mystagogues were to claim that this moment marked the very moment of the crucifixion – the reader is free to believe or not. But from this point the pulse-beat of human civilization changed its epicentre, and the vitality of the ages flowed out of Greece into Rome.

The only other interesting piece of history concerning this tiny spot is probably fiction – though it is pleasant to think it might have been true. Antony and Cleopatra are said to have had a dinner party here on the eve of Actium – where so many of their hopes were destroyed.

What else? The little, flat-roofed villages have water trouble in common with so many Greek islands; they live on cisterns and try to hoard winter rain. But the summers are fierce. There are good little harbours for small-boat owners.

It is in this channel that I have seen, on more than one occasion, the huge plate-like form of the hawksbill turtle spinning languidly about in the wake of the vessel. It can reach a metre in length, this strange animal, and is astonishingly agile in the water. It is only one of a variety of sea-creatures which you may be lucky enough to glimpse as the boat furrows its path on down towards the Lefkas Channel. The land has become poorer towards the east, mountains melting to lowlands.

The heavy-jowled Albano-Epirote mountains have steadily given place, first to bony scrubland, and now to marshlands which dwindle away among malarial lagoons – all very fine for winter snipe-shooting and even the occasional boar – but pestilential in summer, indeed unbearably sad in their desolation, especially after a taste of Corfu. Arta, Prevesa, Missolonghi – they seem to belong to another circle of the Inferno, but of course they are not island towns. Rancid green lakes where water-snakes, flies and green terrapins squirm about – and solitary birds unused to the gun. Trelawny, the keen hunter, found a new Italian Maremma here; Byron skulking about, hunting for remains of the city which was built to commemorate Actium, found a few bits of broken wall. Nobody who visits Missolonghi can help wondering whether it was not an acute malarial fever which carried off Byron. But we ourselves are still at sea, thank heavens.

One should recall another not infrequent visitor to these caves and quarries among the deserted islands; it was once quite a usual sight, but has now become increasingly rare. The little monk seal – a brownish mammal (*monachus monachus*) whose fur is not particularly fine but which has, or had, a delightfully unconstrained manner, presumably because it always found secret coves to breed in and to fish from, and was relatively unmolested. When I was a small-boat owner, I saw the little creature on several occasions, usually in a still summer sea, where it gives the impression from a distance of being a swimmer; but it was always surprising to see one so far out in mid-channel. One seal allowed me to come to within four or five metres of it; of course, I had switched off the motor and approached with oars. Then it submerged, but very slowly, and with an apparent reluctance. Before World War II a small colony of them was reported from the deserted islet north of Corfu, called Errikusa, where they sunbathed on the flat rocks like nymphets, or emanations from some ancient Greek myth. What happens today, I wonder? The fishermen say that mostly they have been destroyed because they had the bad habit of tearing the nets after emptying them of their catch. Perhaps they have disappeared for good? I hope not.

The sad little island of Lefkas (or Santa Maura) has little to interest the modern traveller at its northern end, where its position *vis-à-vis* the mainland suggests a vermiform appendix. The little canal is always silting up, and there has been some learned controversy as to whether it is really an island at all. It has, however, always been taken for a member of the Ionian group, though it cannot vie in natural interest and beauty with the others. There is some pretty inland scenery, but movement is hampered by a defective road system, and nowadays the passenger boats normally do not call in very often. The visitor who really wants to explore it must be prepared for long and stony trudges and longish, bumpy drives.

Whatever the limitations of Lefkas, it has one feature which commands the attention of the world – the White Cliffs from which the poetess Sappho made her ill-fated leap into eternity.

Was it accident or intent? We shall presumably never know, and the ancient authorities are as usual not ancient enough, and somewhat vague in their descriptions of what went on. There was, on the penultimate crag by the lighthouse, a temple of Apollo, and the jump itself was one of something like seventy-two metres from a deeply undercut cliff. Confused legends suggest that the ancients believed that one could leap straight down into the Underworld from here – or at least link up with the River of the Dead, the Acheron. Other traditions say that one could cure oneself of the pangs of disprized love by making the leap, and that this is what Sappho had in mind. The question of intent must rest vague, but the actual leap (unless the whole thing is simply a legend) has struck the imagination of the world. It seems appropriate to the greatness of the poetic star – just like the leap of Empedocles into the crater of Etna. At any rate, it struck a spark in the imagination of young Byron when he was among the islands, and his interest makes one wonder whether he did not have in the back of his mind some idea of emulating Sappho. He was extremely puffed-up by his triumphant swim across the Hellespont, and on the look-out for other deeds as picturesquely suitable to the foremost profligate and love-poet of the day. Suitable or not, he did not risk repeating the Sapphic jump.

As far as Sappho is concerned, it seems that something went wrong. For in the time of Cicero and Strabo the jump was often, and quite safely, accomplished. The priests of Apollo performed it regularly without hurting themselves, and boats were organized to recuperate jumpers. Sometimes plumes and wings were attached to the shoulders of those who chose to leap. The jump itself was called *Katapontismos*, and one wonders if it did not have some ancient propitiatory function. For example, when a whole village had to expiate a sacrilegious act or avert some bad luck, a scapegoat might be chosen – usually the village idiot – who was symbolically beaten with rods and made to repent, before being shoved over the cliff into the sea. If he did not die, he was fished out and from thenceforth treated as if dead; he must choose another village to live in. One of the functions of the temple was probably something of this kind. But the puzzle of Sappho remains – what sort of accident was it?

The fact remains that it is a breathless and bone-cracking excursion up to St Nicholas, where the White Cliffs are. You can see the leap, however, if you have good glasses when the Athens-bound steamer passes *outside* the island. It is perhaps not as distinctive a feature as the White Cliffs of Dover, but nobody celebrated has ever jumped over them and into the Channel.

From the point of view of Homeric references, the cliffs find a recognizable place in the *Odyssey* – figuring, as would be quite reasonable, as a celebrated navigational aid to seamen, rather like the Erice headland in Sicily, or the temple of Sunion. Is it worth mentioning that despite the clearest of textual indications to the contrary, some archaeologists have argued that Lefkas is really the Ithaca of Homer? This ivory-skulled and contentious race of men, each determined to be original, is responsible for almost as much confusion as the ambiguities of history, the intrusions of myth, the disappearance of sources; the poor traveller is bedevilled by their squabbles. One excepts, of course, great seminal dreamers like Schliemann who turned a great poem into a greater reality by proving that it was no invention but a historic fact; one excepts also Evans, with his extraordinary dream-vision of a whole civilization which came true. And we are lucky that in the Ionian there are relatively few bones of contention, so clearly has the terrain been mapped by Homer. A few dates may creak when it comes to the Corinthian War in these waters, or the distinct traces of a flourishing

Mycenean civilization in the form of rich tombs; but relatively speaking it is plain sailing for the most part.

But up there on the white cliffs of poetry, the wind blows with a steady cool drumming on the ears, and the asphodels tremble and nod among the barren rocks with their savage thistles. I once knew an Austrian botanist who spent some time camping upon the central spine of the island – for there are three small mountains in a line, like vertebrae. He was in search of a particular rock plant; he described vividly how, while he was sitting gazing down over the famous leap, he suddenly found himself enveloped in a white mist which had risen from the sea. It was quite a distinct emanation, and condensed into a shape with definite outlines. Inside it, he heard the mewing of seagulls and also the calling of human voices. The phenomenon was so strange that he became afraid and, rapidly packing up, took to his heels. Egon Kahr was his name. A few months later he fell from a high apartment building in Athens and was killed; he was holding a telephone in his hand which had been wrenched from the wall. There was no explanation forthcoming. Should there have been? In Greece, stories like this hang about in the air, somehow pregnant with a meaning that never becomes clear. They seem legendary, undisturbed, complete, meaningless as an echo.

To what point are we the dupes of history and of fashion? After all, there are islands every bit as beautiful as Greek islands off the coast of Yugoslavia, off Scotland, in the Caribbean. Is one just a prey to a facile, poetic self-indulgence? The question will not hang in the air for long, and the answer will be an almost certain 'No'. There is a special kind of presence here in this land, in this light; it is not uncommon for visitors of sensibility to have the almost uncomfortable feeling that the ancient world is still there, at their elbows, just out of sight. It is not the kind of 'feyness' of the Irish; it is not a belief in kelpies; it is something much stronger, akin to panic. Indeed, panic is the very word, and Pan the very person involved – albeit he is supposed to be dead now. The peasants still refuse to sleep in the shade of certain trees at noon, for fear of having their wits stolen away. There are spaces among the noonday silences, while the rough hand of the wind caresses the dry grasses of Delos or Phaestos when you almost overhear the little god breathing. Woe to you if his siesta is disturbed, for he goes on the rampage and sows a Panic fear in all who come his way.

Pan has a strange history, and, as Lawson points out, in his role of patron god of Arcadian shepherd-life, he would have seemed rather an uncouth being to the average cultured Athenian of the fifth century; if it hadn't been for his miraculous intervention in the battle of Marathon, he might never have become elevated enough to have a temple built for him. But on the whole the noontide is his hour. Theocritus writes: 'Nay shepherd, it must not be; ye must not pipe at noon for fear of Pan.' The amusing thing is that he was still active enough to influence the superstitious translators of the Septuagint, for he appears in the Psalms as 'the destruction that wasteth at noonday'. It is not possible to reside long in Greece without coming across peasants who have actually seen the little god; and some feeble-witted children are supposed to have encountered him when walking in the woods.

In all this, there is something faintly sinister, faintly menacing. Little pockets of wind moving about on bare hillsides, the swish of the sea; then an enormous stillness without echo. In the midst of a siesta or in the middle of the night, one is suddenly completely awake and on the *qui vive*, one does not know why. A thrilling moment of anxiety intervenes; as if on the veldt one awoke in one's tent to hear a lion breathing at the entrance. A sudden loneliness assails one. And then, abruptly, the influence, the ghost, the cloud – whatever it is – passes; the wind revives, and the whole island echoes once more like a seashell to the deep reverberations of history. Yes, other islands off Dubrovnik are just as beautiful, but they seem to hold nothing. Here you live in a flower-bed of Greek mythology and poetry, to which sooner or later you succumb because you realize that all these fruits of the brilliant human imagination are not fanciful chimeras but simply facts – the facts of Greek life and nature. And it comes with quite a shock to realize that the roots of our own cultures are buried in this rocky soil. There is no help for it, we are all Greeks, as Shelley once said.

If you set out from Nydri in Lefkas, a pretty little port, you will have to skirt a number of small islets which confuse perspectives and outlines, and will find yourself wondering how on earth the mariners of old ever managed to operate before the first maps were available. They must have depended not only on star-sightings, but a profound memory-ability to remember distinctive features. In these waters it is notoriously difficult, for the island shapes shift with every movement and appear to superimpose themselves one upon the other; outlines mix and cohere, and often what appears to be one whole island turns out to consist of three lying together in the direct line of vision. On the map all is clear. The little stone bundles have names like Taphos (tomb) and Arkoudi (bear).

Ithaca and Cephalonia lie side by side – though the latter is much longer, indeed the largest island of the Ionian group. Ithaca, which reverberates with the Homeric legend, is a delightfully bare and bony little place, with knobbly hills, covered in holm oak, which come smoothly down into the sea, into deep water which is rich in fish. The intimacy of the scale and the rapidly shifting levels make a drive about it as exhilarating as a trip on the old-style scenic railways of a funfair. The channel between Ithaca and Cephalonia is about two kilometres broad, approximately the same as the channel which separates Corfu from Albania. The entry into Vathy harbour will set the atmosphere for a first visit – it is most remarkable as well as beautiful. The bare stone sinus curves round and round – it is like travelling down the canals of the inner ear of a giant. One is seized with a sense of vertigo; will the harbour never come in sight? It does at last, buried at the very end of this stony lobe of rock. It is small and not particularly distinguished, but the clearness of the sky and the purity of the water strike one with a sense of pristine cleanliness. The population of nine thousand is that of a small market town. They are friendly and welcoming people, too, and easily befriend the traveller; which is most useful when one needs a guide to visit the Nymphs, say, or the Eagle Mountain – about the two most pleasant excursions in the island. Nothing could convince you more that this was the island of Odysseus than recalling it while actually on the spot: 'It is a steep little island impracticable for horses, but not too badly off in spite of its smallness. It is good for goats . . .' The harbour of Vathy is obviously the old Phorkys, where the Phaeacians deposited Odysseus on his return home, though they did not escape the wrath of Poseidon on their return to Paleocastrizza – or Cannone, whichever you prefer. It is true that the Grotto of the Nymphs (which requires a small scramble, possibly with a guide) is rather further from sea level than the text suggests, but this is a small point.

According to Homer, Ithaca was the capital island of a group comprising most, if not all, of its close neighbours, and it is well situated to enact this role; it is a dream-haunt for the sea pirate; and, if it had one defect, this was perhaps that it was poor in olives and grain, so that it must always have depended on imported goods. Its position is a dominating one – rather like Hydra's – and Odysseus would have been the right sort of piratical and resourceful king to keep a firm hand on it.

Inevitably, of course, the topographical descriptions in the Odyssey have set the scholars bickering. The Homeric sites are not all a-hundred-per-cent satisfactory from the point of view of identification; but, without being too indulgent or too gullible, one can certainly believe in the fountain of Arethusa and the Raven Cliff which sheers away up some forty metres into the blue sky. One can also combine a bit of home-made piracy with piety and scrabble about in the Grotto of the Nymphs, in the hope of finding something left over from the treasure that Odysseus buried there under the direction of Athena.

The present Marathia is where they say that the piggeries of Eumaeus were situated; but this is drawing a bow at a venture. The most vexing of the topographical problems is the site of the town and the palace of Odysseus. Inevitably, two schools of thought have grown up which hold diametrically opposite opinions about the site. One pitches it at the port of Polis on the north-west corner of the island, and the other at Aetos, right on the midriff, the narrowest point between the two land masses. Meanwhile, a third candidate has started to become manifest with new excavations at Pelikata, which, it is pointed out, is admirably situated from a strategic point of view between the bays of Port Polis and Port Phrykes. All that is certain is that there are signs of settlements which were certainly inhabited at the appropriate Mycenean time.

Does it matter? Yes, in a profound sense it does, even though presumably we shall never be certain of our ground in this game of classical hide-and-seek. The little island is full of atmosphere, and we can enjoy it all the more because of Homer's descriptions and by joining in the paper chase of the scholars. It is certainly the right place in summer to pitch a tent or rent a room *chez l'habitant*; it is equally right to re-read the relevant passages in the *Odyssey* and see what you feel about the sites already chosen. Nobody is happy about all of them – but there are several which can be accepted without demur. The holidaymaker, however, will have most pleasure if he rents a little boat at Port Snow (Hioni) and paddles among the rocky headlands.

While on the subject of holidays in the remoter corners of Greece, there are some bits of important advice to give to travellers.

It will be a long time before Greece becomes sophisticated in the bad sense, and in the remoter country places old-fashioned manners and a cast-iron sense of hospitality, as ancient and as sacred as any in classical Greek tragedy, are the order of the day. Inevitably since tourism came within the reach of every man, there have been influxes of the wrong sort of tourists who did their own country's reputation little good, and whose manners shocked the peasants. There are also problems of travelling alone (especially if you are a woman) or being timorous because you don't speak the language. Nevertheless, hospitality is still sacred to Greek people. In any of the above cases, the thing to do, in order to establish your *bona fides* as a serious traveller who merits respect and assistance, is to call on the mayor of the village in which you have a mind to stay; if he does not speak French or English, he will produce the village schoolmaster, who usually smatters in one or both. Ask the mayor to direct you to a family of decent standing in the village which rents rooms. It is not simply a question of finding a room; the simple act of enquiry not only proves that you are serious, but also puts you under the official protection of the village. From then on, woe betide anyone who lets the village down by disrespectful behaviour of any sort.

The second point worth labouring, for those who come from the north, is that for the most part you will be eating in taverns, not in smart restaurants – which anyway only exist in the very centre of Athens. The *taverna* is cheaper; you can eat well and usually outdoors, and it is as friendly as a club. It is like a seventeenth-century 'ordinary'. The thing to do is to march straight into the kitchen to inspect what is being cooked. Nobody takes this amiss; indeed it is expected. Nor will any fuss be made if you should find the lunch or dinner not sufficiently interesting and decide to go elsewhere. At first this procedure may seem to the traveller embarrassing and rude, but he will rapidly accustom himself to it.

It is Ithaca that prompts this short, and I hope not superfluous, homily; this offering of simple tips that never seem to figure in official guide books, and that make a difference to one's peace of mind and well-being in Greece. Ithaca, the home of Odysseus and therefore of hospitality, is a good place to start this procedure, especially as there is not an over-abundance of hotel accommodation there. The pretty little town of Vathy was savagely knocked about in the big earthquake of 1953, which accounts for its curiously disembodied air; the rebuilding has been haphazard and tentative.

What would be the basic requirements for a sea-dog's lair – the central citadel where the faithful Penelope might spend so many years yawning at her loom? An eminence, first of all, to give as good a view as possible of the surrounding country. The command of one or more harbours. Lastly a place with a bit of green land nearby or round about it where, in times of peace, one could farm a little, pasturing cattle or goats. Alas! These somewhat meagre requirements are satisfied by more than one site on the island – which proves that we still need archaeologists, however exasperating they may seem.

The great journey of Odysseus in the poem by Kazanzaki takes on a heroic and semi-mythical flavour, as if it were an ancient chronicle or a sort of collective poem; its mammoth size creates this feeling. Nor is Kazanzaki the only modern master to write about Ithaca; of all unlikely poets, C. P. Cavafy pitched one of his finest longèr poems here – though in his hands and mind the journey was more a metaphysical adventure than anything else. It was a journey through the whole of his life, and as much an interior journey as anything else:

> As you set off for Ithaca
> Pray that your road will be a long one,
> Full of adventures and discoveries.
> Lestrygonians, Cyclops, rough Poseidon
> Don't be afraid of them, you'll never find
> Such apparitions if your thoughts are high
> As long as the great adventure stirs
> Spirit and Mind.
> Lestrygonians, Cyclops and rough Poseidon
> You won't encounter them unless your thought
> Has harboured them and sets them up.

It unwinds slowly and beautifully, suiting the measure to the meaning. 'Take it easy, don't hurry your journey, better take years, so that at last when you arrive you are old, not expecting Ithaca to make you rich. She gave you a marvellous journey, and now has nothing left to give. And if you find her poor, well Ithaca won't have deceived you. By now you will fully understand what all these Ithacas of men can mean.'

A correspondent, wrote:

On Ithaca I was once accosted by a little man on a donkey who addressed me in good American with the flat vowels of Detroit, where he had lived and worked for half a century. Though old, he was extremely spry, and dark as an olive with clever, twinkling eyes. He said he had come back to die at home, and was proud to show me his humble cottage in a small olive plot. His attitude was extremely aristocratic and he made Turkish coffee and offered me, in regal fashion, a spoonful of the traditional *viscino* – a cherry jam. All he owned apart from his house and a donkey and a couple of suits of clothes was a machine which, by the turn of a handle, could shred down corn cobs. He had planted some corn in a pocket nearby. He said that he was utterly happy to be home and missed nothing and nobody in the new world. He looked indeed blissfully happy to be home at last and I thought of Ulysses. (1971)

The less said the better about the site which popular local folklore describes as being the ancient schoolhouse where Homer learned his alphabet ... though the view is pleasant enough. This time it is the village folklorists who are being tedious. And yet, so vexing is this whole business that one would not be surprised one day to find out that the obstinate village tradition has a glimpse of truth in it.

If one wishes during the calm season to take a passage from Pissaetos across to the island over the way, Cephalonia, there will be time for a farewell drink on the top of Mount Aetos. By now amateurs of classical Greek will have been delighted to see how many place names are marked with an ancient Greek name. (*Aetos*, Eagle; *Korax*, Raven) and so on. Whatever the puzzles and problems of ancient history in Ithaca there is something attractive, even bewitching about the little island, which looks so like a Henry Moore sculpture thrown down anyhow in to the sea.

Nor will the contrast with its bigger brother do anything to qualify its undoubted charm, for Cephalonia is the complete opposite. Superficially it has many of the charms of Corfu; wonderful landscapes, spacious bays. And yet, a sort of reservation rises in the mind even as one is enjoying a swim at one of the finest of all Greek beaches. The landscape is large, massive and kindly – and the hills look polished like a Swiss sideboard. The inhabitants are kindly, if somewhat brusque, and have a fine, long reputation for political intransigence and the will to freedom which endeared them to the heart of Byron. They are good mountaineers and good soldiers, and against them the suavity and smoothness of the Corfiots savours a little of Venetian softness, brought about by the cloying beauty of their island. Here all is rough and energetic. True, there are no sites to visit, and nothing much to do except admire the scenery, but even this is sometimes rather a relief after too much slavery to the guide book. No, there is something which renders it rough and rocky like the accent of the inhabitants. First of all, it seems to have harder winters than the other Ionian Islands – snow really lies on the top of the mountain range where Mount Aetos rises to some five thousand feet. Then the big, raw-boned valleys seem awkwardly disposed, running from north-west to south-east. The island is about thirty miles long, and very broad at the southern butt, while in the north it narrows to a mere three miles opposite Ithaca. There is no doubt about its handsomeness, which makes any reservation sound preposterous. But atmosphere is important, and Cephalonia has not much. It is big-boned, lost, a little wistful; although those who stay become very attached to it, and its natives are the most violently patriotic of all Greeks, reminding one in temperament of the Cretans.

In the folklore of the island, Sir Charles Napier ranks among the demigods; indeed his local fame chimes with the national fame of Byron. The two men got on well during Byron's stay on the island, for they were both warm-hearted. The poet was waiting for his cue from the mainland, while Napier was a servant of the Ionian Islands Administration – a most unenviable job, as he found to his cost. The governors were as foolish as they were pig-headed and, despite the fierce agitation of Napier, managed to frustrate the best of his schemes for improving local conditions. It was not only on the mainland that battle was joined – Napier took on the Corfu administration in a vain attempt to secure approval for his development plans. Meanwhile, he bent his energies to the task of building roads, and the present road system is largely what remains from his devoted work. He is, of course, the Indian hero, famous for his telegram, *peccavi*, which being interpreted meant: 'I have Sind'; but fame meant nothing to him beside his passionate Philhellenism and his love for Cephalonia, and he reverted to the island again and again in memory, and in his extensive correspondence with other 'exiles' from the Ionian.

'The merry Greeks', he wrote, 'are worth all the other nations put together. I like to see them, to hear them; I like their fun, their good humour, their paddy ways – for they are very like Irishmen. All their bad habits are Venetian; but their wit, their eloquence and their good nature are their own.'

Wandering about Cephalonia, one gets the deep impression of a large raw-boned island without much centre of gravity – but this uncertain feeling is largely due to the last earthquake's fierce devastation. (Zante is an even worse case.) The last really big tremor was as recent as 1953; and much of Napier's work, and the stylish buildings of the Venetians before him, disappeared in dust, to be replaced by ugly modern cubes of pre-stressed concrete whose only merit is that it is quake-resistant. The shock runs along the same earth-fault as that which passes through Sicily and ends with a bang at Paphos in Cyprus, after having ripped through the southern Ionian group. Corfu gets the secondary impact in the form of an occasional attack of the shivers, but so far has not had the same bad luck as Zante.

There is nothing imperative to see in Cephalonia except the magnificent scenery; although a few places will earmark themselves in the mind as excellent holiday spots – Assos is one. What is memorable, apart from a few churches of moderate interest and a Venetian fortress or two, is the actual ride by bus up the mountainside – climbing towards the peak of Mount Aetos, the dominating feature of the whole rocky spread.

Looking down, one does, in fact, see fertile valleys and rushing streams which belie the feeling of barrenness. And, of course, in ancient times the whole mountain was covered with a dense forest of silver fir which is special to the island – it is dark green in colour; the wood was much prized for its resilience and lightness, and furnished the hulls of ancient triremes and then galleons, right up to Venetian times and after. Presumably the craft of Odysseus was made from this famous wood, if we but knew. There are a few Homeric quibbles around sites like Sami, but one has the right to ignore them, because there the ancient remains are so scanty and uninteresting that it is obvious that such theorizing will not stand against the wealth of evidence in favour of Ithaca.

Something interesting and strange in the island is a sort of deep circular cauldron about a hundred and fifty feet or more in diameter, situated about two miles from Sami on the eastern coast. At the bottom lies a deep blue lakelet. For a long while there seemed to be no way for one to descend to lake level, and then in the sixties an underground cavern was discovered (rather, re-discovered, for the ancient Greeks knew it), and an access was plotted through the cave known as Melissani. This is now a tourist attraction. What is still more curious, however, is that this lakelet, which is brackish, communicates with the sea near Sami and also, by an underground channel, with the Gulf of Argostoli itself, eight miles away, right on the other side of the island. It was long known that a stream of seawater flowed inland in the Gulf of Argostoli with enough force to turn a couple of sawmills, but nobody could understand where this water went. Now we know that in reality it flows eastwards and, passing by the Melissani lakelet, comes out again in the Gulf of Sami, a singular topsy-turvy journey. Everything about the island and about the island character is obstinately contrary-wise, even the streams. But this reversal of flow carries it right under the so-called Black Mountain (Aetos) which is 5341 feet (1624 m) high.

Subject to wind and weather, the traveller comes at last to Zante (Zacynthos), the younger sister of Corfu. Zante, in the past, enjoyed a reputation for even greater natural beauties than Corfu and for the splendours of her Venetian architecture which, despite the frequent earthquake tremors, manage to keep a homogeneousness of style that made the capital one of the most splendid of the smaller towns in the Mediterranean. Only in Italy itself could one find this sort of baroque style, fruit of the seventeenth- and eighteenth-century mind. Then, in 1953, came the definitive earthquake which engulfed the whole of the Venetian past and left the shattered town to struggle to its knees once more. This it has done, in a manner of speaking; but it is like a beautiful woman whose face has been splashed with vitriol. Here and there, an arch, a pendant, a shattered remains of arcade, is all that is left of her renowned beauty. The modern town is . . . well, a modern town. The thirteen-thousand-odd inhabitants have still however the splendid setting – the sweep of the great bay, with its striking crown of fortress, is as fine as anything in Corfu. The verdant richness of the climate, the fruitful earth, the thrust and colouring of natural beauty are all still there; although for the historian and the lover of the past the present Zante is sad, exhausted, lacking in echoes. One must go to books to recover that past now. The fine Lear engravings of Corfu are matched by those of an artist of less renown but of equal technical finish – Joseph Cartwright, whose *Views In the Ionian Islands* deserves to be available again for travellers. Indeed, a fine album could be made from the work of both men.

The real Zante – famous for its beauties since Pliny first mentioned them – has been replaced with a vague and shoddy provincial town. It is the fault of an age which values riches more than beauty. Yet any regrets may be misplaced, for they centre upon a very recent period, historically speaking. Before Venetian opulence – what?

The ancient Zante was first celebrated as an ideal naval station, from which to keep an eye on the Peloponnesus and the other islands. It lies just outside the mainstream of events, to its great advantage, whether one thinks of corsairs or of the Turkish occupation. In ancient times, all the Greek thrust went into seafaring. When some 140,000 Greeks from 171 city states sailed for Troy to rescue Helen, they sailed in 1186 long ships, according to Homer. It was a huge fleet. The traditions of sea power were already ingrained, and they have never changed much. The big fleet built for Alexander the Great numbered 1800 vessels of every size, and its safe return under the command of Admiral Nearchus was the most famous naval exploit of the day.

World War II took a heavy toll on Greek merchant shipping, but when peace came the Greek fleets once more expanded, with astonishing speed, so that in 1976 the Greek-owned merchant fleet mustered some 4529 ships, 49.9 g.r.t. as the shipping magnates put it, ranking Greece as the leading maritime nation of the world. The bias of Greek history has been continuously in this direction since the Argonauts set off to hunt down the Golden Fleece.

The Greek has lived for so long cheek-by-jowl with not simply adversity, in terms of a poor and rocky land, but with catastrophe, that he has learned how to shrug off the caprices of the merely historic, and hang on to his own internal fibre of spirit which will let him happily dance a dance older than Byzance to an American juke-box on a sandy spit. It is this terrific insouciance and resilience which one feels in the air. Over and over again the country has been stripped by earthquakes, wars, pestilence. For example, we have the names of some one hundred and fifty tragic writers of classical times, but they survive for us in little scraps, fragments cited in essays of anthologies. Only three fifth-century Athenian poets remain to us in any quantity. Of the eighty-three plays Aeschylus wrote, we have only seven full texts; we have seven plays out of the one hundred and twenty-three written by Sophocles. From the ninety-two plays of Euripides, we have nineteen . . . and so on.

Such reflections are appropriate for the wanderer about the streets of the modern Zante with its modernities. The site is marvellously romantic, and the little town, which faces the Peloponnesus, stretches southward along the shore to terminate where the rising ground cradles it, while to the west the wooded steeps shelter it from too much wind. It is an enviable site, and already nature has begun to try to disguise the poverty of the new architecture with its flowers and creepers. Here, in this domain, the island is still a match for Corfu; and indeed the lover of solitude will find better excursions, and a genuine village life quite unspoilt by townism in places like Zante rather than in those which have received their baptism of fire from organizations such as the Club Méditerranée. Moreover, he will realize more clearly what different characteristics the Ionian Islands have from the rest of Greece; they had nearly a hundred years of rest and stability while the rest of Greece, torn with dissensions and sporadic actions against the Turks, enjoyed not a moment of respite in the steady attrition of civil war and internal violence. The seven islands basked in their sunny independence, with a great mercantile power to secure their sea communications, and (with whatever reservations) a fairly indulgent and honest administration to look after their welfare at home. The result was not only commerce, at which the Greek excels; it was also culture in the broadest sense. It was all the furniture of the good life, starting with beautifully furnished and appointed houses and *palazzi* and country properties, and ending with carnivals, masked balls, and a distinctive musical tradition which lingered on in the shape of visiting opera companies that played the three bigger islands every winter almost until the outbreak of the 1939 war. The intellectual life in this small Garden of Eden that was old Zante, if on a more modest scale than Venice, nevertheless had the same lively quality. Three major poets were born here – Solomos, who wrote the national anthem, and was the first national poet of the land, then Calvos and Foscolo. What is even more remarkable is that the Greek of Solomos was learned, for he had been brought up abroad.

When Byron left for Missolonghi, it was like someone during World War I leaving Paris to go up to the front line. Back here in the islands, all was sunshine, and music – strangely enough even today the musical tradition of the Ionian Islands is, harmonically, obstinately European; the Turkish quartertone has, of course, made its way into the picture, thanks to the radio and the popular band, but the real Ionian folklore music smells more of Padua than of Athens.

Zante has all the melancholy charm of that long-lost epoch and, unlike Corfu, has not kept even the frame of reference which made it possible – its architecture. But the land is rich and full of sap, and one could live life fully in this verdant and fruitful countryside. The raisins and olives of the island were well known to the Elizabethan housewife, and there was a steady commerce between the Ionian Islands and London. Zante is shaped rather like a parrot – Cape Skinari in the north being its beak; and the main mountain mass runs down like a sort of spine dividing the inner and outer seas, more definitively than in Corfu. For the landward side (facing the Peloponnesus), there is an adequate road system which enables the visitor to take advantage of the marvellous beaches the island has to offer. Moreover, if he has a mind to visit the unspoiled villages of the interior, he will find that the life of the ordinary peasant has hardly changed since the Middle Ages. The modern inhabitant of the big cities is so used to baths, running water and automatic heat, that he finds the older, slower life-style fascinating; for in a Greek village, water still comes from the spring, and a spring can also serve as a refrigerator (butter and liquids are lowered into wells and cisterns, in baskets). Of course, there is electricity now almost everywhere, but it is still fearfully expensive and usually only the village tavern uses it. The ordinary peasant has paraffin lamps with a wonderful, restful yellow light, and wood charcoal for heat, which is deadly slow; half an hour to boil a kettle in cold weather, one hour for almost any feat of cookery. That has not changed. For campers, the gas bottle is a godsend and also the Primus stove of old, but these are luxuries on the peasant budget. The first thing children learn to do is make a nightlight for themselves with a bit of thread and spoonful of olive oil in a saucer – an ancient Greek light which is still used in nurseries and monasteries.

In the museum there is an architect's *maquette* of the Opera House of the island, and one can see and imagine the musical splendours which have vanished. There are also some excellent prints which deal with past glories, and maps which enable one to site the island in context. It is the third largest in the Ionian group, and is only twenty-five miles from north to south, though about thirteen broad at its fattest point. The northern *massif* of rock – and the heights of Mount Scopus which reach some sixteen hundred feet above the sea – have a moderating effect upon the rough north winds, which in winter blow down from the snow-clad Albanian steeps opposite Corfu.

The patron saint of Zante is St Dionysios – anything Spiridion can do for Corfu, he can do better for Zante. He should be visited and candle-primed with respect – one should not play about with the spring weather in the Ionian. Both saints are, in terms of Greek history, relatively young ones, though the Zante one had a long and acrimonious career, including stages spent in Aegina, and then a battle royal to obtain the episcopal nomination in Zante itself. He retired in a huff after having failed in this laudable enterprise and secluded himself in the uplands – a convent called Anafonitria, dying in 1622. His remains are buried in the atolls called the Strophades. In 1703, he was admitted officially to the register of fully fledged saints. Inevitably enough, his history is intermingled with accounts of Turkish piracy – the convent was pillaged by marauding Turkish pirates and, according to the tourist bulletin available in the island, they put 'some monks to death and others to rapture'. In other words he has seen hard times and is a seasoned island saint, despite his relative youthfulness. It only remains to add that the ancestry of St Dionysios is Norman. By reputation he occupies himself to the exclusion of other preoccupations with the fishermen of the island, and every year he is presented with a pair of new shoes on his feast days.

How to say farewell? It is as difficult a problem as ever Corfu presented; but one should not leave without two memorable excursions – one to the wide-sweeping bay of Laganas, and the other to the mysterious and poetical beach called Tsillivi. Years later, in the pages of a book, the traveller will find a grain of sand from this spot, and perhaps a pressed flower or leaf to remind him of something he has never really forgotten.

The Southern Aegean

*

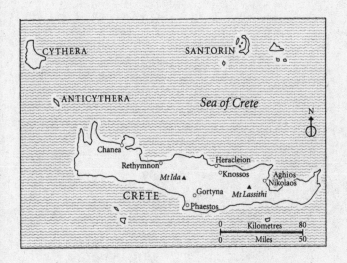

Crete

To the Greeks Crete seems the most authentically Greek of all the islands because of the length of its history and its relative remoteness from the ancient centres of war and diplomacy. Crete, for example, played no part in the Persian or the Peloponnesian wars, during which the rest of the Greek dependencies were almost bled to death; with her crack fleet, she had time to take stock of things from the neutrality of her perch in the main deep of the Aegean.

'The big island' Crete is always called in the colloquial tongue; and big it is, spacious and full of the brooding presence of its four groups of mountains, which have more or less divided it into four countries with four chief towns. The mountains are high enough to be snow-tipped throughout the dour winter, and very often the traveller in the lowlands will have the feeling he is crossing a continent rather than an island. In almost any direction his eye turns, it is halted, not by a sea-line as in the smaller islands, but by a land sky-line, often massive and forbidding. It is sumptuously rocky, though the verdant and bounteous valleys that open everywhere offer no lack of water or shade or greenery; indeed Crete has quite a lot of high mountain pasture, unlike many islands of the same size.

Once you round the broad butt of the Peloponnesus and enter the Aegean, you have turned a new page in the strange, variegated album of Greek landscapes – quite different from those of the romantic Ionian islands. The Aegean is pure, vertical, and dramatic. Crete is like a leviathan, pushed up by successive geological explosions. It is also like the buckle in a slender belt of islands which shelter the inner Cyclades from the force of the deep sea, and which once formed an unbroken range of mountains joining the Peloponnesus to the south-west Turkish ranges. The valleys are the deep faults between eminences. After Sicily, Sardinia, Corsica and Cyprus, it is the largest island in the Mediterranean. In continuity of history and purity of bloodstock, it is probably true to say, as the Greeks do, that it is 'the most Greek' of the islands.

Though beautiful in its spacious style, its ruggedness and its sudden changes of weather make it a disquieting place for the visitor. It strikes a minatory note, which is echoed in all the enigmatic and somewhat vexatious folklore it has accumulated around figures like Zeus, Minos and others – not to mention the famous Minotaur which must still lurk somewhere underground today, like the Loch Ness Monster, waiting to be discovered by television. Yes, it is a strange place, full of echoing wind-haunted valleys and grand glades, of plains full of secret villages which lie baking in the noonday sun, of mountains with holm-oak forests where the charcoal burners stand, like black demons, over their fuming pits.

Its shape is rugged as well, for Crete has been sculpted by a conflict of tides which forever range and gnaw at its cliffs. From the air, it looks something like the case of a violin that has been absent-mindedly cut about with a hacksaw by a retarded child; the whole northern part is heavily indented, yet poor in big harbours. Suda Bay, next to Chanea, is to some extent an exception, but even that is not a really fine commercial harbour. However, smaller craft and yachts will generally find a lay-by, though it is more difficult on the southern coast, for there the mountains rise iron-bound from the deep sea and form great walls against which the sea pounds and shocks and explodes all the year long. The best way into the island and the mood of the island is, as always in Greece, by sea, which gives the pace and the dimension necessary for the traveller to take in what he sees.

But today the traveller who harbours romantic notions of a sort of Greek Tibet will find himself in for a shock. The air-time from Athens is under an hour, and tourism has swamped the island with summer sun-lovers – which has had an inevitable effect on prices, urbanization, and morals. The whole of the northern coast – or a good two-thirds of it – is turning itself into a playground, a place of summer habitation, for sun-hungry Nordics. However, we must make the best of what is left. The Cretans remain dour and gay, which makes one feel slightly better about it; and who could say they are wrong to pine for a higher standard of living – as we all so quaintly call it? In the thirties, when we stayed in a village or camped, we managed without such indispensable things as washing-machines and fridges. Our fridge was the nearest well, or the sea even, into which we lowered bottles and perishables; the village granny was our washing-machine, an excellent one (and glad of the money), even if sometimes we caught trifling children's illnesses like ringworm or Dobie's itch from badly washed clothes. All Cretan housewives would agree that among modern amenities there are real godsends like Buta-gas, insect spray, and washing soaps (it is odd to realize how recently these have appeared on the scene; and even DDT, penicillin and the sulfa group of drugs only date from the end of World War II). Life was quite different without them in remote places like Greek islands. For my part, I would site the island telephone as a worthwhile modern amenity; today you can ring from one island to another, from one hotel to another. You never could before; even pre-paid telegrams did not work. You just had to hope you would find a room when you arrived at your destination.

The Cretans have seen everything – the collapse of the Minoan Empire, the rise of Venice, the slave markets of Turkey, Nazi parachutists and American hippies – nothing has been spared them. If they remain a trifle sceptical and shy, brusque and censorious, it is hardly surprising. One must also realize that they have only belonged to Greece since 1913, though the last Turkish soldier left the island in 1896. The intervening years were years of fragmentation and neglect; they were pawns of the great powers and Crete was split up, as Berlin is now, into sectors and sections. The transition was abrupt, and today one sees new and old rubbing shoulders everywhere. The costumes in the market, at the airport, in the harbour, are a wild mixture of ancient and modern; the music of the juke-boxes is similar, pouring out *bouzouki* music and modern jazz.

Four mountain clumps loom around if one comes by plane into the modern airport. ('Bones of the elephant and the pygmy hippopotamus have been found in geologically recent cave-deposits while deer only became extinct in historic times.') What must it have been like in Homer's day? About this we know a little from the way he doffs his hat to the island in the *Odyssey*, hailing it as a land famous for its hundred cities, its rich and numberless buildings. But the feeling he conveys is that he had not personally touched down here, that he was citing a ready-made descriptive compliment: a tourist handout of the day perhaps?

On the other hand, St Paul (who got into trouble almost wherever he went) had a particularly hard time in Crete, for he told Titus (the first Bishop of Crete) that, to quote a poet, the islanders were 'always liars, evil beasts, and slow bellies'. It is clear that he had gone into a bar in Chanea for an *ouzo*, with a mass of contentious epistles under his arm, and had naturally received what the New York bartenders would call 'the bum's rush'. Much the same thing happened in Cyprus. As for the phrase 'slow bellies', this needs checking with the original; it surely must be a bad translation. How could the saint so assail the digestive tract of the Cretans? Cretans eat faster and more than most islanders. I suspect the passage means something different – perhaps that they were slow to kindle to the faith. At any rate, it is clear St Paul thought the Cretans had not been sent on earth to charm; which suggests he must have been badly treated. The truth is that the Cretans are the Scots of Greece; they have lived through countless crises to emerge always just as truly themselves – indomitable friends or deadly enemies. If their hospitality wavered under the scandalous begging of the hippies, it soon reasserted itself. And even today it is dangerous to express admiration for something, for you will certainly find it in your baggage as a farewell gift when you leave. You cannot refuse. They are adamant. I knew a lady who got a baby this way.

Everyone will have special corners of Crete to which he or she is specially attached, but I think the travel-people are right to insist that the three atmospheric places which one would most deeply regret missing are Knossos, Phaestos and Mallia. The shipping companies have worked out an ingenious week-end manner of 'doing' the two former and finding yourself back in Athens the Monday morning after, but this is only for people *in extremis*. Crete is a big island and deserves at least several days, not merely for ruin-hunting, but also to appreciate its own fair landscapes and enjoy those encounters in remote villages which make all the difference to one's 'feel' of a place. The ideal thing is to rent a small car, for though the new road system only dates from about 1946, parts of it are excellent and almost everywhere is now accessible to the visitor. Of course, the southern coast remains a little remote and out of reach because the mountains run from left to right; but the whole inner coastal run from Chanea right down to Sitia is both possible and thrilling in its variety and ruggedness. Thus you will slip down through four counties, each with its capital town, and glimpse the variety of landscape which exists within this one island – quite apart from catching a sudden sight of a sacred place like Mount Ida, with its white crown. Chanea, Rethymnon, Heracleion, Lasithion are the towns you will pass. Then suddenly cloud-cradled Dicte will come into view, another place sacred to the gods of Crete.

Whatever else has changed, the cast-iron rule of hospitality has not and, if you are lucky enough to rent a remote villa for a few days, you will certainly find that, for during the night invisible hands have placed a basket of fruit or eggs on your doorstep. Nor is it possible even today to pay for your drinks if you are with a Cretan. The far countryside is still remote and savage and intact; the vendetta still flourishes in a manner unknown to the Ionian Islands. In Crete, with its rough accent and manly, chivalrous uprightness of temper, a hero is a sort of Young Lochinvar – a *pallikar* or 'buck'. In a remote village it might even be difficult to get away without eating a whole sheep – including the eye, a great delicacy, which might be offered to you on a fork, with an Odysseian flourish. There are few hazards in such warm-hearted company, but I can think of one. The drink called *tsikudi*, a kind of local *marc* or *grappa*, which has been piously distilled from dragon's bones, fills one with a strange Byzantine effulgence if drunk by the pailful. The resulting hangover makes you feel like one of those sad, haloed saints in the icons. However, these are trifling worries of an everyday sort and are soon mastered under the guidance of a native. In all this blue air and racing sea, everyday life seems easy to live; it is the intellectual problems, caused by the muddle of history, that tend to dismay one most.

What about Minos? He was, in terms of mythology, the old king who ruled Crete during its rise as a seapower and its development into the most important civilization ever to flower in the Mediterranean. It was a stepping-stone between Egypt and Athens, on the one hand, and between Egypt, Athens, and Asia Minor on the other. During the period of its greatest glory, it succeeded in combining and refining dissimilar influences from the neighbouring countries and stamping them with a specific Cretan personality. Yet, as always, accurate dating remains a bugbear; were there many Minoses – was Minos a generic name for all the rulers of Crete? Or did they all descend from one? At any rate, the ancient myth of the Cretan civilization has clung on so successfully that, when Sir Arthur Evans was casting about for a frame into which to fit all his exciting new finds at Knossos, he took the old name and christened the civilization he was examining a Minoan one.

The son of Zeus and Europa, according to the legends, was Minos who, after getting rid of his brother Sarpedon, obtained the throne of Crete with the help of Poseidon. From his capital in Knossos, he developed the island's seapower and overran the neighbouring islands, in which he smoked out the nests of pirates and generally established order. He was venerated for his wise laws and the security his fleet bestowed on the surrounding countries. His wife Pasiphae was the daughter of the Sun, and the children she bore him were called Androgeos, Ariadne and Phaedra. But trouble loomed ahead, possibly due to hubris, or overweening; maybe power had made him too cock-sure about his importance. At any rate, he incurred the wrath of Poseidon for not sacrificing a marvellous white bull which had been sent to him for that purpose. The punishment was dire. Poseidon made Pasiphae fall in love with the bull; with the help of Daedalus she then disguised herself as a cow and the fruit of this union was a grotesque monster with a man's body and a bull's head. It ran amuck and ravaged Crete, so that finally it was locked up in the labyrinth which had been constructed by

Daedalus on the pattern of the Egyptian one, as described by Herodotus.

These legends, with their graphic symbolism to which unfortunately the key has been lost – or not yet recovered – are sometimes more irritating than enlightening. The Minotaur is one of the puzzles; his existence and habits have given rise to numberless differing explanations, but there is no single one which answers all the questions. Equally full of enigma is the maze – did it have a ritual function, a religious function? Did it symbolize the evolution of the individual personality into maturity – after conquering all the stresses and fears of life? Otto Rank, the psychoanalyst, seemed to think the maze was a symbol of the loops of the big intestine of a sheep or a cow – the standard form of divination. Myself, I think that a man sentenced to death was given an outside chance of redeeming his life by crossing the labyrinth and avoiding the Minotaur if he could. Somewhere I have read that, in the old Roman arenas, where so many Christians were fed to the lions, not all the cages surrounding the arena were full of wild animals; and that a slave thrown into the pit was pardoned if he twice opened an empty cage. Maybe the labyrinth worked like this; maybe the trick was to sneak through without waking the monster?

One can scent in all this some of the origins of our own children's infant games, whose history goes very far back. Not to wake the monster ... One remembers the suspense when Odysseus hears the question: 'Who goes there?' It is a breathless and fearful moment, but like a typical Greek hero he is never at a loss; he replies, 'Nobody,' and with this strange, double-take answer strikes the first chord in modern literature – so says a critic. The later history of Minos, the subduing of Athens and the tribute of maidens and boys for the Minotaur, has a more dramatic and historic background offering little satisfaction as to the origins of these fantasies, which at one time must have been capable of a rational explanation. A Mithraic type of bull-culture is strongly present in all the echoes, not only of Minos's own origin but also of that of Zeus – who was originally a Cretan, though of course worshipped later on all over Greece.

It was in Crete that Zeus was born, in a cave you can visit today if you will face a tremendous slog; and here, in secret, he was honeyed into babyhood by two nymphs, daughters of the then king.

He, of course, was a refugee like his brother Poseidon, but he won the distinction of finally mastering his neurotic father Chronos (Time), who had the regrettable habit of putting everything in his mouth and often swallowing it. Phagomania! Chronos swallowed a whole shopping-list of young and unfledged gods, before, at last, he had to give way and allow the Olympian gods to form themselves into a general committee appointed to oversee earthly affairs. But if Minos (a mere man) knew he was supported by both Zeus and Poseidon he must have felt great confidence in himself and his luck; it was like having a couple of friends in Parliament.

I am limiting myself to the affairs of Crete only in these superficial considerations of mythology; I am not suggesting that there is any link between the behaviour of such a polymorph-perverse profligate as the old head-prefect of Olympus and that of the modern Cretan who, like us all, has been bowed down by nearly two thousand years of monotheism and monosexuality. Zeus was not alone in his profligacy. Most of the Olympian heroes were very lightly screwed to their thrones; the mere sight of a nymph or a goddess, and they were in hot pursuit, eager to rid her of every complex, in the most good-natured way. (Inescapable vision of Harpo Marx with butterfly net and bicycle racing about the Paramount lot.) The list of Zeus's own conquests in the Larousse *Encyclopedia of Mythology* is a long one. He left no nymph unturned. Minos had an early tendency to imitate him, and once chased a young huntress called Bryomartys into the sea; but he came to his senses soon enough and sobered up. At any rate, he never managed the vast repertoire of impersonations and disguises of the old god – which must have made Zeus a much sought-after guest at house-parties. The most poetic of these was perhaps Leda's swan; but it is much more important, as far as Crete is concerned, that he turned himself into a bull to court Europa.

As Robert Graves points out: 'In primitive agricultural communities recourse to war is rare and goddess-worship the rule. Herdsmen on the contrary tend to make fighting a profession and, perhaps because bulls dominate their herds as rams do flocks . . . tend to worship a male sky god, typified by a bull or ram.' Perhaps Zeus came into this category. In any case, the bull motif is dense with echoes; and I am sure that a comparative ethnologic and religious study of the Mithraic echoes in the bull-mania of, say, Provence will one day link together not only the sacrificial side of bull-mythology in different countries but also link it with the ritual side of bull-baiting, as shown on the Cretan vases. Certainly, in Provence today a celebrated Spanish bull, after he has been killed, is eaten by the people; I have seen this often in Protestant Nîmes. The head is exposed in the butcher's window with the name of the animal above it, and there forms a long queue of housewives who buy small quantities of the meat – as a token rather than as a meal. If asked, they will agree that the meat is not of the best quality, since it is flushed with blood from the exertions of the battle, and belongs to a creature that has been raised on oats to quicken its temper. The custom is a clear illustration of Freud's *Totem and Tabu* which should always be within reach in the Greek islands! To make my point still clearer: in another part of Nîmes there is an after-the-corrida dinner party of officials, dignitaries and fighters with their trainers. They are solemnly offered a thick soup, made from the testicles of the slain bull. There are similar customs in countries where the bull remains a symbol of force, fertility and the father-complex which might provide more solid material for the student of bull mythology.

Wandering about the quiet and somehow reticent ruins of Knossos, whose proportions and orientation show that their architects had nothing to learn from ours, one wonders whether the matter will not one day simplify itself and bring the Minoans into much clearer focus for us. When the king gave judgment, for example, did he place the great bull's head on his head and shoulders just as an English judge dons the black cap? And was the labyrinth both an execution ground for malefactors and a training-device for young gladiators – or even a place where initiates had to learn to find a way through the muddled penetralia of their own fears and desires? In these quiet precincts, which in fact may be simply administrative buildings, but which exhale the kind of equanimity and poise of an architecture at once beautifully proportioned and not too sweet, one feels the presence of a race that took life gaily and thoughtfully. What a pity we have not yet found something of interest in the scripts so far deciphered; it is tantalizing – wanting to work out their philosophic or religious views from something like an income tax declaration.

A few thoughts on the Olympians might help to identify the Cretan mind or soul during the periods about which we know, if not everything, at least a bit. Hesiod has set out the history of the gods in fairly neat trim and there is no reason to distrust his pedigrees, for the little group finally, after mastering more tribulations than ever Odysseus faced, formed itself into the Parliament of Olympus and took an eager interest in what was happening on the earth. First of all, says the historian, there was no difference between the two lots, gods and men; they sat down to the same table to eat. Gradually they became differentiated – gentlemen versus players; though even when Olympus became a workable headquarters and the gods a going concern, there seemed to be little qualitative difference between the two groups. The gods had more power, that is all; they were not morally superior or in the possession of any special nuclear secrets – apart from the thunderbolt of Zeus. They behaved, however, like rather irascible and unstable uncles – one never knew when they might go off at half-cock and cause trouble. So it was best to keep them soothed with frequent sacrifices. Of course, this was long before anyone worried about cruelty to animals, and anyway, it is now generally agreed that the tremendous bloodshed of all these sacrifices was simply a way of feasting the whole community at the expense of the taxpayer. In every village festival where sheep or pigs turn whistling on the spit, the indigent can claim first place for a serving; and lots of beggars virtually live like this. There is little doubt about the ancient origin of today's *panagyri* – and anyway, Xenophon has described the whole matter in detail.

The trials the Olympians had to undergo before consolidating themselves on the mountain whose secret magic is still with us today – as anyone who has got lost on it (almost everyone does) can testify – would make films look trivial. First the Titans had to be smashed, then the blubbering giants, and finally, just when all seemed plain sailing, the super-monster known as the Typhaeos came upon the scene and had to be dealt with; this composite horror was finally put to death and buried under Etna in Sicily, where one can still hear it writhe and roar when an earthquake arrives. After this, one might say that the reign of the Olympians really began, at the point where Zeus at long last managed to master his own father Chronos, whose pronounced phagomania had done for so many of his offspring. Poseidon also escaped the fatal gobbler-sire and settled down with his brother Zeus for a long and successful reign. They took their place naturally among the twelve major deities.

Hesiod, the old herdsman-poet, has roughed out the historic pedigree of mankind as his age knew it – and this roughcast view must correspond to ancient traditional belief. There is no need for it to be wrong. The various ages succeed one another – ever degenerating, ever declining I fear – until they reach our own degenerate and senescent epoch. First of all, in the Golden Age, men lived like gods, free from worry and fatigues, unafflicted by old age; they rejoiced in a continual felicity and festivity and, though not then immortal, they died happily, as if falling asleep. Then came the Silver Age, which was less happy, for the inhabitants of the earth were feeble, inept people who obeyed their mothers (a matriarchy) and lived by agriculture. The Bronze Age brought in new races, with men as 'robust as ash trees' who delighted only in oaths and warlike exploits. Alas, they came to a smart end by cutting each others' throats; but this age of stress was marked by the discovery of metals and the first attempts at what we call civilization. Then came the Iron Age – but no, it is too depressing to continue.

Gradually the separation between gods and men became more critical, though they still resembled each other in many ways – not always the nicest; indeed it took the gods some little time to pull themselves together and play their roles of mediators between man and the universal forces which menaced him from every side. Meanwhile, of course, there was a good deal of pretty hot skirmishing for maidenheads up on Olympus, and sometimes the inhabitants of the earth got caught up in the centrifugal force of a god's actions. This interpretation makes the Olympians more human than other gods, but vastly increases the confusion in terms of earth-history.

The days of the gods passed in permanent merry-making; they had an eternal dinner party round golden tables, on which they were served limitless supplies of untaxed nectar and ambrosia. In their veins flowed, not blood, but *ichor*, so they never wore out physically. As they feasted, they had pleasant whiffs of roasting pigs and cattle from the smoking altars on earth below. Yes, they were a queer lot in early times – parent-size copies of their children, the earthlings. If they had no 'character' in the psychological sense, they had clearly marked attributes and reasonably precise functions.

Perhaps that is claiming too much, for they certainly lived, just like modern Greeks, from impulse to impulse; a way of life that kept, and still keeps, reality fresh and totally unpredictable. Nor were the impulses always praiseworthy – pique, jealousy, lust, cunning; the gods ran the gamut, and were pleasantly free from self-reproach or the gnawings of guilt. Yet (and it rounds off the notion of a parent–child relationship) one must emphasize that they were vastly bigger in size than their earthlings. Ares's body when stretched out on the ground was seven *plethra* in length – over two hundred yards.

The story of these ancient divinities is touching in its way; a story that little conceals the longings and desires of the earthbound peasant spirit of that epoch – and indeed of ours also. One can see Olympus for the glorified *taverna* that the popular belief must have made of it, full of good smells of wood-smoke and lamb. And then those golden tables! They make one think of a Hollywood 'vehicle' bearing, as they did, all that Disneyfied ambrosia and nectar – unremitting fare indeed; it was like being forced to live exclusively on caviar. What better heaven could a *taverna habitué* think up to solace himself against the poor harvest below, which was so often his lot?

These thoughts about the gods will not seem entirely out of place if you find yourself sitting in the main square of a Cretan hill-village today, watching the quiet drinkers and players of tric-trac; past and present are joined by so many fine threads.

You will see, for example, an elderly peasant fill his glass and, before raising it to his lips, let fall a few drops on the earth floor of the shop. The libation is a contemporary thing, as is also a muttered exclamation in the order of 'Good Luck'. The old man may not be conscious of the age of the gesture or of its origins. In Crete – indeed in Greece – the scale of things is so small and human that the old monuments and the contemporary scene seem to have been hatched from the same strange egg.

The green glades, so dusty in summer, echo to the drilling of the *cicada*. But if you happen by chance on a mulberry village you will hear another kind of drilling, which sounds like musketry or a forest fire, so intense is it, despite the small scale. This is the death-feast of the silkworms as they quash their way through the mulberry leaves which cover them. When a mulberry peasant goes to the town to shop, she makes for the shoe shop and cadges all the empty shoe boxes she can find – they are perfect for her purpose. In these she places her leaves and her worms. Later, in some other village, you may see the butter-yellow, butter-soft loops of the raw silk being drawn from the hissing cauldrons hanging from their tripods and wound slowly and piously on to a hexagonal frame of wood ready for the looms. How ancient can this art be?

The persistence of things is a striking factor in the life of modern Greece; very old beliefs are sometimes left undisturbed, just like a vase in the ground, waiting to be unearthed by some historian, but still believed. Take saffron. My wife, when she went in search of some in the town of Alsea, was told that it would need a doctor's prescription to obtain, and that it was only on sale at the chemist. Alarmed but intrigued, she went through the drill and an unsmiling doctor gave her a prescription, and in due course also her modest condiment. When she asked the chemist why such precautions were necessary, he replied that it was a powerful aphrodisiac;

this ancient belief had somehow managed to climb into the prescription book of the modern chemist. I seem to have read about the aphrodisiac qualities of saffron in the pages of Athenaios. It is only one example of a belief that has survived.

The interior organization of a small Greek village today – such a one as you might pass through on the road to Phaestos, say – has not changed substantially since ancient times, despite electric light and concrete. The village square may be the delivery point for goods like flour and rice, but the threshing floor is as active as ever and, when not in domestic use, serves as a sort of theatre for speech days and open-air festivals; it is, I suspect, the prototype of the first theatre. It is always beautifully sited for wind, because of the winnowing, and in consequence is fine for voices or music. I have seen it everywhere used for festival purposes, in villages of medium size. Nor would it take one very long to divine three other communal points which serve as electrodes, so to speak, for news, opinion, argument – the factors upon which the intellectual life of a village reposes. There is the bakery, first of all, which, as there are no private ovens, has a specially large built-in corner for personal bakings – where for a penny one can have a dish cooked. The ten minutes or so before midday, or the evening shortly before the baker opens up, is a prime gossip time for the women. Another community centre is the village spring, where water is drawn and clothes are washed. There is no need to repeat stories of haunted springs and the prevalance of Nereids in modern Greece – their origins reach back to Olympus and perhaps far beyond. And the men? They have the café where their intellectual life is spent drinking *arak* or *ouzo* and staring mindlessly into space.

One modern Cretan obsession which is striking in its ubiquity is the passion for high leather boots, upon which the modern peasant will spend quite large sums. Everywhere there are bootmakers crouched, in little shops, over their 'trees', their handicraft proudly on show in the window. The boots! Everywhere they are worn, or are on order, or are being tried out with that famous Cretan strut, or being worn with an old-fashioned and dignified costume. They set off to perfection a pistol in the sash and dagger at the hip (now uncommon, except on dress occasions like important weddings).

Whether it is true or not that Crete is the most Greek of the islands, its history is certainly more continuous and more revelatory than in any other island. It is more revelatory chiefly because of the discovery of the Minoan civilization and the brave attempt to date history backwards almost into the Neolithic Age, around 4000–3000 BC. Knossos and Phaestos are the most important places to show us these discoveries; but apart from their historical interest, both supply an aesthetic experience which cannot be matched elsewhere. I would stress here that a visit to Knossos must be followed by a browse through the Heracleion Museum where so many of the treasures from the site are housed and admirably displayed.

The two fixed stars in the firmament of Greek archaeology are Heinrich Schliemann and Sir Arthur Evans, who trod hard on his heels. The German had all the luck and the optimism of the great romantic – indeed his life is a romance; he spent it realizing a childish dream. Nobody before him had thought of the *Iliad* as more than a poetic fantasy. He used it as a guide book, literally dug up the reality behind the document, and set all our thinking about ancient history by the ears. He was both lucky and determined; everywhere he planted his spade, treasure hoards sprang out of the ground. What is piquant is that he even had his eye for a while on those enticing green *tumuli* on the knoll at Knossos, and even tried to get permission to open up the site; but administrative problems with the authorities proved too vexing and he turned aside to make discoveries more important, though slightly less spectacular, at Mycenae –

the famous shaft-graves which were useful historical echoes when it came to placing and dating the finds from Knossos.

Sir Arthur Evans was less flamboyant but no less a dreamer. He had been in the island already, hunting for seals with pictographic markings, and in some curious way he was able to predict that when Knossos was cleared and assessed, they would find specimens of Minoan writing. Was it premonition? Or had the disposition of the seals he found given him a clue? He was more plodding than imaginative – though he wrote an excellent travel book about Yugoslavia when a young man. Looking backwards it seems that everything lay at hand, ready for him – a whole civilization which pushed back the old frontiers of prehistory. Cautiously he waited until he could buy the whole site and deal with it carefully, at leisure.

So the great adventure began. Evans's findings were carefully checked against the typology of objects already unearthed in Egypt and Asia Minor. Egypt was especially helpful, for the desert is an admirable conserver of everything, even papyrus, and the history of this ancient land is more smoothly continuous, less tempestuous than that of the Greek isles where invasions, wars and shattering earthquakes have erupted so often. Egypt was the touchstone; with its help Evans began his, at first, vague and hesitant back-dating of Minoan history. Even today, when the time-chart (still open to correction according to findings) pushes the history of the place back to 3000 BC, one can feel how momentous the discovery was – and also how difficult and unsure the intellectual act of trying to sort and assign all these fragments. What would be the impressions of a Minoan archaeologist, picking over a heap of mud in a London devastated by an atomic attack – a heap which yields him objects as disparate as a teddy bear, a Father Christmas, a Rembrandt, (was England full of monkeys, and at what epoch?), an Iron Cross, an income tax return . . . and so on? How would he sort them out historically and assign a purpose to them? Were the English believers in a bear totem? And was Father Christmas a sort of Zeus? The margin of possible error is disquieting, and should put us a little on our guard against the 'certain certainties' that T. S. Eliot refers to.

However chilling the time-chart is to those who hate dates, the thing is well worth a glance. For, in fact, it records the slow emergence of cultural man – with so many failures and collapses, not all of his own manufacture – from a cave-lurker of Neolithic times to a warrior, a priest or an architect, capable of abstract thought and the use of a tool which did duty as an extension of his arm. Completely different animals, one might say. Here is the chart in all its grimness.

NEOLITHIC	4000–3000
EARLY MINOAN I	3000–2800
EARLY MINOAN II	2800–2500
EARLY MINOAN III	2500–2200
MIDDLE MINOAN I	2200–2000
MIDDLE MINOAN II	2000–1750
MIDDLE MINOAN III	1750–1580
LATE MINOAN I	1580–1475
LATE MINOAN II	1475–1400
LATE MINOAN III	1400–1200
SUBMINOAN	1200–1000

What all this proved was that the first centre of high civilization in the Aegean area, with great cities and sumptuous palaces, highly developed art, extended trade, writing, and the use of seal stones, was here in Crete. From the end of the third millennium BC, a distinctive civilization came into being which gradually spread its influence over the whole complex of island and mainland states. During the late Bronze Age (c. 1600– c. 1100) this civilization contributed a kind of cultural uniformity to the Mediterranean scene, which was characterized by the interlinking of cities and the exchange of goods and artworks. The gradual sway exercised by the kingdom of Minos made his capital Knossos one of the great cities of the world, and Crete the most powerful island, enjoying a pre-eminent central position in the Aegean with links to the north and to the south.

Yet history cannot be side-stepped – what goes up must come down. Gradually the *thalassocratia* of Minos degenerated, lost its absolute sway, and finally surrendered its supremacy to the more powerful mainland states. About 1400 BC, the centre of political power shifted to Mycenae. Evans dates it from the destruction of what he has called 'The Last Palace'; subsequent palaces were never to equal this one in size and splendour, and after it was destroyed all new buildings were small and meaner. This is partly because Knossos had also been the administrative centre of a highly complex and developed system of military government on the Spartan pattern. The great inscription found at Gortyna makes no bones about the slave culture it defines and delimits; citizens are divided into full citizens, serfs, and slaves. In 1400 BC *all* the palaces in Crete were destroyed simultaneously which makes it reasonable to surmise that enemy action rather than an earthquake was the cause. This is not Evans's view, however; we will discuss that later. Whatever the cause, the land was over-run, and Mycenae took over the political and commercial contacts with Egypt and the Middle East that had once been the prerogative of the Cretans.

Of course, it is not possible to simplify, since so many unknown factors pop up at every turn of the road. It is perhaps wiser simply to tread the quiet precincts of Knossos and catch a glimpse of Mount Juktas centred between the so-called 'Horns of Consecration'. The question of Evans's restoration will inevitably arise; I personally find it insipid and in poor taste. But then Evans was trying to illustrate the relative position of things, and this purpose is fulfilled. The treasures in the little

museum, however, are a better guide to the spiritual temper
of these faraway Minoan people, who sometimes make one
think of China and sometimes of Polynesia. Bright, fresh and
pristine are the little faces from the frescoes or from vase decorations. Candour and a smiling self-possession seem to be the
characteristics of these people, but of course they guard their
secrets very well. The snake goddess with her snake cult is an
example; *was* it a cult? Snakes that are not venomous (which is
true of those on Crete) are easy to play with. The Provençal
couleuvres – grass-snakes sometimes two metres long – provide
the same sort of fun without developing into a cult. At every
harvest time the newspaper has pictures of people snake-
teasing; but they let them go without harming them. And the
snakes in the *garrigues* of the Midi are positively cheeky. The
situation may well have been similar in ancient Crete, with no
question of snake-playing being a religious rite.

If the Minotaur, the labyrinth, and the double axe are sym-
bols, they are harder to interpret. Is it fair to suppose that the
Minotaur symbolizes some great event – perhaps the arrival of
men from far away – who brought with them a terrifying and
puissant animal which had never been seen before: a bull?
(Imagine the terror of seeing one's first bull!) And then a bull-
culture, bull-obsession displaced whatever had been the native
pastoral cults? It is not too far-fetched if one remembers the
superstitious horror combined with delight that our grandfathers felt on sight of the first devil-car, and recognizes to what
a degree the invention of the petrol-engine has changed and is
gradually strangling our whole culture. This is an obsession if
ever there was one; and soon the tourist organizations of all
Mediterranean countries will be forced to print and issue a map
of all the marvellous beaches ruined by oil slicks.

To return to the labyrinth; is it relevant that the famous
double axe was called *labrys*, and that the name of the labyrinth

was derived from it? Earlier folklorists, such as J. C. Lawson, were perfectly content to see the double axe as a sort of nuclear sceptre wielded by Zeus who, as top god, had the right to inflict top punishments. It represented the lightning which is such a feature of the Greek winter, a winter which specializes in extra-ordinary electrical storms of almost tropical intensity; trees are stripped with a single ripping noise like torn calico, balls of electricity roll about along the ground. Both in Corfu and Rhodes, and once in Kalymnos, I left the house open during a storm, and these violent balls of haze rolled softly through it and out into the garden again. The peasants fear these storms very much, not only because one could get struck by a lightning flash, but also because sometimes they turn to hailstorms, with huge chunks of ice capable of wounding a mule and knocking you senseless. Zeus, in modern belief, has given place to the word for god, but is a sort of personified god they think of, for when it suddenly thunders, a peasant will say, 'God thunders, god lightning-flashes.' Indeed he is not very far from Zeus, the modern peasant's god. Well, in earlier days the double axe seemed to explain itself along these lines. More sophisticated, and perhaps more penetrating, is the observation of a recent archaeologist (Jacquetta Hawkes): 'Its shape, the double tri-angle, was widely used as a sign for women, and the shaft sunk through the central perforation affords an effective piece of sexual imagery.'

The subject is still bedevilled by controversy. I write these lines in an attempt to present a more or less coherent picture of the issues raised by the discovery of Knossos.

An anecdote which is pleasing, beguiling, and perhaps instructive, concerns the marriage of Schliemann, who in mid-career suddenly felt the need for a wife by his side. He had nobody particular in mind but, with his heartfelt passion for Greece, felt that the ideal would be a Greek wife. He pondered the matter, examined all the statues in the museums, and finally announced that he would offer his hand in marriage to the first girl who could recite the *Iliad* entire, without a single fault. He was taking a chance, but the whole of this noble German's life had been built upon such chances – right from the day when he heard a drunken miller in a grog shop recite some lines of Homer, and felt the strange stirring in the breast which comes only to those who have heard the voice of their vocation speak. Now all Athens was in a ferment, for the Greeks love lotteries, competitions and challenges. The *Iliad* went out of print; everywhere was heard the humming of voices as the girls of Athens started to learn their lines. Many were pipped at the post, many were faulted on a caesura or thrown by a rough breathing, as that queer microdot above an initial vowel is called. The list grew shorter, until at last Schliemann's future bride appeared on the scene, to recite the whole poem at one go, perhaps even without drawing breath! She was not only word-perfect; she was one of the most beautiful girls in Athens! His luck had held firm.

Though he was getting on in years, Schliemann was regarded as a great catch; his fame was world-wide, and in Greece he had become almost as much an adopted national hero as Byron. It is understandable – he was restoring to the Greeks the true historic image of themselves as descendants of the ancients; a role that had been denied them for centuries. Suddenly, here was the truth – the real Agamemnon, so to speak, and not just a dramatic figment of the imagination. The wedding struck a sympathetic spark in every Greek breast. Schliemann had given the lie to the otiose Professor Fallermayer who, in his celebrated essay, 'stoutly maintained that the modern inhabitants of Greece have practically no claim to the name of Hellenes, but come of a stock Slavonic in the main, though crossbred with the offscourings of many peoples'. According to him the facts of the case could not be slighted. From the middle of the sixth century onwards, successive hordes of Slavonic invaders swept over Greece, driving the local populations into the more remote corners of the land. Slav supremacy lasted until the end of the tenth century but, already in the middle of the eighth, the great pest of 746 had caused such depredation that the historian Constantine Porphyrogenitus says categorically 'the whole country had become Slavonic and was occupied by foreigners'. J. C. Lawson, in his admirable essay on the modern folklore and ancient religious beliefs of the Greeks, counter-attacks strongly as follows:

In the islands of the Aegean and the promontory of Maina, into which the Slavs never penetrated, the ancient Hellenic physical types are far commoner than in the rest of the Peloponnesus or in northern Greece. Not a little of the charm of Tinos or Skyros or Mykonos lies in the fact that the grand and impassive beauty of the earlier Greek sculpture may be seen in the living figures and faces of men and women. If anyone would see in the flesh the burly black-bearded type idealized in a Heracles he need but go south to the Peloponnesus . . . where he will find not merely an occasional example but a whole tribe of swarthy warriors.

You will find many an echo of this observation in the villages of Crete, even though you are briefly passing through; and if you have the time and patience to attend a Greek wedding or a Greek funeral with its terrifying keening, you will have no doubt that these people are the descendants of the ancients who have kept their ethos and their spiritual salt intact because of the purity and intricacy of their native tongue.

Even if your time is limited, if you use it properly, the impressions you gather should fall into place and permit you to see beyond the tragic 'modernization' of the towns with its ugliness. A traveller of modest means and limited to a few days in the island should go to Heracleion and find a modest perch in a small hotel. He will find that Knossos is a longish walk, but five miles or so is nothing if one is curious to gather one's own impressions. There is of course a bus, nowadays there are taxis galore. The distance of Phaestos need not daunt him either, for there is an early-morning bus there from Heracleion and a late-evening bus back. It is about twenty miles away on the southern shoulder, but it has the added attraction that the journey there will make you pass through a magnificent section of the Cretan countryside. Of the two sites it is, for me, the most evocative in its brooding stillness, in the light airs from the sea which cradle it, and from the shadows of high cloud which roll across it. It is uncomfortably full of suggestive mysteries, which produce a feeling that the guide book with its careful, factual approach does not suggest. To camp out here in a fierce thunderstorm, and to awake frozen in a dense dew which has condensed on your blankets like a sheet of mercury is the sort of experience which every camper will relish, but the swift tinges of rheumatism that follow from damp clothes is no joke. By the road among the olives, a peasant has lit a fire with olive trimmings; he jovially welcomes you and helps dry your kit, plying you the while with gasps of *tsikudi* and slabs of brown crust. When you are ready to set off you offer him money; he looks shocked and aggrieved, and puts your hand away as if it held a sword. The quiet ruins rest on your tired shoulder-blades as you march in the deep dust – you feel the weight of a message from the past which you have not been able to decipher. The experience is dense and exciting, but you would be at a loss to say why or in what manner. Phaestos! It is one of those places which mark you.

To revert for a moment to the vexing question of the labyrinth, it is important to make a distinction between a man-made maze and a labyrinth constructed by nature; and the natural geological labyrinth situated near Gortyna has for long been a candidate for the honour of being the original lair of the Minotaur. Sceptics have declared that it is simply an abandoned quarry with a few corridors but, while I have not completely explored it myself – for lack of an Ariadne and a ball of thread – I think it is more suggestive than that.

The most succinct and accurate description of this singular geological formation comes from the pen of that energetic and endearing Victorian divine, the Reverend Tozer, whose detailed, factual travel books enjoyed a great appeal during the last century. He says:

> Our host, Captain George, undertook to be our guide and accordingly next morning we started in his company and, fording the stream close under the Acropolis of Gortyna, ascended the hills towards the north-west and in an hour's time reached the place . . . It is entered by an aperture of no great size in the mountainside, where the rocks are of clayey limestone, forming horizontal layers; and inside we found what looks almost like a flat roof, while chambers and passages run off from the entrance in various directions . . . We were furnished each with a taper and descended by a passage on both sides of which the fallen stones had been piled up; the roof above us varied from four to sixteen feet in height. Winding about, we came to an upright stone, the work of a modern Ariadne, set there to show the way, for at intervals other passages branched off the main one, and anyone who entered without a light would be hopelessly lost. Captain George described to us how for three years during the late war (1867–9) the Christian inhabitants of the neighbouring villages, to the number of five hundred, and he among them, had lived there as their predecessors had done during the former insurrection, to escape the Turks who had burned their homes and carried off their flocks and herds . . .

I can vouch for the accuracy of his description and also for the fact that the place is known as 'The Labyrinth' in the local speech. To the best of my knowledge the whole of it has never been explored, though the villagers thereabouts claim that the internal network of corridors spans an area of some ten square kilometres. One must, as always, subtract a bit of peasant exaggeration, but nevertheless the place is impressive – in places like a series of small cathedrals – and so well ventilated that I am not sure one could not trace the corridors with smoke, which always follows the direction of the air. Once again, however, there is disagreement among scholars about the true history of the place. Of course the whole surface of these volcanic islands from Sicily to Cyprus is simply a cap of metamorphic limestone, punctured everywhere by successive volcanic explosions, and pock-marked like an old piecrust. It is not the only cave system in a Greek island – I know of a dozen. But there seems to be nothing of the same size, in such tantalizing juxtaposition with a historic reference – nor anything as worthy as a Minotaur's haunt. (The limestone crust over most Greek islands certainly accounts for the way that sound carries over great distances; the whole place is like a drum, responsive to every snatch of noise.)

It would be an exciting thing to explore this Gortyna labyrinth with professional care; perhaps by the time these lines are printed the Speleologists' Club of Athens will have done so and printed their findings.

One last brief thought before leaving the ancient history of the island with all its conundrums – a thought devoted to the scripts. Here again one wishes that the whole subject had been fully explored, and the findings clearly tabulated. Alas! Despite all the great enthusiasm for the Michael Ventris 'breakthrough' into an interpretation of the script called Linear B, opinions seem still to be divided as to its veracity.

Nothing could better illustrate the sharp division of thinking about the history of Minoan Crete than the fact that the *Encyclopaedia Britannica* carries two articles concerned with it, one of which clearly accepts the authenticity of Ventris's discovery, while the second seems to cast doubts upon it. The ordinary reader or visitor will not pay much attention to these learned differences. But if Ventris is right, it is most exciting to find, among the deciphered words, ones which are in daily use in any Greek village today (*toson* meaning 'so much'; *kreesos* meaning 'gold'; *eruthros* meaning 'red'; *selinon* meaning 'celery'). There are also some proper names which strike a chord – Theseus, Hector, Alexandra and Theodora. Myself, I hope that Ventris is correct though I have not the scholarship to assert that he is.

The earliest seals, tags or tallies, with their pictographic signs, hinted at an Egyptian influence. Linear A and Linear B came later, and are thus probably more sophisticated. While A remains undeciphered, the brilliant suggestions of Ventris gave great hopes for a decoding of Linear B, and some progress was made along the lines of his suggestions. The real disappointment has nothing to do with the accuracy or the errors of his interpretation – it is that what has so far been decoded is relatively uninteresting. We have so to speak tumbled into a Minoan stockroom, among registers which tabulate the stock held in these depots. No poems, alas, or proclamations, or religious documents, which might give us a clue as to how these far-off people thought or felt about the universe.

If history is eloquent though mute, the poets themselves are far from mute, and the Cretan poet deserves to be heard on his native soil. Here is one whose name is now world-famous. 'This Cretan landscape seemed to him like good prose; well-fashioned, economical, shorn of excessive riches, powerful and controlled . . . It said what it had to say with manly austerity. But between its austere lines you could discern an unexpected sensitivity and tenderness – the lemons and oranges smelt sweet in sheltered hollows, and beyond, from the boundless sea, came an endless stream of poetry.' The writer is Kazanzakis,

perhaps the most representative Cretan mind of today, expressing strange yearnings for mystical revelation, and a stranger
belief in the heroic future of man. There are few Cretan writers
or artists who have done work of European stature. This is not
the fault of the Cretan soul and mind, which is both poetical
and productive; it is the fault of the history that has torn up the
land, annihilated the populations, driven the clans into hiding.
There has been no peace, in which the arts of leisure and introspection could flourish; it is hard to be an artist with a loaded
pistol in one hand. Nevertheless, whenever chance offered the
Cretans a breather, they took it, and men like Kazanzakis and
Prevelakis, though they spent much of their maturity abroad in
Athens and elsewhere, remained obstinately Cretan-souled to
the end. It is doubtful whether someone who is not an ardent
Philhellene will find much literature to read about Crete, except
the really great book *Zorba*, which is a marvellous evocation of
a landscape, and a sketch of a temperament as validly Greek as
that of Odysseus himself. It is a captivating book, which should
be read in the island if possible or immediately after returning
home.

There are other good books about the island, but they are
mostly by foreigners. The home-grown article is good in quality
but, apart from one very big novel by Prevelakis, there is not
much of it. The average reader or traveller will probably not
surmount the longueurs of the national poem, *The Erotokritos*,
though he will, if he dips, find much to admire in it. Nor does it
seem strange that this is a poem of courtly love, which might
have been made in Toulouse by French troubadours. The heroic
style is Cretan *par excellence*, and the village poets, often blind,
wandering bards, have carried it all over the island with them –
and far afield, selling the texts of their songs and recitations in
little chap-books printed in other corners of Greece. They sing
of courtly virtue – *levendia*, which is simply the modern word

for Homer's *arete*. And the feminine version of the word describes the virtue of a girl not only supremely beautiful but valiant and heroic – a real mate fit for a *levendis*. It is a beautiful word – *levendissa* – and when a Greek wants to compliment you on your wife or your sister, or express a genuine and profound admiration for the noble stamp of her mind, he will use the word. Without girls of this heroic mould it is doubtful whether Crete, or for that matter Greece itself, would have kept on constantly renewing its poetic image, and in the long wars and insurrections there are as many women heroes as there are men – whose exploits were no less dazzling than those of their men.

This can best be appreciated in the folk-poems, which sometimes lilt and swing, and at others are cobbled by the patient drone of the bagpipes. The verse, with its long hopping lines – the words are so long in Greek – sounds as if it were skimmed across the tongue, like pebbles skimmed upon a calm sea. The imagery is all taken from the much beloved scenes around the singer – the Cretan landscape. He writes of what he best knows and feels.

The rhyme-schemes and imagery have that sweet, pastoral quality which we tend to associate with Theocritus; but if Cretan verse seems somehow wilder and less sophisticated, that is because of the musical intrusion of Asiatic quarter-tones. What is particularly interesting to the student is that so many of the words are ancient ones, still doing duty in the spoken demotic of today; words which might have strayed out of a Greek anthology. Apart from the marriage and christening poems, and the straight love poems, there are others that are darker, sadder. There is quite a tradition of poems devoted to exile, which is not surprising, for Cretans were often carried off and sold into slavery just like the African negroes. I am reminded of the haunting, negro songs of exile when I hear these long, sometimes sobbing, tunes about *xenitia*, and I am also reminded that exile is one of the most painful things to inflict on a Greek. *Pace* the Turks who extorted their yearly levy of young boys just as the Minotaur did long ago – the impoverished economy of Greece in general forces people to go abroad to earn a living. But they always come back. Songs like these are also mixed with a group of songs called the *Amanedes* – or 'Alas' songs, adapted from Turkish models and expressing a sort of hopeless *Weltschmertz* of a romantic kind, that is associated with every kind of deception and disappointment. (In common speech, too, one hears 'Aman-Aman' said often, with a wagging of the head; it is sorrow with a wide-angle lens.)

Of the most ordinary and popular rhyme-forms, the *mantinades* corresponds roughly to our popular limerick, and copes with all moods and behaviours. The Greek rhyme is competitive, too, and every village has its prize versifier, capable in an open contest (liberally dosed with wine or cognac) of 'capping' a rival's lines and carrying off a trophy for his village. In the villages of Cyprus, the Cyprus Radio organized fully fledged Eisteddfods up on the mountain of Troodos, where once a year there was a cup-tie, so to speak, involving all the bards of the island. It was an impressive sight, for the old singers dressed up in full rig, just as the Scots pipers would in similar circumstances. Microphones were provided. There were times, too, when tempers frayed under a particularly nasty satirical thrust, and one was afraid that one of the contestants might receive a crack over the head with the microphone-boom. The contest was widely followed, and each champion took a dozen bus-loads of fans with him for the finals. The red thick wine *Commanderia* is excellent for oiling the gullet and the creative soul, and we made some memorable films of these contests for our archives.

Cherries for lips, then, almonds for skin turned white under the stress of passion, olives for dark eyes, the night sky scattered with stars like flour, young men in embroidered waistcoats with waists slender as violins dancing the handkerchief-dance before a chosen girl . . . All this is still there today – a delight not only to the visitor but also to the philologist. The dialect is strange, the accent rocky and abrupt; you can know Greek quite well and still not understand what a Cretan villager says to you.

You may be safe in thinking that it is always something hospitable; usually it is a summons to have a shot of *tsikudi* in the local tavern and recount all. In the old days, when a stranger entered an island village, he was confronted by a Homeric scene; the clients in the café crowded into the street, holding their chairs, and sat down in a semicircle, involuntarily turning his entry into a kind of theatrical performance. Embarrassed and flushed, ashamed of his inadequate Greek, and full of good intentions, he strayed about like a lost camel in front of fifty pairs of beady dark eyes – feeling like some enticing dwarf for whom they had waited a century. Then he would notice that in front of the theatre two chairs had been placed, one for himself, and one for his wife. Beckoned, he would weakly sit down. It was then, in the tones of a herald in an ancient Greek play, that the mayor (or the oldest among the oldsters) would address him with the historic, 'You are a stranger?' 'Yes!' 'What news from *Europe*?' This has happened to me almost everywhere in Greece; the smaller the village, the more I expected it. What is most striking is the reference to 'Europe'; as if Europe were as far away as the moon. And, when conversation became general, one was always astonished to find that one had to do with thirty old gentlemen who were up to date with the happenings of that strange world, Europe. They knew when a Government had fallen, and in their own pronunciation they knew the names of Attlee, De Gaulle and so on . . . It seemed somehow strange to find oneself involved in an argument about the fate of the pound sterling or the franc in a place like this – a mountain village, say, in Crete or Rhodes, with eagles combing the high

heaven and a blissful northern wind painting Chiricos everywhere on the main deep. How strange and thin it sounded – the
fate of the British Labour Party amid all this glamour of nature!

Life in the small villages is as horrible as the same sort of life
in far Wales or far Scotland; full of bigotry and ignorance, and
the perennial low IQ, which spells death to art. It is a horrible
life, not only full of physical privations but of intellectual stran-
gulation, the life of a remote village in Greece. If I never regret-
ted it, and really managed to enjoy it, this was because I was
fascinated by the language and the people, and buoyed up by
the marvellous classical landscape which is so full of magic that
it wallpapers even your dreams. People who don't have precise
things to do or study, or who are in need of outside stimulus
and crowds, will find that life in a Greek village will turn them
claustrophobic within a year. It is quite understandable; for a
Greek villager, life in Surbiton would do the same. Here I must
add that the Greek race is the only one I have so far come across
in which people can actually pine away and die from home-
sickness; I have witnessed it more than once. Nostalgia, by the
way, is an ancient Greek word still in full use. Pronounced *nos
tal ghea*, it still means what it says. The penultimate symbol is
long.

Home is where the heart is, says Euripedes, and even Greece,
that rocky heap of wave-worn grey stones, welcomes its children back with open arms. The Cretans will remind you that a
fine style does not depend on riches: indeed if you knew the
mean yearly income of the old Zeus-like gentleman in the pub
who insists on paying for your drinks, you would feel humbled
by his vehement assertion that, for the Greek, strangers are
closer than brothers, and life must be taken aristocratically, by
the horns.

Atmosphere for atmosphere, I feel much more mystery and
splendour about Phaestos than Knossos. I think most people

would agree. The site is a honeyed one for summer breezes, and hard by on a westward tack lies the little close of Hagia Triada in its green curves of sward; there is a wisp of a Byzantine chapel and a few sketchily dug-up houses. The view is as good as from Phaestos itself, and through the verdant plain below a small river called Giophoros – 'earthbringer' – prettily potters. This is apparently the St Ives of the Minoans; here they built a villa and sent the children to spend their summers. This impression seems right when you are there, and it is supported by factual evidence, since many of the richest and most elaborate finds have come from hereabouts. These include the mysterious Phaestos Disc, which is so strange and beautiful; inevitably, it too remains undeciphered, and the scholars think it came originally from Asia Minor. About seven inches in diameter, it is imprinted with pictographs on both sides, which move inwards, spirally, upon the centre. Date about 1600 BC. Does it have to do with Babylonian astrology? Is it a mandala? That it has magical powers I am sure; a Greek painter friend blew up a photograph of it and incorporated it into an icon for his island house. He assures me that one can wish upon it with success, and there are several people who claim that their lives (maybe a misprint for 'wives') have been completely changed by praying to it. I cannot vouch for this claim; but the little disc is so beautiful that I am surprised artists have not made more play with it, as an illustration to brochures – in the way they have with the gold mask of Agamemnon. More interesting still, it is an almost unique example of printing signs with movable type.

The rain has stopped, the clouds have broken; the vault of blue spreads out like a fan, the blue decomposing into that ultimate violet light which makes everything Greek seem holy, natural and familiar. In Greece one has the desire to bathe in the sky. You want to rid yourself of your clothes, take a running leap and vault into the blue. You want to float in the air like an angel or lie in the grass rigid and enjoy the cataleptic trance. Stone and sky, they marry here . . .

HENRY MILLER

It is always the light that gets them.

It is fair to say, though, that if we find so many puzzles and enigmas in Crete, the modern peasant, pressed by the economies of life into becoming a waiter, has to snatch up a sort of phonetic ghost of a foreign tongue which is often the cause of diverting mistakes – though not for him. In Aghios Nikolaos, a barman tried to find me a pair of blue jeans, which he insisted on pronouncing 'gins'; I paid no attention at first, and then in a later conversation I suddenly saw that this man, who spent his life pouring out pink gins, had conceived a perfectly rational echo-association with blue jeans. For him the Anglo-Saxon soul hovered between the two poles of pink and blue gins; it was his form of Linear B. And of course we make the same sort of mistakes, or worse, in Greek. You will not have spent long in Greece before your children ask plaintively why it is that the Greeks seem to talk of nothing but teapots; it seems to be a national obsession, cropping up in almost every conversation. The truth is that the absurd Greek word for 'nothing' is 'tipoty'.

I first saw Chanea in April 1940 during a perilous voyage in a shaky, leaky *caique* which was down a bit by the stern; I was one of about fifty refugees from Kalamata, and my destination was supposed to be Egypt via Crete. It was a miracle we were not Stuka'd during the night, for our engine belched clouds of sparks into the sky and must have pinpointed us clearly. Many similar craft on the same journey that night did not have our luck and were sunk with all hands. However, my daughter snoozed in her basket like a loaf of bread between two badly wounded men we had picked up; and I was later too preoccupied with washing her nappies at the public washery in Cythera to give much thought to Venus Anadyomene. Chanea was in a state of disarray, or at least our forces were; except for the New Zealanders who arrived in top trim, with oil rags round their bolts, hats on, and a good book under their arms. There was little to be done, and I was glad when we were whisked out into Egypt some time later; but I won't forget the cruiser *York* lying almost on her side in Suda Bay, firing at the Stukas with the last usable big gun. As a small-boat owner, and a sketchy but adequate sailor, I found this an ignominious way to arrive in the kingdom of Minos; and I longed for a chance to visit Crete in a boat – a wish which so far has not been granted. However, during the last war, I learned so much small-boat lore from the people who were putting agents ashore or collecting them at all times, night or day, in winter or summer, that I realize no account of the island would be really complete without a warning about its navigational problems. Crete is a devil for small boats, and an anxiety even for largish ones.

I must insert here a warning from somebody far more competent to give one than myself – Ernle Bradford, that enviable mixture of sea-dog, poet and scholar who has really made the Mediterranean his own back garden, and whose books are captivating. He writes:

Compared with many a smaller island, Crete is still a difficult place for those who come here in their own boats. There is Kissamo, Chanea and Suda Bay (of evil memory) to the west, then there is little between Retimo and Heracleion. To the east, in the gulf of Mirabella, there is the anchorage of Spinalonga, where a friend spent a whole winter repairing his boat. I have not been to Spinalonga myself but if solitude and primitive conditions, coupled with a good anchorage appeal, then it is a fine place to stay. On the south coast I know only Port Matala, ideal for visiting Phaestos . . . As always along the southern coast one must keep an eye out for clouds gathering on the mountain peaks. Squalls white or black, bursting down from the islands are a regular feature in the Aegean. But the Cretan squalls are something that no-one who has experienced them is ever likely to forget.

So much for the sea; as far as the land is concerned one should offer an honourable mention to the two hideouts of Zeus, without taking sides. Between the White Mountains and the Lassithi ranges, there is only a sort of symbolic difference which is the result of the poetic echo which *Ta Lefka Ori* give off to the Cretan. This great harp of rocks is a-dazzle with snow all winter – the chief peaks crowd up to over two thousand metres – and it spells the secrecy and silence which lie at the heart of the Cretan soul. Solitude, silence and whiteness; this is the inviolate stronghold of the Cretan spirit, and thus the most likely nursery for Zeus. The whole western end of the island is dominated by them, all skylines bend to their whiteness, all ballad singers tune in to their image.

The great massif is the largest single mountain block in Crete; and high up there, hidden from the plains, is a plateau which seems like the roof of the world. It is some five kilometres in diameter but seems much more. It is surrounded by a semicircle of angular, stony, limestone hills like wardens. This is called Omalos and, while no springs burst into the charmed circle, the winter rains are drained off through blowholes set like gills at the northern end, where the road enters through a forbidding pass. Through another short pass one comes to the mysterious gorge of Samaria, which has always had a mixed reception from visitors; some think it is just a natural feature and without interest, others find it one of the most sinister corners of Christendom – as I do. I can't recall anything as long or as spectacular in Europe, though perhaps Switzerland may have something like it. There is a twisting path down to the sea which is eighteen kilometres in length and which varies in diameter, its narrowest being three metres; the walls close in and, if your donkey is heavily laden, they will scrape and strip him. Why is there no great legend (Eurydice-like) about this singular Hades-like descent into the gorge of Samaria? Or is there one I don't know about? At all events the walk is both long and a bit dangerous because of the surfaces. One day, one supposes, all this area will become a national game reserve where tourists, with trained ghillies, will spy on the shy chamois. Halfway down the gorge is deserted little Samaria, with its silent, backwards fourteenth-century church of St Mary. Light a candle. Cross yourself.

As far as the towns are concerned, both Chanea and Heracleion have a few choice corners, but in the main I have always found them charmless; they are dusty and windy, and fairly throb during the summer heats. In Heracleion, the old town is still clearly demarcated by the Venetian walls, though they are now almost overgrown in parts and have been pierced for wider roads. Indeed high up on the battlements, a crazy colony has grown up, where people live in shacks with their livestock and even manage a spot of market gardening. It presents an improbable sort of picture (sometimes a donkey appears in the sky), which has much of the charm one associates with those refugee towns which sprang up around Athens after the Asia Minor disaster – all fashioned in old kerosene-oil tins, but beautifully planned and contrived for simple gypsy-style life.

You will, however, have more to do with Heracleion than Chanea because of the museum and the proximity of Knossos; not to mention the fine little Cretan Museum which has a marvellous display of costumes with intricate Byzantine-influenced decoration. Sumptuous and bold in style, yet exquisite in taste, these marvellous creations of the peasant mind fill one with respect.

Once you have made yourself familiar with the Mycenean treasures and enjoyed the ruins of Knossos, you may find yourself faintly doubting the authenticity of the later restorations. In fact, there has been a good case made out against Sir Arthur Evans, not for falsifying but for exaggerating when it came to restoring frescoes. He had fallen in love with his dream-child – and of course there is no doubt of the greatness of his discovery from an historical point of view. His critics have claimed that he jazzed-up the site with unwarrantable and specious reconstructions, and that he attached far too great an aesthetic importance to things Minoan. The Minoans did not produce (or so far have not) one single sculpture which seriously rivalled the best that Egypt or indeed the Greek mainland had already done. The little snake-goddess is charming and pleasant as a piece of folklore but not really impressive as sculpture. The jewelry does not compare with Egyptian, nor with the hoards found at Mycenae, in aesthetic value. What remains? The artistic reputation of the Minoans rests upon the frescoes, and it is here precisely that the criticism falls most sharply. Evans used two ghosts (one might say spectres) who faithfully copied down what he told them to; one was Dutch and one Swiss. Their work smells of the twentyish *art nouveau* which was the rage in Paris when they were young – a rage which cubism finally blitzed, though it still hung on furtively as the cobwebs do in the back of an interior decorator's mind. At Knossos the Evans restorations so much took on this style that Paul Morand was excited to find Russian ballet choreography had been influenced by Crete (the opposite was true!). And now, just as *art nouveau* seems to us *passé*, so do the ladies of Knossos.

Knossos is worth a second visit to settle your mind. Did Evans exaggerate unpardonably or not? It is something worth troubling about, though this is a purely aesthetic consideration in no way reflecting on the greatness of Evans or on the value of his work.

Whatever doubts one may have about the order in which successive waves of men came washing into Crete, the Minoan finds constitute a great historical anchor for the historians. The codification of the laws is one department in which the Cretans made history, for the earliest written legal document in Europe (though of course of another period) is the great inscription on stone of the Law of Gortys. Its discovery was one of those splendid accidents which I always feel are predestined. In the wall of a water-mill near the ruined church of St Titus at Gortys, a visiting German antiquary discovered a large stone with a long inscription which he copied out. Succeeding visitors found more stones embedded in the water channels and, after a long fight with the recalcitrant peasant who owned the land, managed to assemble a reasonable text of this great code. The inscription was written in twelve columns, each originally five blocks high, of which we only have four. Each column was about five feet high. The text consists of a series of laws relating to citizenship, marriage, tenure of property and inheritance. Though incomplete, it gives us an incomparable insight into the way people lived at a remote time (they are dated the first half of the fifth century BC). Many of the laws found their way into the elaborate Roman code and thence into our modern codifications. For example, the property rights of women, both married and divorced, are clearly enunciated: a wife's dowry and inheritance remained subject to her control and could not be sold or used as a security by her husband. Divorce was the right of married couples, at the instigation of either party, and seems to have been relatively common – as with us. A divorced wife could, if the husband had been the cause of the divorce, claim back any property which she had brought to her husband, together with half the produce from her own property. The rights of both serfs and slaves were carefully defined.

Important too is the safeguarding of property interests. In

cases of adoption, for example, the rights of inheritance were precisely defined; an adopted son could become sole heir if there were no legitimate sons; otherwise he took a daughter's share in the estate. The division of the population into age groups, before and after puberty, and the age of full citizenship, was laid down clearly. Regulations were promulgated for the membership of the Dorian tribes and of the brotherhoods. Sharp distinctions between the various classes were the order of the day – as can be seen by the variations in the scale of fines payable for the same offence. Legal credence given to witnesses varied with social status – that of free men being the only evidence acceptable in certain cases. The culture was one in which the dice were loaded in favour of privilege. For example, for an offence such as rape, the fine levied was far heavier for the violation of a free woman than of a serf, which in turn was heavier than for that of a slave. On the other hand most offences were punishable by fines or by restitution, and no barbaric penalties seem to have been envisaged by the code. There is no mention of the death penalty.

Traditionally, Chanea is the home of the quince, and its quince *compote* has always been a famous local comestible. I also remember Chanea as greener and less dusty than other towns. There are small and pleasant prospects, where one can sit over an *ouzo* and think about nothing – just feeling the sunlight on your fingers, and tasting it in your glass. Traditionally, too, its inhabitants are thought more cosmopolitan and outward-looking than most Cretans. Certainly, they are sufficiently evolved (to use a word in its French sense) to make jokes about the duller aspects of the island character.

One of these, which illustrates Cretan hard-headedness, can be told with decency since it comes from a Cretan himself. During a parachute course in the Middle East the instructor, jump-training a group of commandos from various islands, saw one of them fumble with his harness and hesitate to advance into the bay for the jump. Incautiously, he made a pleasantry – asking if the novice was scared. The response was unexpected. 'Scared?' cried the young man. 'You dare to tell a Cretan that he is scared? I'll show you who is scared.' He unhooked his safety harness altogether and jumped to his certain death. So be careful what jokes you make when you are in Crete.

The Cretan is famous for his stubbornness and his national pride, which almost matches that of the Spaniard; he feels about Athens very much what a Sicilian feels about Rome. If in some remote village, you happen to strike a fiesta evening with some village dancing, look out for the Butcher's Dance (*Hasapiko*) which is performed with every sort of knife, even those big ones shaped like cutlasses. Advancing and retreating, the dancers clash knives until the sparks strike, and they utter roars and snarls which suggest that their enmity is not imitated but real. *Hasapiko* gives you a disturbing insight into the savage buried passions which stir the breasts of the villagers in these remote corners of the big island. Hundreds of years of sieges and battles and famines have gone to make up this unyielding and obdurate character, with all its limitations as well. I once asked a friend who had spent two whole winters as a commando in Crete what had made the job he had done hardest. I expected some stock answer – the cold and chilblains, or fear of the enemy. But no; the hardest thing to cope with, he said, was the lack of conversation. There were only two permissible topics for men – the performance of pistols or small arms, and the cut of boots. This was worse than the Cavalry Club, he added; and went on to say that if one dared to open a book, there would be alarmed looks all round – you must be sickening for something; a friend would ask, 'Feeling off colour, old man?' But I doubt if remote village communities would be any different from those of the Cretan shepherds living on Mount Ida.

A modern Greek poet has called the Cretans a people of stone – but he didn't mean stony-hearted; one must remember that the crop-area of the island amounts to only three-eighths of the total space, and that the remainder of the country is unsuitable for any sort of cultivation. This bony land, with its uncompromising mountain slopes, pastures three-quarters of a million sheep and goats, which forever scramble and munch among the rocks of the thin *garrigues*. Hence overgrazing with all its dangers, and whole sectors of good land invaded by unpalatable spiny plants and shrubs. The high mountain pastures cannot be used in winter because of the snow, so that lowland grazing is obligatory. In addition to the half-million flock animals there is a further quarter-million of domestic sheep and goats, approximately three per farm family. These chosen members of the caprine world are, by contrast, cosseted; they shelter under the family roof at night, and by day they are towed about by the children and fed upon whatever greenery comes to hand. Hence the enormous damage they inflict upon the land. However, they provide enough milk to meet the family requirements in dairy products like cheese and yoghurt. It is a tragic situation, for the goat is the scourge of Greece, and there seems no way that it can be abolished. At any rate, just after World War II, I saw a re-afforestation plan for Greece which was, I think, sponsored by UNRRA or some such international body. It was an extremely comprehensive study; it clearly promised that the Greek forests could become as they were in ancient times within the space of some eighty years, and the plan argued great financial prosperity for the country if carried out. The only proviso was that the goat must go but the Athens Government could see no way of bringing this about without risking trouble with the public.

I remember, too, trying to discuss this plan with some villagers, when I visited, many years ago, the island of Spinalonga
(Longthorn), where I was surprised to find some good wine in a
tavern and some fresh mullet. The idea was greeted with con-
sternation – and the promise of long-term benefits with utter
scepticism. It was an autumn day of high wind and racing
clouds, with a thunderhead sea; I did not at that time notice the
harbour amenities of Spinalonga. It used in the past to be a
leper colony; when I first went to Greece there was a significant
number of leprosy sufferers, and there were several little settlements for them. Spina was one. After the last war the disease
seemed to decrease dramatically, perhaps with new treatments,
and the island returned to itself again. There is a pleasant Venetian fortress on an islet which protects the bay opening. Here
we waited for a squall to die away with the evening calms, while
our skipper found a chapel to pray in and to make advances to
the local saint whose name I forget. By dint of much crossing
himself backwards, as is the Greek Orthodox fashion, he
managed to prevail upon him at last and we had a smooth
passage.

Recalling that forgotten saint, I am reminded that I have said
nothing about icon painting – a vexing subject, though one
which should not be completely ignored, since Crete has of late
come to the fore with her recently discovered (they were always
there, but nobody cared before) church paintings and icons. It
is difficult to know exactly how one should evaluate and
appreciate an icon; certainly not in the same way as one does an
Italian primitive or a Renaissance church painting, because
there one is dealing with individual artists. With icons, one is
dealing always with a school; its range of impact seems much
less, and much more remote, than that of Italian painters. Icons
convey a delightful smokiness to the dignified interiors of
Byzantine churches, with their massive displays of convoluted

silver and copper decorations and candlesticks; and I can well understand one wanting to have a fine icon or two on one's own walls. But just what criteria one uses in judging them I do not know, and I have a feeling that the subject has not yet been opened up by critics, whose judgments might help us to form our own taste and appreciation for these delightful *eidola*. Myself, I always see them with Olympian rather than Christian protagonists, and I think they must have hung as charms in the ancient Acropolis – to be coaxed, invoked and implored. Or threatened, as they are still. Ask St Spiridion if he hasn't been threatened more than once, or St Nicholas or Poseidon (there is little real difference to the peasant mind).

Saints, like men, can become lazy and fail in their duties; it may be necessary sometimes to call them to order. As late as the last century in the Italian Abruzzi there lingered a custom which sounds very ancient. When the weather was not what it should be, or when a harvest turned out particularly badly, the statue of the village saint in the local church was carried out into the fields and ceremonially whipped. Nor were these Italian peasants the only ones to retain the sense of magic in their dealings with heavenly matters. Much the same sort of thing must have gone on in the mind of an eminent English archaeologist of whom I was told. He lived in Greece before the last war. He always carried an ash-plant in his car; for the slightest defection he would raise the bonnet and administer a smart thrashing to the engine. He seriously claimed that this treatment worked nine times out of ten in cases of dumb insolence, to which cars of that remote epoch were prone. The defect was remedied by the chastisement. Someone a little more modern might perhaps have thought of thrashing the chauffeur instead.

I am hunting for the right tone of voice in which to attempt to convey the strangely ambivalent attitude of the Greek peasant towards his patron saint; it is a compound of the personal and sceptical which contains no hint of irreverence or whimsicality. He scolds his saint when things go wrong, as one might scold a business partner who has not been pulling his weight. And he feels so close to his saint that he can allow himself the luxury of a joke at his expense which, to the casual eye, might suggest disbelief in the powers of the *eidolon*. Not so. We spend our time in beseeching our saints and praying to them; the Greek wishes on his saint, and by a man-to-man attitude seeks to coax him into, the appropriate state of mind to grant the wish. He is particularly irritated when he has actually invested something like an *exvoto* in gold or a jewel, and the saint does not come across. I have even heard saints referred to in a most opprobrious fashion – sometimes as 'that stinking old cuckold in the niche'. This is not irreverence, but a kind of superstition that one should not utter praise aloud for fear of igniting the devil. It is on a par with the Evil Eye drill; when you see a beautiful child you must spit thrice and mutter the formula *Na meen avaskathi* ('May she not be bewitched'). In ancient times certain deities had to be approached counter-clockwise, so to speak; there used to be a shrine to Heracles in Rhodian Lindos which could only be approached by walking backwards, throwing stones, and uttering the worst curses and blasphemies. The god would not respond to any other kind of blandishment.

It is not likely that you will take your leave of Crete with the happy feeling that you have come to grips with, and solved, any of the tantalizing problems it presents – whether those concerned with Minoan dating, the invasions of Mycenae, or the date of the Dorian epoch. It is pitiable how scanty and enigmatic, not to mention self-contradictory, the available materials are. But this provides a rich and muddled compost in which archaeologists and prehistorians can flourish; and they must be kept employed, for the best of them bring us enriching theories and discoveries. Nor from the world of fables and semi-fictions

will you feel that you have nailed the Minotaur, or really eluci-
dated the scientific discoveries of Daedalus. It will not be your
fault for, even as far back as Homer, the muddle and overlap-
ping seem pretty constant; he speaks for example of 'a land
called Crete in the midst of the wine-dark sea . . . and in it
many men beyond number and ninety cities. And there is a
mixture of tongues there. There are Achaeans there and stout-
hearted Eteo-Cretans, Cydonians and the wavy-haired Dorians,
and illustrious Pelasgians.'

If he lived at the start of a slightly less muddled epoch, this
was because of the power of the written word. Now, exactly
when the Greeks started to write instead of to pict is still a
matter for speculation. Some recent evidence suggests a date
around 1400 BC. But the flashpoint came when one day they
took over the Phoenician alphabet; the actual borrowing process cannot be either described or dated with any accuracy, but
it signalled the beginning of something momentous – literature! This brings us ourselves closer to the Greeks, for the whole
beginning of our intellectual life and culture is rooted in the
two great poems which sprang from this take-over bid. The
deliberacy and rationality of the act seem beyond doubt, for
the Phoenician sign-system was not simply copied, but adapted
and modified to fit the needs of the Greek tongue, which was
unrelated to the Semitic family group to which the Phoenician
belonged. The pre-Greek invaders of the land had brought with
them a language which belonged to a group of ancient languages; among them Indian (Sanscrit), Persian and Armenian.
Through this vast mesh of historic influences, accompanied by
countless changes and trends and overlappings, the Greek language finally precipitated itself like a rare calx – and then with a
masterstroke one day appropriated an alphabet in which, as if
in a mould, it could marmorealize itself. Written, it also became
a channel for psychological elements of the national character to

stabilize themselves – to clothe themselves in myth and poetry. But here I must catch myself up sharply, for I have referred to a 'national' character quite inadvertently. A quotation from a Cambridge scholar M. I. Finley must put me in my place:

In one respect the ancient Greeks were always a divided people. They entered the Mediterranean world in small groups and even when they settled and took control they remained disunited in their political organization ... Greek settlements were to be found not only all over the area of modern Hellas but also along the Black Sea, on the shores of what is now Turkey, in Southern Italy and Eastern Sicily, the north African coast and the littoral of Southern France. Within this ellipse of some fifteen hundred miles at the poles, there were hundreds and hundreds of communities, often differing in their political structure and always insisting on their separate sovereignties. *Neither then, nor at any time in the ancient world was there a nation, a single national territory under one sovereign rule, called Greece (or any synonym for Greece).*

It recedes and recedes from us, this strange land, until it starts to take its place among historical figments and myths and metaphors – with not reality but a haunting dream as its morphological envelope. It becomes as unreal as a Minoan Age or a Minotaur or a peasant crossing himself backwards, or the old men whose baggy Turkish-style breeches have taken their shape because one day a new saviour will be born of a man and one must not risk bruising the infant's head when it appears ... There is an extraordinary tangle of legends ancient and modern which somehow have the right sort of plangence when you are there, on the spot, sitting in some battered café in Chanea drinking *ouzo* and watching the sun slowly setting upon these grave, poetical abstractions. The stout walls are Venetian. Yesterday, walking by the shore of a small viscous lagoon, I noticed an overpowering smell of rotting iodine; and then herons rose and clanked awkwardly away to the further marshes, uttering their desolate cry which was supposed to be a Turkish word once – but what word had slipped my memory. It is also hard to imagine a siege of twenty-two years, or the extraordinary beauty of hundreds of parachutes falling out of the sky, Icarus fashion, in 1941. Everything exists in an eternal present locked in this extraordinary historic dream which is Crete, which is Greece – a country which has never existed.

By now the visitor will have made his first experiments with the Greek cuisine – so variable in execution that it can convey the impression of being anything between horrible and good-to-fair. Poor countries do not have the money to turn out great chefs but, though one can eat abominably in many parts of Greece, there has been of late a remarkable improvement over-all. The range of choice is limited of course, though the raw materials (as any visit to the fish or fruit market will convince you) are as good as in Naples or Marseilles. What happens to them? There is no general rule. One must work to find one's own palatable restaurant in whichever place one is, and put one's trust in the Greeks only when by some accident of nature they come up with something really good. Though limited, the cuisine has a number of really delicious dishes to its credit. The problem is to find them well cooked, and presented reasonably warm. It is not true that all Greeks are born without taste buds: there are a number of fancy feeders in Athens, who spend their time running from one place to another hunting for that delectable dish they ate last week. It is really astonishing too how the wine can vary from bottle to bottle, how taverns can vary from week to week in their fare. You should always be on the *qui vive*. If you fall upon *sofrito* (meat stew) well done in Corfu, or *souzoukakia* (spitted entrails) in Rhodes, you will catch a glimpse of what would be possible if there were money and time – for the fruit and vegetables and fish are as good as anywhere. Cooks vary, and one needs the patience of Job to put up with this. Yet why does this little character-defect not seem to matter too much? You get over your first vexation rapidly and sink into a resigned mood where you accept whatever comes with equanimity – and so much is really good that does come (lobsters or crayfish in Hydra are examples).

I always remind myself how the peasantry lives between fiestas. When young I shared many an agricultural worker's meal in the shade of a tree. Consisting then of two or three cloves of garlic, a hunk of bread, and a gullet full of wine, it was astonishingly nourishing – particularly the garlic, which chases away all fatigue. There is another reason why the Greeks are confused in their kitchen: tourist authorities have convinced them that northern peoples like the Swedes, Britons or Germans will not come to Greece if there is garlic in the food (and of course it is sometimes true). So the meals come up as shoddy imitations of British Railways' *haute cuisine.* For people who dream of dancing peach to peach on the sun deck, garlic is of course a hazard. What is to be done? I do not know; this non-garlic scourge has now hit the south of France where in the Langue d'Oc the cuisine in the small hotels has become a shambles, because of a few bus-loads of somnolent Swedes or subfusc Germans. Mass catering, they call it, and the hotel keepers (who *do* know how to cook) are up in arms but will do nothing to harm their custom. How will the Greek ever improve his cuisine at this rate?

But the real test is what the Greeks eat at home, and here there is no doubt that they fare well and show both skill and taste. Whenever you are invited to a private house or to an engagement party, say, you are astonished at the variety and tastiness of the food. But it takes a great deal of preparing; always in the background, there is the hovering figure of grandma who has been up since four to start cooking for the feast. The general preference for food in Greece leans a bit towards the *meze* or *amuse gueule*; which is understandable when nearly all the food you eat is partaken of outdoors under a vine. The Greeks like a dozen little dishes with a dozen different things *à la Chinoise*, rather than the heavy structured meal which the French, say, prefer. Moreover their idea of real conviviality is that you and your friends should dip in the same dish . . . The notion is a sound one.

As for drink, the controversial *rezina* has been discussed so often that it seems invidious to do it again. *Rezina* may well taste 'like pure turpentine which has been strained through the socks of a bishop', as someone wrote to me; but it is to be recommended most warmly. You should make a real effort with it, but be warned that it is never as good bottled as it is fresh from the blue cans of the Athenian *Plaka*. It is a perfect adjunct for food which is oil-cooked, and sometimes with oil not too fresh. Its pungent aroma clears the mind and the palate at one blow. Yet it is mild, and you can drink gallons without a hangover; nor does it ever provoke the disgusting, leaden sort of drunkenness that gin does – but rather, high spirits and wit. If you drink *rezina* you will live for ever, and never be a trial to your friends or to waiters. If you really cannot take any pleasure in it, you will find today several good little wines, white and red, which are not only stable but very good to taste. I think immediately of *Santa Elena* (white) and *Naoussa* (red), which are available almost everywhere because their production is high. But some of the monasteries also have good small wines which do not travel. In Santorin I remember once a red wine that came from volcanic soil and was faintly fizzy. It is worthwhile experimenting with the local brew wherever you are. You simply have to present yourself at a wine shop and say gravely, 'I want some samples,' and a glass is produced and you are invited to sit down. Whole mornings can be passed in this delicious sport when once you have tired of ruins and thirsty, dusty valleys.

Confused memories will remain of the rich groves of orange, lemon and almond, and the darkness of the tall cypresses which rise everywhere, self-seeded it would seem. The two varieties – the slender and the spread-out variety – are supposed by the peasants to be the male and female of the tree; whereas in truth the cypress is *monoecious* with the male and female flower on the same tree. What else? Yes, the stands of Aleppo pine along the hilly seashore – so often attacked by the Processionary caterpillar, the larva of the moth, whose untidy web-like nets can be seen in the branches. If you camp, watch out for the hairs of this caterpillar which are highly irritating to the skin and can indeed cause blindness. Other trees are the elm, the eastern plane and the white poplar (now alas dying of various fungoid diseases which they cannot as yet cure). Most curious among trees is the Tree of Heaven which, imported into France from China in 1751 as a garden plant, suddenly decided it liked Crete and has naturalized itself. It grows rapidly and seeds itself with winged seeds – which can travel twenty metres. In June and July it is covered with a riot of huge crimson flower-like leaves. However, the peasants hate this tree despite its beauty and call it 'Stinktree' – the leaves smell bad, and its seedlings invade their holdings.

It is hard to leave Crete, yet, if this book is ever to end, I must. I have things to say about vampires and volcanoes, but I will keep them until I reach Santorin, which specializes in both. As a cliff-hanger I will just mention that Sir Arthur Evans did not believe in the 'invasion' theory as an explanation of the final destruction of the palaces. He believed in a 'natural calamity like an earthquake'.

Later I must discuss this theory in great detail, but again the proper place to do so is in the tremendous crater of Santorin. Was it this great quake that finished off Knossos and the Minoan culture?

Cythera and Anticythera

By some of those vagaries of pure chance, which in retrospect
often seem meaningful, I first heard the words uttered by a girl
student one afternoon, in the swimming, grey aquarium-light
of an Athens museum. She was leaning forward through the
reflections thrown by the glass cases, in order to read a show-
card referring to an exhibit which had already caught my attention. Its empty hand is what somehow impressed me in the
little statue; it lay there in space, lightly and effortlessly curved
around some lost object – a ball, an apple? The empty space
itself conferred something like a signature. It seemed symbolic
of Greece itself, where so much vital information has vanished,
leaving only these tormenting black spaces, clues from which
one must try to fashion a mould into which we can pour our
notions about these forgotten peoples and times. The apple of
truth perhaps?

She read slowly with a strong provincial intonation: 'Bronze
statue of a youth *circa* 240 BC. The extended right hand seems
to offer something for it is as if curved around some object. It
has been suggested that he is a Paris, the work of Euphranos,
shown as offering the apple of discord to Aphrodite.' It had
been part of a shipload of statues wrecked off Anticythera *en
route* for Italy.

The apple – *was* it an apple? – had been sucked out of the
hand by the sea. As for the hand, it haunted me as a sort of
symbol too: the Apple of Discord, the Apple of Oblivion, the
Apple of Eden, or of the Hesperides – eternal youth! The statue

alone knew the truth, and it stood there silently, inhabiting a unique moment of time, limbs tense as music yet full of controlled desire, full of the sufficiency of their own pure, primal weight. To give him a name, to call him Paris, would hardly disturb the smooth surface of the sculptor's thought. It was balanced there like a bird. Its precious apple lay fathoms deep off Anticythera, an isle about which I then knew hardly anything. Yes, once a fisherman had said that there was an islet somewhere near it called Egg (Avgo) which had a marvellous marine grotto with stalactites and a colony of seals. (The seals all look like Proteus; that is presumably why he was appointed to be keeper of the Olympian sealery.) Not many months later I found myself coming into Cythera for a dawn landfall, as a refugee on my way to Crete and Egypt. I thought of the little statue.

But it is not for any personal reason that I feel it right to add a note about these two unprepossessing little islands. They have today little charm and less to show in the way of ancient monuments. Some good, safe anchorages for small craft are about all they have, unless you count the two mediocre churches and a sort of nondescript barn of a building which suggests a maritime *lazaretto* or a *dogana*. However, Cythera marks the halfway point between the mainland and Crete and, during the long centuries before steam, almost everything either touched it or passed close in, using the island as a convenient lee against the swing of the main deep, or a shield against wind. Yes, that is all, except for one singular and arresting fact, namely that Aphrodite was apparently born here. The small Phoenician trading post, which has now completely disappeared, imported her worship from the Middle East, and it was from here that she went back into Cyprus to lovely Paphos, and forward to the eagle-patrolled heights of Mount Erix in Sicily. In comparison with these two magnetic sites, Cythera seems a dowdy little place to be born in, but then Aphrodite enjoyed a multiple personality and no doubt in each place she took on a separate identity. In Erix – so grim is the place – she must have come in her savage and pitiless version. There is still a whiff of sulphur about the mountain, and obscure hints in the texts of human sacrifices and incredible fleshy orgies. Of course the scholars keep reminding us that she is Asiatic in origin and not Greek, and warning us not to be taken in by bad puns on words like *aphros* meaning 'foam'. This is all very well. Once she was adopted, re-cycled and structured by the invincible Greek tongue – that alphabet crisp as a laundered collar – she became, and will for ever remain, the Greek goddess of love – older than Greek, perhaps, but always as young as first love. Under her title Urania, she stood for pure and ideal love; as Genetrix or Nymphia, she was the protector of lawful marriage and favoured all serious unions; as Pandemos or Porne she was the patron of all prostitutes and favoured all lust and venal love. Everything to do with passion, from the noblest to the most degraded, came within her scope. It is her completeness, compounded of many attributes, which wins our hearts. With her, loving had a comprehensiveness that accepted every human foible, good or bad.

Nor was she averse at times to using her powers mischievously – as when she took it into her head to light a short fuse under the chair of Zeus in Olympus, which gave him one of the worst attacks of skirt-fever ever to win a place in the Olympian version of *The Guinness Book of Records*. Was there nothing sacred, he asked her, all lit up like a Christmas tree? Yes, she must have answered, everything is sacred, without distinction, even laughter. Especially laughter.

It was natural that men should come to worship this graceful blonde pussmoth of a goddess, with her grey eyes and the smile they always mention as playing about her lips – that memorable smile! Of course Hera and Athena were also pretty girls, but they had other qualities which made one feel they were fragile, this-side-up-with-care sort of people. Haughty Hera inspired respect, while Athena's severe beauty arrested desire. Aphrodite only had to look and one was enslaved. She hovered somewhere between the impossible and the inevitable. But even she had her moments of weakness for, when Zeus returned the compliment and put the Indian Sign on her, she too was forced to fall in love. He had 'inspired her with the sweet desire to lie with a mortal man'.

If you should happen to make an excursion to Mount Ida, spare a thought for the Trojan Anchises, for he was the lucky man upon whom her eye fell. He was reputed to be easily as handsome as any of the immortals, and there must have been something to it, for she was overwhelmed. He was there, pasturing his flocks on the holy mountain, when he saw this extraordinary apparition come towards him across the shocks of mountain grass. Aphrodite knew she was looking her best, for she had just come back from visiting her shrine in Paphos, where the Graces had anointed her body with fragrant and incorruptible oils and adorned her with her most precious jewelry. 'Her veil was more dazzling than flame, she wore bracelets and ear-rings, round her throat there were golden necklaces, her delicate bosom shone like a moon.' Anchises was dumb with amazement as he watched her calmly climbing towards him, with her retinue of shaggy wolves and lions and sleek panthers which frisked and played about her. Who could she be?

She told him that she was the daughter of Otreus, King of Phrygia, and that she would like to be his wife. Still speechless with amazement he led her to his rough cot, which however contained a comfortable bed covered with the skins of lions and bears. So: 'A mortal man, by the will of the gods and of Destiny, slept with an immortal goddess without knowing who she was.' They say it happens to all of us, but usually only once.

Next morning when she woke, perhaps quite inadvertently, she showed herself to him in all her true splendour. The terrified shepherd fell down before her, fearing the premature old age which is promised to all mortal men who dare to sleep with a goddess, even unknowingly. She reassured him on this score and promised him a son like a god (who proved to be the pious Aeneas) – but he must promise never to reveal the name of his mother. This was her most perfect love-adventure; after it she seems to diminish in size somewhat. Why, for example, did she give herself to the graceless, churlish hunchback called Hephaestus? As a marriage, it was a failure from the beginning, and she sought refuge in other loves like Ares and Hermes. I do not profess to follow her later career with so much interest. Perhaps we do not know all the facts. It would be interesting to write a book which explained all these rather capricious changes of mood. But think what happened to her victims when the spell of her passion was on them. Medea and Ariadne betrayed their fathers; Helen abandoned her home to follow a stranger; the incestuous desires of Myrrha and Phaedra came from her; also the monstrous and bestial passion of poor Pasiphae. It is useless to ask her image about this; all one has in reply is the marvellous smile. 'When she appears,' cries Lucretius, 'the heavens are all assuaged and pour forth torrents of light; the waves of the sea smile on her.' I do not pretend to understand, but I feel the weight of her enigmatic, smiling presence. Her goodness is terrifying because it is so absolute.

The Germans had almost reached Kalamata when a consular *caique* appeared and proposed to offer us a safe passage to Crete and thence to Egypt. We left by night and travelled right down the stony sleeve of the Mani, until we reached the very end just as dawn started breaking. By extraordinary good fortune, throughout this whole adventure we had an April sea of silk, while the nights were starless and without moon. The vessel was crowded with refugees like ourselves, a number of them British, and was a defective old tub slightly down to port. The real danger however was that her wheezy engine uttered showers of bright sparks up into the sky.

Cape Matapan (ancient Taenaron) was the very last toe-hold on the peninsula; after that the black bitumen of the night sea which took us to Cythera. It was a poor harbour, indeed hardly one at all; but the divine stillness of the sea made it safe. The whole village came down to see us as we tied up. They had all the reserve and pride of the Maniots – the proudest of Greeks, for their peninsula has never been conquered by a foreign nation – but they were hungry for news. Cut off like this by the mountains, there was no contact with the outside world except one little radio which had died on them. We were in hardly better case, but we shared what news we had from the stricken Kalamata we had left. We had to wait for dusk again before tackling the next leg of the voyage, and I remember in what calm and ease we passed that day – reorganizing ourselves, tidying up the boat, checking provisions and so on; then swimming and washing and sunbathing on the warm pebbles. The whole world seemed to be in a state of suspended animation, the whole turning, sunlit globe. No sign of aircraft, nothing upon the sea. The bountiful peacefulness of that day had a dream-like flavour. Towards evening our hosts proposed to feast us before we left with the darkness. The last two lambs of the village had been killed; tables were laid down the main street as if for a wedding. So we sat in the warm, buoyant, late sunlight and toasted each other calmly and with love, for we did not expect ever to see each other again. It was a typical Greek feast in this classic simplicity and formality. Boys of rifle-bearing age (around fourteen) were seated with the grown-ups. A few conventional expressions of hope and good cheer were uttered by individuals, but there were no prepared speeches. Yet our hearts were full. Where did it come from, this smiling calm, this simple confidence, this warmth of plenitude? We had no right to feel like this, for the world had come to an end. Why then this happy fulfilment of quiet talk and laughter?

The reason is that a word had been uttered, a single small word for which the whole of Europe had waited and waited in vain. It was the word 'No' (*Ohi*) and Greece had uttered it on behalf of all of us at a time when the so-called great powers were all cringing, fawning and trying to temporize in the face of the Hitlerian menace. With that small word Greece found her soul, and Europe found its example. A small, almost unarmed nation, internally self-divided, once more decided to defy the Persian hordes as it had done in the past.

I think we were filled with a secret relief that at last the word had been uttered, for it brought us the certain knowledge that now, however long the war took, and however many of us did not return from it, it would finally be won. It was the premonition of that distant victory and return of peace which filled us with such tranquil happiness. As dusk began to fall, we took our leave of this little faraway village, cut off from everywhere by its ring of mountains. They waved us goodbye with the same smiling certainty as they had shown all day. The sun was just below the rim of the horizon, the world was sinking through veil after veil of violet dusk towards the sheltering darkness.

There came a shriek. 'Look!' Wildly, one of the crew pointed up into the sky above us, and we craned our necks to see a flight of Stukas in arrowhead formation moving above us. Instantly the skipper turned the boat in under the high cliffs where it would present a difficult target for dive-bombers. There was a moment of high excitement and near panic; but it ended in roars of laughter, for the wretched aircraft above us turned out on closer scrutiny to be an arrowhead formation of wild duck, doubtless heading southward to Egypt for their familiar haunts on Lake Mareotis. The darkness came now, the night became chill, and we turned in a little ashamed of our panic. At dawn we wallowed into Cythera.

Here we ran into a group of deserters from the Albanian armies, mostly Cretans, who were in an ugly mood. Their craft had fallen apart just as it reached harbour and was a total wreck – indeed how they had got so far was a mystery, no less a mystery than the route they had taken. There they were, lying among the rocks like mastiffs dressed in bloody rags and soiled sheepskins. They were armed too, which put us at a disadvantage during the long diplomatic discussion that followed. They proposed to take our boat and maroon us on Cythera. They had urgent work to do in Crete, they said, they had to execute a traitor, a general, whose name I forget. It took us nearly all day to dissuade them from this course, pleading our women and children as an excuse. Finally they relented and allowed us to go, provided we took three of their badly wounded fellows, which we did. But we cleared the harbour bar rather smartly, long before time, lest these grumpy warriors should change their tune.

Mercifully we were neither bombed nor machine-gunned, though a number of boats quite near were. The darkness was alive with boats heading for Crete; you could hear the drumming of their engines, and here and there you might see a spark of light from a cigarette. In comparison, we were almost a travelling firework display, and it is a wonder we were not marked down for machine-gunning. Tired and cramped and folded up like soiled towels, we at last climbed ashore at Chanea to stretch our cramped legs. The town was full of troops in various stages of undress and disarray, and in the far distance some mild rifle-shots echoed and subsided in a desultory, haphazard sort of way, as if some idle boy were shooting at rooks. Once again, despite the relative commotion, the movement of soldiers and so on, there was a sense of hiatus, of suspended animation. I set about finding lodgings, a decent enough berth for my wife and daughter, with some kindly Cretans who were delighted that we spoke a little Greek. There were a few air raid alerts and, I suppose, a few air raids; but the planes were not over us – they were after Suda where the old *York* lay right over on her side, with only one viable gun slanted up at the sky. However, a lot of the muck sprayed down over the town in the form of sparrow-shot and shrapnel; we could hear it clattering upon the tin roofs of the tavern lean-tos when we were having a quiet *ouzo*. Nor were the elements of Grand Opera lacking at this moment, for not only was the King on the island with his entourage, but also the Greek Government, whose Minister of Interior I saw emerging from a hole, clad in a tin helmet and looking like a giant rat. (With them of course would be Seferis the poet.) In fact the whole of Athens was there, and despite anxiety there was a slight feeling of euphoric fiesta in the air. All my friends were there, and I kept meeting them, either improbably clad (Peter Payne in a digger hat) or manifesting a sang-froid which was rather out of place (Alexis Ladas in beautifully cut riding-breeches).

We were finally carried out into safety by an Australian transport, which appeared in some miraculous fashion as evening began to fall and proposed that we should go aboard with the coming of night. It was to be my first farewell to this vehement island with its rugged beauties and ruggeder men.

It was in a street of Chanea – I was hunting for some Carnation Milk for the baby – that I came upon a detail of some Greek regiment busy about some internal matter of proper equipment. They were shortening webbing or something like that, and all at once I saw the bronze form of the Paris statue from the Athens Museum; the same pose, the same stance. Moreover it had the outstretched hand, though now this was not empty; nor was it to Aphrodite, but to his fellow soldier that he was proferring, a Mills bomb. This sight somehow assuaged and illuminated the faint disappointment I had felt about the empty hand of the statue. I felt vaguely that there might be a worthwhile short story in it; but I have never been able to manage the short story form, so it had to go on slumbering in a note book or in my memory until now, when I produce it here in its unfinished state.

In the morning we were in Egypt.

Santorin

It is hardly a matter of surprise that few, if any, good descriptions of Santorin have been written; the reality is so astonishing that prose and poetry, however winged, will forever be forced to limp behind. Perhaps only in the more fanciful reaches of science fiction will you find anything quite like this extinct volcano of white marble, which blew its head off at some moment in the Bronze Age, and must, by the most reasonable modern assessments, have partially destroyed, or at least deeply modified, a rich and elaborate culture of the Cretan type. The tidal wave alone must have caused floods as far away as Syria and Spain, while the rain of volcanic ash, the scholars surmise, may have been what finished off the Minoan civilization once and for all. Such theories are not mere fanciful suppositions – the most modern scientific evidence goes far to support them. And Crete is only sixty miles away. If the craters of Milos and of Nisyros, both of them extinct volcanoes, contributed secondary bursts, the whole Mediterranean must have been affected. All early traditions speak of a world-engulfing flood at some early time. As for Plato's Atlantis – traditions of which came to him perhaps from Egypt – nobody who visits Santorin today can help being half-convinced by the relatively modern theory that it was here that it was situated.

What happened? A deep fault in the earth's surface opened, and with a roar the whole sea was siphoned into it directly on top of limitless beds of molten magma, the earth's core, causing an explosion of steam which was prodigious. It was the size of the eruption which counted – for there exists much early evidence of volcanic activity, recorded by the seismologists and historians of all epochs. Strabo records one in 196 BC, when a whole island was thrown up. Later again, in 1570, the island of Mikra Kaumene and, in 1770, Nea Kaumene, lifted themselves into the air. And once you sail into the huge bowl which the Santorin explosion created – eighteen miles round the inner rim – you find yourself confronted with something quite unlike the rest of the Cyclades. The smell of sulphur and the pit still seems to hang in the air, giving a diabolical flavour to the scenery which, without too much imagination, could conjure up a backdrop suitable for a stage hell. Chunks of pumice still float about and knock against your hull, as if broken off still warm from some sudden push of white-hot lava thousands of fathoms below. And then the cliffs, which rear up with their ravaged-looking ghost town on the crest – where has one ever seen such colours, seen rock twisted up like barley-sugar, convoluted and coloured so fancifully? They remind one of the oil marbling on the endpapers of Victorian ledgers. Mauve, green, putty, grey, yellow, scarlet, cobalt . . . every shade of heat from that of pure molten rock to the tones of metamorphic limestone cooling back into white ash. And off the crest, like the manes of horses, little spurts of white ash drift down into the bay from the silent white houses. Sunset and sunrise here put poets out of work. The lines of men apparently carrying immense rocks on their shoulders are only handling pumice which is as light as air.

As far as the creation of the island is concerned, the modern scholar has a useful yardstick in Krakatoa, where the largest volcanic convulsion in recent history provided measurable data for study: it occurred in 1883. The shock wave produced by Krakatoa was fifty feet high and it destroyed towns and villages hundreds of miles away from its epicentre. To compare this with Santorin, I quote a modern writer whose authoritative and carefully argued book will provide the traveller with all the arguments that I must briefly summarize here: 'The Santorian caldera (the deep cauldron-like depression of a volcano) is thirty-two miles in surface, and 160 to 220 fathoms in depth. It is therefore five times greater in volume than that of Krakatoa; the thermal energy produced was therefore about three times that of Krakatoa ... Occurring in the middle of the Aegean, a relatively densely populated centre of Bronze Age civilizations, it could hardly have been forgotten ...' (*Atlantis* by Galanopoulos and Bacon, 1969.)

Approaching from the north, you first touch the island at Oia, where there is no real harbour; all landing has to be done by bumboat, as our grandfathers used to call it. The real capital, perched on its glittering white crest, lies midway down the island, right opposite the smaller island of Therasia. The whole assemblage is composed of the scattered volcanic fragments of the marble mountain after its eruption, and indeed there are still frequent twists of smoke and ripples of water-surface around the two smaller and most recent islands, while the sea itself seems, if not actively to smoke, at least much warmer than the rest of the Aegean. The yachtsman feels uneasy when he decides to anchor for a few nights – to wait for full moon, say, when Santorin glimmers like the City of the Dead in Cairo under the cold, flaring white light. It also smells of the devil, and consequently it is no surprise that in the modern folklore of Greece peasant superstition has picked on the island as a specially favoured home for the vampire. Vampires in retirement, vampires who have shot their bolt, vampires wanting to get away from it all – they find a haven here. In fact in the demotic, there is a saying which closely parallels our own proverb about taking coals to Newcastle. 'He who takes vampires to Santorin' is performing a particularly redundant function. There is almost no shade on the blazing escarpment where the present capital lies. There is also precious little agriculture, apart from small tomatoes; and the vines which produce a characteristic volcanic wine containing just a suspicion of fizz, a *pétillant* spark of life that sets it apart from most of the red wines of the Cyclades.

The town is nine hundred feet above the jetty where one lands, and where a draggle of surly mules awaits to hoist visitors up a seemingly endless staircase into the sky; a staircase with many a perilous zigzag from which you find yourself staring down into the turquoise eye of the sea below. It is an adventure.

The old Atlantis Hotel has been pitched in a perfect strategic position on the top, and here you can restore your shattered nerves with a pleasant *ouzo* or brandy, drunk while gazing into the middle distance of a view, the like of which . . . It is so much the high spot of the Cycladean journey that even rhapsody is out of place, as it must be when one is dealing with a real experience, an Event and not a mere Happening.

The superstitions of the place make you feel that something lingered behind after the great explosion and disappearance of a whole culture. More than vampires, there are ghosts in the island about which it would not do to be ironic. Here is a peasant's account of them taken from *Voyage To Atlantis* (Mavor):

Evangelos Baikas of Akrotiri had this comment to make upon the excavations just concluded. He said: 'This summer my family could not work in the fields because of the ghosts. In the mountain that came from the sea there are ghosts where now they make excavations. I saw them. One morning when I went to collect the tomatoes and it was not yet sunrise a big white light covered a great ghost, covered with a shield. There were many, all in movement, yet they looked firm. They went toward the sea in the direction opposite from the sunrise to escape from the light which goes towards the west.'

This is almost on an Irish note, and in much the same key. Lawson, that admirable folklorist, records finding an old lady making rain up on the mountain, and he noted down some of her pious incantations. She discussed the matter quite reasonably with him in a matter-of-fact tone, but admitted that it was easier to make rain start than to get it to stop. And thunder was quite beyond control – could he help? He must have been the first Oxford don to be asked to make rain and control thunder. There are witches and apparitions in plenty on this strange island. A friend of mine tells me that when she was a child, she spent a holiday near Thera (the capital) and one day the peasants called out to her to come quickly and see a little man who was hiding in an olive tree and playing on an instrument. They surrounded the tree and three or four people attested to the existence of a 'devil' or a *kalikanzaros*. My friend could not see him, but she heard the faint quirky music of a pipe, and also the clicking of his little hooves in the branches. Then he jumped down and they all fled screaming.

A visit to ancient Thera calls for stamina and a touch of intrepidity; it is muleback and walking for some three hours – or you can drive as far as Pyrgos, which is pretty, though the last earthquake knocked it about somewhat. The ancient site, itself also some thousand feet above the sea, lies on the east coast on the exposed flanks of a barren range. From the very top on a clear day one can see Crete.

I do not think ancient Thera alone would justify a visit to the island, although it is impressive; but the Delos temples, though smaller in scale, have greater atmosphere. The reigning divinity of the place was not the Delian but the Dorian Apollo, in whose honour the festivities of the youth took place. *Apollo Kourotrophos*, the 'boy raiser', was the patron of the *palaestra*. The celebration was called the *Gymnopaidia*. A few inscriptions and epithets have a slightly questionable ring to a Protestant mind –

though Seferis the poet, who was not particularly interested in naked boys, wrote a beautiful long poem about the event, as classical as a star. Once up here, in this brilliant light, it is worth treading the Sacred Way and trying to imagine how life was once lived in this windy fastness, so high above the sea. On one of the walls, you may be amused to see a highly serviceable-looking phallus engraved and, under it, the inscription 'To my Friends' . . . Surely this is the best bequest one could give or receive in the name of friendship?

At dusk, when the sun falters and starts to tumble down in ruins, the islands go black and seem to smoke all round the central cauldron of the harbour. Always you wonder if perhaps tonight, in the middle of the night, will come the premonitory rumble which means that the volcano is on the rampage once more.

A glance at the little museum in Thera is worthwhile, for it contains good things recovered from various island digs – notably some interesting Minoan ware and some geometric vases.

Only one or two foreign residents brave out the winter here, for it can be fierce, and, because of poor anchorages, the island is frequently cut off by heavy seas from the mainland. That means that, by the middle of October, when the cruise lines stop calling and the ferries close down, the whole place reverts to silence and grimness – is given over to ghosts once more. Santorin!

The Southern Sporades

*

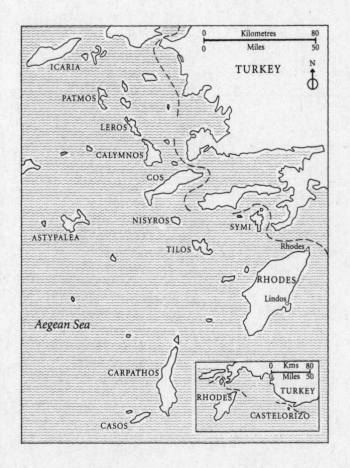

Rhodes

To understand the modern town of Rhodes one needs to recall that one year before Crete was allowed to re-join the mother country in 1913, Rhodes and the whole group of so-called Twelve (Dodecanese) Islands (a misnomer, they are fourteen) were handed over to Italy; they were to remain an Italian dependency for thirty-six years. To the Duce, when he arrived on the scene with all his addle-pated notions about Italy's supremacy in the Mediterranean, the island of roses was especially important because of its strategic position. It is, after all, the third largest Greek island in area after Crete and Euboea. Not only that. The Black-shirts, in the first burst of auto-intoxication, drunk on the new folklore, believed that they were in some sense the inheritors of all the martial traditions of the Ancient Order of the Knights of Jerusalem. This order had once reigned supreme here, withstanding the full weight of the Turks for more than two hundred years; and when at long last they were forced to yield and evacuate the island, the six hundred knights of the order had repulsed the attacks of an army numbering one hundred thousand for more than six months. This was a story of heroism and devotion which naturally appealed to the Fascists, who wanted to enshrine the exploits of the knights in some visible way. The Rhodes of that epoch, they decided, must be reconstructed as accurately as possible so that no one would forget such a heroic period in the island's long history. The reconstruction was admirably done, with all the Italian's pleasant taste for greenery and décor. Indeed, it is none the worse for looking like a film-set ready for the cameras.

It is inevitable too that the Italians should be more interested in Roman than in Greek history. However, here the archaeologists have played fair; Lindos, Cámeirus and Ialysos, the ancient cities, bear witness to their scrupulous honesty and thoughtfulness. And the huge nine-volume *Clara Rodos*, printed on the Government presses (which I directed for a blissful two years), also pays as much scholarly attention to the Greek as to the Roman past. (I had the pleasure of distributing this work – slightly larger than Evans's Cretan work – to all the libraries in Europe and the United States.) Nonetheless, if we carp at the jazzing-up techniques of Evans in Knossos we could apply the same sort of criticism to Rhodes. Indeed it is amusing to think that if it had been Crete and not Rhodes which had been given to the Italians for thirty-six years, Crete would probably look not unlike this, with the Venetian bastions of the towns restored and the old Venetian quarters of Chanea and Heracleion completely made over . . .

The Italians also wanted Rhodes to be a tourist playground – perhaps even more delightful than Capri. It was partly with this in mind that they produced a healthy budget, and the Fascist rulers of the island began their lavish restoration work. Inevitably the restoration is very much of its period, but the little town of Lindos is beautiful with its little toy fortress and its magnificent medieval walls. Moreover, it is an accurate reworking of the great original which still has so much left in place in the way of armorial bearings and escutcheons that its newly restored authenticity never seems in doubt; only the absence of ruins gives it its faintly fictitious appearance. There are courtyards and fountains and sunken gardens and galleries which are a great delight, full as they are of flowering shrubs and lemon trees. The bees hum and circle in the dense summer heat, the waves of perfume climb the stairs of the Grand Master's Lodge, punctuating the steady surge of *cicadas* from the market gardens which occupy so much of the ancient moat. In the silence, a few quarter-tones from a café radio are suddenly cut off, as if someone has taken it by the throat. A boy goads sheep along the narrow Street of the Knights with a thin, bored whistle. The sheep's hooves curdle the afternoon silence. It is time to be going down to the sea for a swim.

Never was there such water. For two lucky years I was able, by virtue of my job with the occupying force, to swim at the Albergo Della Rosa beach and to inhabit a tiny studio buried in flowering hibiscus hard by – at the shrine of Murad Reis which still exists, though the old Mufti is dead and the cemetery terribly unkempt. (Ah, those beautiful Turkish tombstones – showing the same wild melancholy and poetry of the Eyoub one outside Constantinople!) Rhodes had been suffocated by the Germans. Such thorough mining and festooning with barbed wire I have never seen. (Of course they had months to do it in, and they were trapped.) Then once we had made them prisoner, we co-opted them to help us de-mine and de-fuse and unwind wire together with our own sappers. As we watched, the famous town came to life again daily. First the harbour was cleared by the Navy for food convoys, then a post office opened which put the islanders in touch with the outside world. Then transport re-started. Some of the demining was done by the sea – I remember beaches where the winter surges had been so severe that a whole field of Teller mines had surfaced, like teeth in a gum, to show their ugly white steel faces. In some cases the little fisher-boys learned to defuse them and would crawl over minefields at risk of life and limb to rescue some of the explosive for fishing expeditions. Once, on a picnic with a rather tipsy staff officer who professed to know all the minefields, we suddenly found we were in the middle of one near Mount

Phileremo which gave no signs of having been cleared. The officer had got his facts wrong; we had been drinking white wine and eating bully beef in an uncleared area. How to get back to the road was the problem – which we solved with the most ludicrous and comical precautions, swearing at our friend all the time for having lured us into such a dangerous place.

Of all the 1900-odd Greek islands, I feel I know Corfu, Rhodes and Cyprus best, simply because I have had the luck to reside in them for a couple of years. I have also camped in them at every season and covered much of the ground on foot. Of the three, Rhodes is the most compact and manageable for the visitor, though not the most lovely. Corfu and Cyprus are each more beautiful in their own way. It would take a lifetime to reside in all the islands for any time – and even the number 1900 does not take account of the mere atolls, quite uninhabitable, of which there are so many. Rhodes is specially interesting to me because I first arrived in it just after a fierce though short siege, which enabled me to visualize how the place must have been just after the greater sieges by Suleiman and, earlier still, that great siege-master Demetrius Polyorcetes. The British made one attempt to seize the island but the Germans showed their teeth and threw us into the sea. It was therefore decided to let them starve until they submitted. In the interval an attempt by the Italian forces to make their allies surrender led to a battle which was followed by a wanton massacre of their troops around the defensive positions of Phileremo. Then starvation set in, which was unfortunately shared equally by civilians and soldiers. We arrived in time to save most of the civilian population, but not before most of the livestock, both domestic and personal, on the island had been devoured by the Germans. It was strange to see pets tied to the front door knob, lest they escape and be picked up by the troops which scavenged everywhere; cats, dogs, hamsters – anything they could find went into the cooking pot. But the Germans were obstinate and were losing some three hundred malnutrition cases a day when at last they caved in.

So Rhodes awoke once more like the Sleeping Beauty, though it took more than a single hairy kiss from the incoming army administration to wake her. The confusion was unimaginable. Many of the Italian civilians wished to return to Italy, as did the four or five hundred Siena farming families who had been co-opted to settle and farm the central parts of the island. It was thanks to them and to the high tourist budget that the island had been so beautifully re-afforested – though of course the work of modern forestry experts had produced something quite unlike the forests of ancient Greece. Pines and eucalpytus were as much in use as they are in Sicily – and the work had been very thoroughly done. Rhodes is naturally fertile, but the Italians succeeded in increasing water and greenery and for this they must be much commended. That there is a slight feeling of theatrical deadness about their Rhodes reconstruction does not diminish its interest for those who would like to refashion in their minds the sort of backdrop against which the Crusades were launched. The museum is a model of its kind, and the envy of curators on other islands. I spent some time trying to persuade the Greek authorities that these august precincts might make an admirable small university, which would attract pupils from all over the Middle East. But local visions did not stretch further than a casino, which does not yet exist. The quiet streets of this romantic quarter are a pleasure to saunter among; while hard by is a huge tree under which kindly Turks have made a café where you can still hear the bubble of rose-water in a *narguileh*, or smell the sweet-leather smell of Lakadif tobacco smoked in churchwarden-type clay pipes – which are becoming rarer today.

It is curious the number of names under which the island

went in ancient times – each seeming to represent a facet of its protean character. Rhodes is shaped like a maple-leaf or an obsidian arrow-head, whence the name *Stadia* to denote its ellipsoid form; Mount Atabyros, the chief mountain, supplies another name; while *Olyessa* denotes that the island was always earthquake-plagued. *Poeissa*, referring to its richness, is more justifiable; *Makaria*, the Blessed Isle, is all right too, and *Asteria* which describes its star-clear atmosphere. The only odd name is Snake Isle, apparently suggesting that it is the home of snakes. I saw no sign of these creatures although they proliferate in most other islands. If there are snakes around, they tend to emerge during the first sunny days; the tarmac warms up and they come out to sunbathe and warm their stomachs. Snakes are voluptuaries, just like cats, and often fall asleep, sun-drugged; and as they are also deaf, one often runs over them in a car. In a rich island like Corfu – at the southern tip near Lefkimi – they slide across the road all the time, in Crete as well. But in Rhodes I was not struck by the number of snakes. Probably most of them are not strictly speaking poisonous, though I suppose the adder and the horned viper must exist in the marshes here as they do in metropolitan Greece.

The ancient history of Rhodes is compact and shapely. Originally there were three capitals, Lindos, Cameirus and Ialysos. The accent was on trade and sea-power, just as in Crete, and the Rhodian sailor was as famous as his Cretan neighbour for his skills. Some of the old battles are interesting to read about in the pages of Torr's history, but the sieges are the most fun and would make a book in themselves, full of details about extraordinary mechanical weapons. Demetrius, with his crazy elephantine towers and other kinds of ballista, makes wonderful reading – especially as one can follow the engagements as if one were reading a staff map, thanks to the reconstructed fortress which is unintentionally also a good guide to the ancient quarters of the town. The early history is made up of the usual intricate collection of tribal invasion stories. However, most unusually, the three major cities decided to pool their resources and found the city of Rhodes, on its present site. This was in 408 BC. What is striking is that the new city had no good harbour; that of Lindos was infinitely superior, and indeed Lindos lived on in splendour for a long time because of it. Nevertheless Rhodes, on its bull-necked spit of land, was fixed as the new capital. Gossip has it that the town was planned by Hippodamnus, who also laid out Alexandria when it became a rich *entrepôt* for trade. This gossip of course has been contested on several grounds, most of them well founded; it was perhaps a piece of local snobbery to pretend that the man who laid out both Piraeus and Alexandria was also responsible for the layout of the ancient town of Rhodes. The absence of a harbour was a problem, which was dealt with in a surprisingly amicable way by the three investors in the maritime future of Rhodes. (And how well it turned out for them!) Apparently they equipped the town with no less than five harbours, all to some extent artificial. Three were of handsome proportions and made use of the indentations on the east cape; hard by these was an elaborate complex of bays for dry-docking – in fact, a well-found naval yard. When the whole operation was at last finished and the result put into action, the astonished world woke up to the fact that Rhodes now had the best equipped port in the Aegean. Prosperity was not slow to follow, though the elegant natural harbour of Lindos did not die immediately. The magnificence of the exploit inspired Timosthenes to write his treatise *On Harbours*, a sort of *Mediterranean Pilot* of its day.

In 1936 the Italians published a detailed plan of the city, recording thirty-four classical and Hellenistic finds within the area demarcated by the medieval walls. But the westward suburbs, rising very steeply to the Acropolis (now Monte Smith), give much clearer evidence of the street grid and the dimensions of the buildings of antiquity. Already, between 1916 and 1929 – long before the craze to restore the Crusader castle – extensive Italian digs had revealed the foundations of temples to Zeus and Athena Polias, a stadium, a small theatre, a gymnasium and a temple to Apollo. The whole of this site dates from the second century BC. It is an easy stroll from any of the hotels, and you can lie in a rock tomb eating cherries and watch the night fall over the straits – for Turkey is only eighteen kilometres away from this eastern spur of Rhodes. The theatre is now completely restored and has a summer classical programme of plays and recitations – a delight in those crisp, crystalline nights with the sky full as a hive of twinkling and shooting stars. Aerial photography, developed during the war, has clearly revealed the chief parts of the ancient city's ground plan. Whoever executed it was a master architect. The famed rectilinear plan with its uniform houses and thoroughfares retained its decorative force from nearly every visible angle and, together with the three thousand statues for which the city was famous, made it rank beside Athens itself and Syracuse in spaciousness, dignity and aesthetic beauty. When one tries to visualize such splendour and catches a whiff of the blazing whiteness of marble or salt or whitewash which somehow seems to symbolize the Greek thing, one cannot help feeling that the world which followed – Venice, Genoa, Turkey – exemplified something meaner and crueller ... History running down like a tired clock, beauty being bartered against gain.

With the birth of Rhodes city and its harbours, the island was able to afford itself the best fleet of the age, and its rise to power in economic terms was extraordinarily swift and complete. Moreover, they were diplomats, the Rhodians, as well as tough sailors, and they managed to play the surrounding states off against each other and thus keep their freedom. They were also far-seeing enough to recognize the powers of young Alexander the Great and to throw in their lot with him; they helped his forces destroy Tyre and then, as the conquests of Alexander swiftly succeeded one another, it fell to the lot of Rhodes to dominate rich markets – Cyprus, Cilicia, Syria and Egypt. Taking full advantage of this, Rhodes became the richest and most peaceful of all the Aegean islands of that time. It appears that Alexander himself was so great an admirer of Rhodian institutions that he was later to try to introduce them into Alexandria around 331 BC. He even had the little island opposite the harbour christened Antirhodos.

But the situation was not to last. Even though Rhodes had been masterful at trimming its sails according to the prevailing winds, it found with the death of Alexander that the whole pattern of things in the Middle East had begun to fall apart. Within a decade dissident generals began to emerge as the kings of warring states. There was nobody sufficiently strong to back. Which way should they turn? Ptolemy's Greek kingdom was in Egypt, Seleucus's in Asia, Cassander's in Macedon; Lysimachus held Thrace . . . and so on. Antigonus was the only ruler with the will and the sea-power to try to restore the unity of the Empire, and his efforts went as far as the creation of a new league for the Aegean Islands. Rhodes stayed clear and independent still – happily so, for Antigonus was smashed at the Battle of Ypsos in 301 BC. But the island was not forgiven for her supercilious attitude, especially because, before being smashed, Antigonus had nursed schemes for an attack on Ptolemy and had asked Rhodes for an alliance – which the island refused on the grounds that Egypt was their main trading partner. Thus, when the son of Antigonus, Demetrius, set out upon his military career in the vain hope of imitating Alexander, he decided to teach the Rhodians a sharp lesson, and assembled a large force with which to do so. The gloomy

Rhodians found that they had to face some forty thousand men excluding cavalry and sailors and sappers. The armada which carried them was 170 ships strong and filled the straits, while 200 men-of-war convoyed them and guarded an innumerable flotilla of small craft carrying provisions of all kinds – plus the inevitable swarm of scavengers who smelled loot and booty.

What Rhodes could muster was heartbreakingly small. About six thousand troops with a thousand aliens in the city represented the hard core; then they armed the slaves which gave them another sixteen thousand men. Crete and Egypt sent help, so that the final score was about twenty-five thousand men versus twice that number. However, the figures take no account of the machinery which Demetrius had brought.

Today this machinery may seem faintly comic, but any study of the science of siegecraft of that time can only impress the reader with the complexity and efficiency of the weaponry they used. 'Sophisticated' is the *mot juste* and, when one thinks of the sheer presence of the giant *Helepolis* as it hovered up over the walls of Rhodes, one wonders why the Rhodians did not simply give in without firing an incendiary arrow. This famous assault-tower was nine storeys high, was propelled on oaken wheels, and reared up above the high towers of the city. It had catapults, grappling irons and drawbridges which could be lowered to release a stream of skirmishing infantry upon the bastions. It took an operational force of some 3000 men to propel the thing. The whole structure was given a thick outer skin of osier and hides, enough to stop arrows; the top floor was a nest of archers who could shoot down into the town. Diodorus says it was fifty metres high, and the careful Vitruvius calculated its weight as 125 tons. This dreadful contrivance gnawed away at the walls of Rhodes and succeeded in causing extensive damage, though not to the morale of the defenders. They held firm and drove back repeated assaults. After a year of inconclusive

operations, Demetrius received a pigeon from his father ordering him to return to his home; he was, however, told to sign a
treaty with Rhodes before leaving. As this was rather generous
in its terms, the Rhodians were relieved and signed it.

Demetrius, though something of a lout, had a generous side
to his Macedonian nature; no doubt too he felt a bit of a fool
for not having done better with all his toys. At any rate he left
the famous assault-tower as well as all his siege equipment,
ordering that it be sold and the proceeds donated towards a
statue which would commemorate this great siege. The Rhodians accepted the terms, and thus the statue of the sun god
Helios was born – the original Colossus of Rhodes. Work on
the statue began in 302 BC by Chares of Lindos. It took twelve
years of his life to complete, and when it was finished stood
some thirty-five metres high, all in bronze. The precise site of
this huge figure is still subject to argument; as is its pose also,
for it was never described by reliable eyewitnesses. It served as a
landmark for all vessels as they neared the island, and by superstition it became the protector and guardian angel of the city.
For sixty-odd years it stood there until the earthquake of 227 BC
toppled it over. Could it have straddled the harbour as some
people said? It does not seem likely. At any rate when the statue
fell it fell on land, and lay there for centuries, as famous in its
ruin as it had been when erect.

According to rumours and legends Helios was supposed to
have been displeased with the statue, and his oracle forbade any
attempt at restoration. No Rhodian therefore dared touch it
once it fell and the huge thing lay there for nine hundred years
until AD 635, when it was taken off by Saracen marauders and
sold to the Jewish merchants of the Levant.

So foundered the fame of Demetrius Polyorcetes leaving only
a footnote in the history books. It is just, for he lacked
the magnetism of the truly great man. In him you smell the

personal ambition behind the deeds. The boy Alexander, on the other hand, gives the impression of being a sleepwalker of genius pursuing an ever-receding dream of human unity. Nor is there anybody very interesting in the bead-roll of the generals and kings who, like termites, chewed his fragile dream-empire to pieces within a decade.

So the Colossus crashed down, and gave a chance to the superstitious to read into it omens of divine displeasure. When finally it was carried off, piece by piece, popular rumour said that it took nine hundred camels to do so. Does that seem excessive for 125 tons of scrap? I know nothing of the habits of camels; perhaps it was. Another rumour, which sounds like the work of an ironist, insists that Rhodes got back her Colossus later, during the siege of 1522 in the form of cannonballs fired by the investing Turks.

The glory and intellectual fame of Rhodes can hardly be exaggerated; and it endured for many centuries, through flourishing schools of rhetoric and fine arts. It is pitiful what little remains today, of what is recorded by Pliny and praised by Pindar. Her fame held on into Roman times, and famous Romans like Caesar, Brutus, Antony, Cassius, Tiberius and Cicero all studied in Rhodes. Some contracted a great affection for the island with its wonderful winter climate, and Tiberius spent one of his exiles in the island, transporting his entire retinue of concubines, catamites and conjurers; for once, at least, the comparison with Capri seems reasonably apt. The mystic Apollonius was another who made several stays in the island; there was also a host of other poets and painters who are now just names, attached to empty plinths or broken chips of vases.

The Rhodians evolved a code of laws which was, in its time, world-famous and was later adopted by the Antonines; parts of it were later absorbed into the Venetian sea code. In addition, the island played a very powerful part in commerce; spices, resins, ivory, silver, wine, oil, fish, amber, from every point of the compass, came to her and were sold in her marts. Yet, though the Rhodian fleet was considered the best in the Mediterranean, it seems not to have numbered more than fifty ships of the line.

However, history is cruel. There was no deep economic or military reason for the decline and fall of Rhodes. Rome was jealous of the island's riches and out of spite declared Delos a free port – which dealt a fatal blow to the Rhodian commerce. Then, in 42 BC, came an unexpected physical assault by Cassius, who stripped and destroyed the town and butchered most of its inhabitants. Kaput the glory and power; and there was no way to recover them. Of her thousands of statues, buildings and harbours, nothing remained – or hardly anything. The invaders left no stone upright upon another. The pathetic relics are there in the museum – among them my favourite stone jujube-woman (the marine Venus), a statue as much the work of the sea as of a sculptor. Mostly such things were fished up from the harbour or discovered by accident during recent excavations. The story-book town in the story-book island has vanished.

But what you do not know you do not miss; the present beauty of Rhodes, together with its buoyant blue sea and crystalline air is more than enough to delight the visitor. Although Swedish tourism seems to have turned it into a Swedish town if one judges by street signs, menus etc., this does not really matter. The afternoon prowl round the four kilometres of bastion is an unfailing delight, ending as it does with a coffee or a *mastika* under the spreading tree which shades a little café (Barba Jani's it was when first I went there). Then it is pleasant to saunter out through the great barbican and on to the waterfront, where the little harbour of Mandraccio has a handsome line of outdoor cafés at which you can read a paper, send off incoherent postcards, and do the hundred and one things that tourists feel called upon to do.

The modern architecture of the administrative buildings and the cinema is suitably chocolate-box, but the little Turkish-style market place is a success because of its layout and because the Italian tenderness for trees makes certain that shade is not lacking. The sunset, as seen from the top of Monte Smith, is worth the short walk, and will probably put you in a mood to round the crest of the hill and push on until you reach the ancient stadium in the midst of green glades starred with flowers. The spring flower riot in Rhodes is easily as splendid as that of Corfu; and after spring rain there is one hill on the right just before you reach Lindos which turns blood red, covered as it is in sheets of anemones. The town has little architectural merit but its wide streets and general impression of space lavishly treated are pleasant, and also enable it to be kept clean; after the insanitary uncleanliness of so many provincial Middle Eastern towns this is particularly striking.

I had the luck during my stay on the island some time ago to be a Foreign Office Information man on loan to the Army, and the Army treated me well. I had an office jeep – or rather a captured German Volkswagen which looked a total wreck but remained valiant, indestructible and faithful right to the end. With this whizzing old thing, I was able to get to know Rhodes over two and a half years as few people did soon after the last war. They were the happiest two years of my life. My duties were not killing, and continually interesting. Since the war was over and Enosis was heralded as the right and true end of Rhodes, the Greeks were all amiability. The Army relaxed, dreaming of Wimbledon and Winchester. Strange to say, a lot of people there didn't think the climate of Rhodes was a patch on that of England – which proves the truth of the old proverb attributed to Euripides, 'Home is where the heart is,' a proverb that no Greek would disapprove of.

Fate was even more lavish with its gifts to me, for I was accredited not only to Rhodes but to the whole Dodecanese group – the fourteen islands. It was assumed that these fourteen islands were crying out for the rich and copious information which I had to offer. My saddle-bags were crammed with syndicated intellectual fodder, and since the Greek is so greedy for news, I had a marvellous client to serve. Moreover, when I presented my case to the Navy, I was allowed to declare myself an official passenger and travel, when I wished, by naval craft of all sizes. What an experience this form of travel offered! It was infinitely more speedy than the lagging inter-island *caiques* which, like a slow train, put in everywhere. I continued to take *caiques* when in search of local colour, or when hunting for a friend, because it gave me an invaluable sensation of leisure; I wandered about, calling in at the various islands for a drink, so to speak, and wandered away again having transacted my business.

The sea has no timetable, and one may be locked into ports for days at a time when the weather turns sour. Nothing to do but play cards and drink and watch the barometer. This is why seamen have such unwrinkled faces; they co-operate with the inevitable, they let Jeeves cope. When young, I travelled much in these waters and have vivid memories of being locked into harbour for as much as ten days, with very little to eat or drink; at such times Ithaca, Patmos, Mykonos, Leros, Calymnos, seem to raise themselves from the ocean floor with the spray exploding all over them, and smile, their fingers to their lips. The winters in Greece are really more marvellous than the summers ... but you need to be young and fit to enjoy the necessary struggle against cold and wind.

It is partly poverty that keeps the Greeks so happy, so spare and in tune with things. There are no psychoanalysts in Athens; they would not be able to make a living. The Greeks act things out with total abandon. No sooner is something felt than it's done; there is no room or time for gloomy self-questionings and lucubrations. When you know that you might die of starvation this winter, when you feel your ribs stick out, what point is there in indulging your Oedipus complex? If he is mentally troubled, the Greek sets himself a long pilgrimage to some distant monastery and consults a local sage. He makes a real thing of his religious problems – and fundamentally (apart from lesions) there is no problem of mental health which is not in the last analysis a religious problem.

I linger a little before leaving the town of Rhodes where I spent such happy post-war years, locked into the secret garden of Murad Reis. I was indeed living in a Turkish cemetery of such beauty and silence that I often longed to die and be sealed into one of those beautiful forms; to lie there dreaming forever of Eyoub and the great ladies who drowse away time in the vehement silences of the Turkish heat, with just the sound of the leaves falling. In Rhodes it was the leaves of the eucalyptus, like little propellers, spinning down. My table in the garden rotted with heat and spilt wine; sometimes I made notes on it or drew something. Everything ran with sweat, wine and heat. Then visiting friends wrote messages on the table when I was absent, and finally started to write poems. The yard was completely surrounded with flowering hibiscus – the most beautiful, tenacious and feminine plant there is. What a joy, like a drink of cold water, to see it bursting from the throat of a riverbed, or from a nest of burning stones, in full summer. In my dreams women have always been mixed up with flowering hibiscus! Obscure thirsts are nourished by such images.

There is a persistent factor in Rhodes's history which seems to repeat itself over and over again. This is the Rhodian's taste for all things outsize. Think of the three thousand statues, for example, or the gigantic proportions of the statue of Helios. When they had a siege it was the biggest ever, and Demetrius produced his *Helepolis* for it. When they possessed a philosopher, he was greater than Solon. It is interesting that this preoccupation with size emerged again during the period of the Crusades. Not content with having the biggest-ever sieges against the biggest-ever armies, they decided one day to go the whole hog and build a Titanic of a boat – the biggest man-of-war ever seen afloat. It was called *The Grand Carrack* and descriptions of it suggest that it really was all that they planned it should be.

It had eight decks and so much space for stores that it could keep in the sea for more than six months at a time without touching land to re-provision, even for water. It had huge tanks of fresh water aboard. Nor did the crew get along with mere ship's biscuits as was the custom of the day. They ate the whitest of white bread, for the ship's bakeries turned out two thousand loaves at a throw, using freshly ground corn milled in hundreds of hand-mills. This great sea animal was sheathed below water with several layers of metal, riveted with bronze screws which do not rust like iron ones. 'With such consummate art was it built that it could never sink, no human power could submerge it.' (One recognizes the authentic note of hubris – the Greek sin of overplaying one's hand, the sure road to catastrophe.) The armoury was equipped for five hundred men. Cannon of every sort and kind figured in the armament, while fifty of the pieces were of extraordinary dimensions. But what crowned all, according to the chronicler, was that this enormous boat was incomparably swift and manoeuvrable; it required little effort to reef or veer her sails and she was speedy in her revolutions. A crew of three hundred managed her, while she had two large galleys of fifteen benches each, one lying in tow and the other aboard. 'Though she had often been in action and perforated by many cannon balls, not one went directly through her, or even passed her lead work.'

The ancient cities can be visited comfortably in a day; leaving the town by car at nine, you can lunch, lounge and swim at Lindos, call in on Cameirus at about four, and after a visit to the site of ancient Ialysos return to the town by dusk. This is thanks to an excellent motor-road which the Italians provided and which is still the most important tourist factor today. In sunny weather it is worth taking an early morning stroll round the market before setting off and filling your saddle-bags with fruit, melon, peaches and tomatoes – a sort of spare lunch in case Lindos should let you down; or worse still, lest some horror to suit the palate of some barbarous nation be forced upon you. Moreover, with a picnic you can crawl down to the sea and eat on the beach between bathes, than which there is no sweeter moral exercise or richer psychic balm. But first the assault on the citadel should be made otherwise you will not be worthy of your food, eaten beside this water which from the top of the cliff looks like a peacock's tail spread out below – so brilliant and so various are its hues in sun and shadow. Your mind will say, 'Go on then, jump!' and for a long moment you will hover between the worlds of the dead and the living, hanging like a fly to the edge of the citadel. It is an extraordinary place, the temple of Lindos; so light and aerial, so pure and in tune with the sky above. One longs to know what statues stood up here. It is far more impressive than Sunion or Erix in Sicily. Here one regrets the intrusion of Byzantines and knights – everything sweaty-Christian should be scraped off, so that the pagan soul of the place can float free, as a reminder of the time when the aspirations of the human mind acknowledged the powers and terrors of nature. The site echoes with its past like a chord of music which the mind only can hear.

The little town below, with its intricate cobbled streets and blazing whitewashed walls, lies very still. There seem to be few taverns, few open spaces under a plane tree where one can put a table and a chair. The main *taverna*, however, is beautifully situated just outside the citadel entrance under a tree, and others have sprung up in recent years. You can rent rooms in the town of Lindos, which drowses its life away, hardly troubled by the coming and going of the big buses with their sightseers. Strangely enough, the fishing is poor and one sees few fishermen. I made friends with one of the rare people with a small boat, a sort of absurd moralist called Janaki, and was pleased to see that the gift of philosophic reasoning was far from dead – indeed had been transmitted directly from the chief sage of the region, Cleobolus, who was, so to speak, the ancient Greek ancestor of Janaki. There is a marvellous water-labyrinth off the tiny beach below and while we explored it, Janaki, rowing while standing up, and dragging me softly along behind the boat in the cool water, would give way to profound moralizings upon nature. He took everything in dead earnest. Once we were arguing about the respective rights and roles of men and women in society and Janaki said, 'The nature of the man is to bring a hammer down hard on a stone, that is his role.' I said, 'What about women?' For a moment the question perplexed him and then his face cleared with relief. 'Her role is to hold his trousers up,' he said. 'If ever she should let go our whole civilization would fall apart.'

It was in deference to Lindos's top sage that I called my little studio in Rhodes the Villa Cleobolus. Nothing of the old boy's teaching remains, but we know that, like Pythagoras and Buddha, he believed in admitting women to the work, and allowed his own daughter and wife to become his students. Janaki had not heard of him – his education had stopped with the catechism. Yet I would regard Janaki as an educated peasant,

for he knew his saints, his trees, and his sea. We spent after-
noons in the little bay where St Paul touched down once
(another epistle, another thrashing), and Janaki regaled me
with his Lindean culture, which as a matter of fact, contained
some interesting elements – such as the sunken cities. There
were, he said, three cities which had been submerged far out to
sea, off the point of the citadel, and sometimes in still weather
one could look down into them and see everything very clearly.
Being so used to this kind of Atlantean folklore I paid little
attention, thinking that he had heard an account of the three
Rhodian cities of antiquity, of which Lindos was the most famous, and that he had jumbled it all up in his head as peasants
do. But I repeated this tale to a flower-hunting soldier who used
to botanize in the island and he told me that one day, walking
on the great bronze cliffs above Lindos in summer weather,
he had seen the sea curdle and become still far out and had
perceived, as if from an aircraft, dim forms which looked like
Janaki's city, far out to sea. The idea stayed with me and I once
tried to work it into a play.

Janaki was a dynamite fisherman – since the coming of
dynamite the fish have moved very much further out to sea and
have become more scarce. Today the Aegean is full of fishermen
who are thumbless, because of a faulty priming; the standard
lazy man's weapon being a cigarette tin packed with explosives
and primed with a short fuse which makes an explosion in
about two fathoms. Before the time of dynamite the fish were
not only more plentiful but stayed close in to the land. Now
they have to be pursued much further out, which explains why
in poor ports where the men cannot afford good boats and
tackle there is a dearth of fish. This is certainly the case with
Lindos today.

I am much on my guard against chronologies which seem
too water-tight, and against statistics. Theories of gradual

evolution may not be infallible. An entirely new species could, I have always felt, emerge by an accidental jolt or jog caused by the elbow of a sleepy god. The infinite millennia so often posited are the dream-boats of numerologists. As for the science of statistics, I must report respect tempered by scepticism. There was a fine example in Rhodes, where I was saddled with a clerk who went to exaggerated lengths to secure statistics of sales for our little newspaper. Of course you must know who buys your paper and where, for distribution purposes, so I did not discourage his ardour. One day he came to me in some puzzlement and showed me the sales for one small island off Leros, which startled us. Apparently we sold five times more copies than the total population of the island, on which there was only one tiny hamlet. Moreover, I knew from a friend that there was almost nobody except the priest who could read in the place. How then came these prodigious sales?

On my next trip north I called in and the mystery was revealed to me. The price of ordinary brown paper, such as tradesmen use for wrapping, had become very high, because of shortage; they were using my precious newspaper to wrap up their fish because it was cheaper than any other. It was not the prose or the layout or the information which it carried that made them buy; it was a godsend to them for *wrapping fish*. This was a salutary lesson and I often think of it when I study the circulation of a big London paper. Who is wrapping fish in it? Every editor should ask himself the question at least once a day.

Another factor in evolution that interests me is human adaptability. It need not take centuries for an entirely new thought to come into the human mind and create a fashion which runs counter to all that was accepted before. I experienced an example of this too in Rhodes. The Turkish community had no newspaper and we were asked if we could oblige with a small weekly. We had no Turkish founts at the Government Press. Dear old Gabriele, the Venetian head printer, mulled over the problem for a while and then came up with a suggestion. Since Ataturk had romanized the Turkish script, we could set up almost everything they asked us to; but there were two or three gaps – letters with a cedilla, or an apostrophe. The old man said he thought we might find a substitute for the missing letters by turning some of our existing vowels upside down or on their side. It sounded to me most impractical, and a nightmare to hand-set. Gabriele, who loved his plant and everything about print and paper, implored me to let him try, and so I did. The first number was a surprise, and my critics in the administration accused me of trying to give the Turks strabismus and sick headaches. I also got a mild Turkish protest or two. By the third number everyone was reading our new improvised Turkish quite easily and the paper enjoyed the desired success with the community. Come to think of it, the Greek post office has become quite used to receiving and transmitting texts in transliterated Greek. Indeed, I seem to remember that somewhere in Asia Minor there is a community for whom a special edition of the Bible was prepared in transliterated Greek, because though Greek by birth they had never been allowed to learn the alphabet; they had preserved the spoken language phonetically.

When one thinks how systematically and with what tenacity the Italians tried to suppress and undermine Hellenism in these islands for thirty-six years, one is amazed at the resilience and endurance of the Hellenic tradition. It is claimed the Italians were much tougher even than the Turks; they were certainly set on stamping out the embers of Hellenism in order to secure their propaganda pre-eminence in the world at large. I was therefore astonished to find that, though everything had gone under cover, hardly a year passed before the whole trappings of feasts, holy days and religious observance had once more taken possession of the island, for all the world as if they had never been suppressed. The brilliant Byzantine colouring of the Orthodox rituals, the country fairs, the weddings and baptisms emerged with renewed impetus and vigour. It was touching to see the ancient Greek island awake from its long sleep, with an indication that after so long it might be united to metropolitan Greece.

But has Greece ever 'fallen asleep'? It is worth mentioning (in order to stress once more the primordial continuity of things) that just under Lindos, as under the Acropolis in Athens, there is a sacred grotto which is still invoked in prayers – though the present incumbent is called 'The Virgin' (*Panaghia*) instead of Athena. She is equal to every emergency – from plagues, or national disasters of any kind, to sterility and even human illness. The Christian overlay is less than an inch thick. Moreover, with the liberation of the island, all the Orthodox saints popped into the daylight, one after the other. St Nicholas, once Poseidon; Demetrius, once Demeter; Artemidoros who was once Artemis the huntress; Dionysios about whom the less said the better. Sitting in the tavern, under the blaze of whiteness – the heart of light – which is Lindos's citadel, I often heard the saints invoked by Janaki and his friends, and it always reassured me that they should spring so naturally to the lips of these inventive, generous and dispossessed modern Greeks, who had all the same virtues and defects of their long-ago ancestors.

It was here too that I came across the Rhodian version of Pan – the modern orthodox devil which has become his contemporary replacement. For some reason I could not establish, he is called by a different name – *Kallikanzaros* – and he is the chief mischief-maker in the peasant's world. He is a curious mixture of differing attributes. His chief trait is the mischief-making that is already so well expressed in the folklore of

Ireland – or of Germany for that matter. He turns milk sour and generally makes life a misery for the incautious housewife who forgets to put out the traditional battery of charms needed to neutralize his wickedness. In physique he resembles a diminutive Pan or Christian devil. In another sense he is stupid, his behaviour as inconsequent as it is often loutish. He can cause miscarriages or kidnappings – every kind of peasant mis-adventure. It would be fair also to describe him as some sort of changeling, for in the terms of the Orthodox Church (which tacitly accepts his existence) those couples who have intercourse on 25 March will certainly have a *kallikanzaros* child born to them on Christmas Eve! He exists side by side with his more sinister cousin, the vampire, who is less evident here than in Crete, Santorin and northern Greece. Sometimes – an inevit-able result of the historic distortions produced by these long-lived personages – their lines of conduct get confused. In some parts a *kallikanzaros* pops out of a tomb and leaps on to the back of an unwary peasant whom he forces to run across country at breakneck speed until he drops down exhausted by setting a cross of bramble over a suspect tomb.

The Orthodox *vrykolax* has his own sphere of action, and many are the stories told about him and the grim ceremony of staking a suspect body while an anathema is pronounced. One old priest, who told me about two ceremonies of exorcism he had personally witnessed, said that the physical results of the prayer were remarkable – the body literally flew asunder and the joints made a fearful crackling noise, which he imitated vividly by shuffling spittle about in his mouth. He also taught me to look for the sign of a vampire – in case I ever needed to offer a diagnosis. One never knows what might happen in Greece, so I accepted his lesson with grateful attention. The corpse when revealed is particularly bladder-round and fully fleshed, though deathly white. The lips, however, are ruby red, and the lower lip pends, round and thirsty-looking. I have never had a chance to apply all this strange lore; only on one occasion did I ever get near a vampire and then I arrived weeks after the ceremony and the reburial of the corpse. But I was introduced to a small boy who had once been the brightest boy in the village but was then a hopeless idiot. What had happened was this. When they opened the grave of the vampire – a particularly unpleasant villager, a moneylender – they found not only that the body was quite fresh after over two years of burial, but that the orange he held in his hand was still ripe. Incautiously, the child peeled and ate it. It turned his wits and there he is now, a pitiful reminder to us of the demonic powers of the vampire.

I for one firmly believe all this rubbish – there is something about the atmosphere in a Greek island which renders one both superstitious and indulgent towards attacks of ancient Greek aberration disguised in the modern folklore. Nor is it wrong to invoke the psychological power of faith in matters of this kind; I am thinking of the numberless faith-healers in the villages of Greece, and also the diviners who can take a dip into your future – often with remarkable perceptiveness and accuracy. Twice I have had correct fortunes told from my hand – the palm full of ink on one occasion; and I have come across numberless cases of faith-healing for minor ailments. Moreover, there is a pleasant mystery about that strange race of women healers called 'the good women' (*Ai kales gynaikes*); most villages have one, usually a widow or an elderly nun. They have an extensive knowledge of simples and herbs, and often perform remarkable cures. Their work very much intrigued our army doctor, a sceptical Yorkshireman, who wrote a monograph on them for *The Lancet*. There is no knowing where this information was gathered; there is no school for good women, and besides, many of the best healers are illiterate. I remember the

Edinburgh-trained doctor being particularly struck by the fact
that though they were good at massage they knew how to spot a
tuberculous bone and leave it alone. The islands are full of such
little mysteries.

As you swing up out of Lindos the temperature drops with
the change of air and you are cooled by the mountain air. Along
to the north, the country gets harsher and bonier, until you
reach the little end villages around Siana, whence the ascent of
Atabyros must be undertaken. It is the old god-mountain of
Rhodes and echoes Mount Ida on Crete across the way. The
country is abrupt and farmless, and the only reward you will
get from climbing the chief mountain is a stupendous view.
Atabyros has its history also, but it hardly differs from that of
the many mountain sanctuaries of the islands. Once a great
shrine, a few tentative references suggest that human victims
were among its sacrificial offerings – burned alive in a huge
bronze bull. From Siana you curl round upon Monolithos, with
its shocks of mountain grass and spring flowers and great boul-
ders stuck up against the sky. The sea flashes below among the
trees – blue as a kingfisher's wing. It is a splendid corner of the
island for a picnic, or even for a weekend of camping. There is
nothing to see now until you get to Cameirus, which should be
with a westering sun, in a late hot afternoon with bunches of
cicadas strumming their music to the golden airs. Cameirus is
situated like Lindos at the midriff of the island, but on the
opposite side. There is a tiny little harbour, but it is for rowing
boats, and it is clear that even ancient Cameirus did not enjoy
the same maritime advantages as Lindos.

The atmosphere of Cameirus is wonderful. I make no special
plea, but write with the opinion of one who has camped there
winter and summer. The ancient town was never fortified,
which suggests that Cameirus was never invaded and reduced;
it lived on forever in this bronze summer calm with its

orchestra of insects and the whiffs of resin from its pine groves, quite out of time. It lay in the sheltered lee of the island, while Lindos took the brunt of battle and commerce and pirate invasions. Its quiet limestone slopes were ideal for building, and excavations have uncovered the groundplan of a prosperous but somewhat secluded town, which lay here above the sea, its face turned towards Cos and Kalymnos. There is an impressive arrangement of water cisterns which fed the old town; but they suggest not so much sophisticated plumbing as a need to combat water shortages, which are all too common in the islands. The land hereabouts is brown and white limestone. In the summer, the sea becomes a sheet of enamel with an enamel sky above it. One smells earthquakes and takes refuge for a siesta among the pines whose resin perfumes the still air.

The winter rains are of such density, albeit short-lived, that they form tiny torrents that roar down into the ditches dug by the archaeologists. They wash away whole slices of wall so that when they stop you find whole walls that have 'teethed' pottery like a baby's gums. It is tantalizing to see the handles of tear bottles or *amphorae* protruding from the brown soil, which you must not touch while everything is wet for they would snap off. You wait for the sun and let them cook slowly; then one day when the trenches are nice and friable you start with a small brush to dust away and clear them. It is exciting, and demands great patience. During my stay, I uncovered several small bits of pottery for the museum, though nothing upon which I could erect a new theory of Rhodian culture, unfortunately. Meanwhile, what has been uncovered at Cameirus, so I have been told, is only a tithe of what remains to be uncovered in the surrounding foothills of the site. My only regret is that the Germans plonked down a military cemetery on the hillside below, hogging the view of the old town, which was not necessary in an island with so many wonderful corners for military cemeteries.

The little winding road up to the town and, by the same token, to the shrine must have been decorated once by trees and punctuated by statues, and perhaps a fountain. In fine weather the little beach below might take a boat the size of a *caique*, and was undoubtedly a good deal more animated than it is today. The place has its peculiar magic, which never lets you down; and when you sit there on the edge of the hill to watch the sun setting over the deep, you feel the whole weight of evening descending on you, pushed by the penumbra of the turning world. It is time to light that small campfire and unpack the sleeping bags and the other kit. To brew a billy among the stiff, listening pines. From here, the run on into Rhodes town is no great matter in terms of time or distance; and all the more pleasant if undertaken in the evening glow, early enough to allow you to call in at ancient Ialysos and take a look at the Valley of the Butterflies – a curiosity which is well worth a moment's attention. As for Ialysos, now prettily transformed into Mount Phileremo, its history suggests that long before the Greeks it was settled by Phoenicians. However, apart from its role as one of the three capital cities, there is little to tell about it; except that in the Middle Ages a frightful dragon dwelt hard by in a cave, and was finally despatched by a gallant knight, the Chevalier de Gozon, who later joined the knights. The only thing of interest is that in almost every invasion of the island the invader has first landed here. Suleiman was no exception; for the great siege, he pitched his tent and raised his standard here, using Ialysos throughout as a headquarters.

The Valley of the Butterflies (the Petaloudes) is further west, under the little feature called Mount Psinthus, and may be too far to include in the usual one-day itinerary. But it is very strange and worth a visit. A series of narrow, shady ravines have been chosen as a dwelling by this small butterfly; there would be nothing remarkable about this, except that they exist in such numbers that they flow in and out of the ground and among the trees like a soft cloud of dark-winged moths. I say 'dark-winged' because they haunt the shadows of the ravines, but with the slightest touch of sunlight they turn out to be in fact red-winged. The best time to visit them is June or July. For what it is worth, I will add their scientific pedigree, which took me some trouble to unearth. They are day-flying moths (*Callimorpha hera L*) – a variety of the red and black Jersey tiger-moth. Since no eggs or caterpillars belonging to the moth have ever been found in the valley, or for that matter anywhere else in Rhodes, it has been assumed that they are visitors from the Turkish mainland; though why they should choose to congregate in this particular corner of the island rather than any other corner, is a mystery. Once, while I was there, a young Greek entomologist collected a number and took them back to Rhodes town in the hope of breeding them, or at least of finding out whether there was any special herb or perfume which had lured them from so far away. He had no luck with them, as all his specimens died in captivity. So the mystery still remains, though the firework display of the little things continues unabated and is a perpetual delight for visitors to the island.

One of the pleasant features of the Rhodes of the knights was that they encouraged or perhaps even introduced herds of deer, leaving them free to roam at will upon the wooded slopes of the Profeti Elias. In modern times the Italians followed suit, and I once saw some photographs of these pretty animals moving slowly like tiny stars on the side of the mountain. By the time we occupied the place they had disappeared, no doubt into the cooking pots of the Axis troops.

There are many corners of Rhodes that have not been swallowed up by the tourist development – which has largely restricted itself to the butt of the island upon which the original town of Rhodes was constructed. There is a pleasant little spa at Callithea which is a longish walk from the town, but a good place to picnic – a place with medicinal springs which the Italians had hopes of turning into a health spa. Then there are wonderfully peaceful corners like the old stadium or the grove of pines at Rodini. One night, up in the stadium after dark, while we were having a late night drink after a bathe, we saw lanterns and torches moving about – a group of half a dozen young men it would seem. They were looking for someone. The night was starless. Then one of the figures cupped his hands around his mouth and uttered a cry, calling out the name of a girl with an anxiety that stirred the blood. Or perhaps what really thrilled the blood was the name he uttered – 'Eurydice!' It is a cry that echoes on through world literature: 'Where are you?' Moreover he pronounced it in the Greek way as 'Every deechi' with the accent on the third syllable. He only called once. The little group moved on slowly over the brow of the hill and were lost to sight. But the name seemed to echo among the dark shadows. Nor did we ever discover who the young men were, or whom they sought.

When steam replaced sail, Rhodes like the other big islands became less important, and at the time of writing it seems that only brisk tourism will keep the island's economy balanced. The Greeks have wisely kept a customs union with the Dodecanese which confers a wide margin of autonomy as far as prices of commodities go; it was to cushion the fall of the island from the relative opulence in which it lived under Italy against the privations of an impoverished post-war Greece. The plan worked well and is still in force. Tourists also benefit in terms of cheap drinks and smokes.

There could not be a pleasanter place to buy a cottage for the summer; I venture to think that of all the island climates I know, the Rhodian climate is the best in every sense – though Greeks get so passionate about their favourite islands that one hardly dares to say anything like that to them. Compared with the other big Greek islands – Crete, Cyprus, Chios, Samos *et al.* – I think I am right. My memories of its winter weather are still sharp after more than thirty years of living in various other places. It was always with a pang that we took ships to leave Rhodes; the farewell siren echoed up there on Monte Smith and among the green glades of Callithea and Rodini with heartbreak in it.

Carpathos · Nisyros · Casos · Tilos · Astypalea
Symi · Castelorizo · Cos · Calymnos · Leros
Patmos · Icaria

After Rhodes it is fair to call these islands smaller fry. This may seem somewhat opprobrious for a section devoted to such smaller beauties as Carpathos and Castelorizo, even though they are definitely poorer in monuments than the larger key islands whose modern reputation has reflowered under the impetus of tourism. Yet it is necessary to stress a change of scale, for lack of communications makes these islands a little remote. They are for those who seek out quietness rather than ruins, or for those who have work to finish which needs concentration mixed with sea-bathing. Carpathos is an ideal hideaway; and it is not so very tiny, being some forty-seven-odd kilometres in length with a ten-kilometre midriff in parts. It is mostly orchard and vineyard, but rich in trees with plenty of water and shade. The little harbour is pleasant but not memorable: only when one moves inland and strikes villages like Messochori and Kilion does one realize how delightful it might be to rent a room with a family and stay on for a bit. Just a few words of Greek would do the trick – though, as in all these small islands, there is someone who has spent twenty years in Detroit and is hungry all over to talk English again.

From Pigathi, the harbour, you can rent a boat to visit Casos – a smaller, stonier version of the same sort of thing. Or you can ask the harbourmaster to cadge you a lift on a passing *caique* with stores to unload here and there, and thus catch a glimpse of some of the other members of this scattered group.

One of these is Nisyros, a rocky little islet with an extraordinary volcanic crater (diameter four kilometres) punched into its stony armature. According to the ancients Poseidon, in a giant-killing mood, scored a near miss with his trident on a giant called Polybotes; irritated by this he chunked off a giant stone from Cos and hurled it at his enemy, thus crushing him into the ground. Is the crater the product of an earthquake, a volcano or a meteorite? The question remains open. Nisyros is a depressing place, with its burning stones and lack of shade; so you will not be sorry to carry on towards Tilos and Astypalea. Neither of these will seem a patch on Carpathos, even if Astypalea has a somewhat more distinguished history and once harboured the Roman fleet in its spacious bay. Astypalea is also no nest of rocks but relatively fertile, and its Venetian fortress is most picturesque though recently restored. Nevertheless, the charms of Carpathos usually carry the day – I have taken several people there in the past for a few days' holiday.

If these islands seem rather remoter than they should, it is because they are in the main deep, and voyaging among them constitutes a real journey, rather than a bit of pleasure-boating. You can get blown into harbour by a change of wind and locked up for a long weekend, to wait for the weather to change its tune.

The most picturesque, though the most grim at the same time, is Symi, which stands between Rhodes and the coast of Turkey, thrust up like a pitted menhir. Yes, pitted is the word, for the whole island seems to be alveolate – honeycombed rock; at any rate it gives that dramatic impression, especially in winter, during the lulls between the heavy storms which play about in this region, pushed up from Africa or Crete. Rounding Symi close in, I remember the noise made by those underground grottoes and blowholes: a prodigious slobbering and snoring, wailing and swishing – as if a thousand whales were holding a political meeting of supreme importance. It was a most awesome and melancholy sound, and gave the little island in midwinter an extraordinary feeling of strangeness and remoteness ... as if it were a sort of Tristan, lost in the far Atlantic surges. Also, down here the islands in and around Rhodes are relatively unprotected from the north wind and the cross-surges of the main deep. If you start moving north, on to Cos and Calymnos, you find calmer seas and more protection from the mountains of Turkey; you also travel on the inland waters, between the mainland and the island in question, just as you do in the Ionian, and this makes for safer and more reliable navigation. I have vivid memories of being taken aboard naval craft as a passenger, and scouting these channels with maddening slowness behind that curious instrument called a paravane, which pushed on several hundred yards in front of us to tangle and set off mines. A nervy sort of operation which justified the occasional touch of pink gin all round.

It would not be fair to move north without casting a friendly glance at the remotest of the little islands, which would make an excellent honeymoon paradise. This is Castelorizo, which almost touches the coast of Asia Minor. It is spare and neat in its scenery, with just enough history to intrigue a visitor without overwhelming him. The bathing is wonderful, the sea of dazzling clarity, and in this remote nook the underwater fishing is excellent. Another pleasure, too, is the small population – under three hundred – which gives a visitor the feeling of intimacy that one has in a small village. One knows everyone by sight in a day, and intimately in a long weekend. The island, however, is completely dependent upon Rhodes for its supplies – apart from seafood – and its needs are covered by a twice-weekly ferry service. It is a long thresh – seven hours in calm seas, and perhaps more in rough ones. When I first saw it (the word 'thresh' was deliberately chosen) the link was assured by two lumbering tank-landing craft which chewed their way back and forth across the stretch of open sea with the provisions needed by the island folk. Perhaps now communications have improved in speed and organization, but the journey was what the Navy used to call an 'open leg' of sea. You lumbered along the coast of Turkey all night; remote mountain villages twinkled up and disappeared like fireflies. Then, near dawn, you rounded a tall black shape and the harbour burst into view, with its rectangles of light. All the inhabitants were down at the port waiting for us; they had heard the engines far away.

As may be imagined, a small, undefended island in such a remote corner, overlooked by the Turkish mountains, has had a long and chequered history of invasions and conquests; it has been owned by seven different nations, and yet had managed during quite long spells to become affluent through skilful use of its fine harbour. Once, towards the turn of the century, it even owned some three hundred vessels, but it lacked the capital to convert to steam quickly enough. The island's power declined. Then, during World War I, the whole fleet was sold at a blow to the British for use in the Dardenelles campaign; the inhabitants were rich in gold sovereigns for a while, but that did not halt the economic decline. Now there are more island immigrants in Australia than there are residents in Castelorizo itself. They proudly call themselves 'Kassies' and frequently come home on visits, as all Greeks do. The last world war proved unlucky for the place, as an ill-calculated attempt at a landing by the Allies provoked a German bombardment of exceptional severity, and a whole quarter of the town was razed. Once the population was some 14,000 strong; now the majority of citizens are Australian.

You can swim across the harbour and climb to the little museum, which houses quite a number of mementoes of the island's past. Among the most singular are the pictures of the harbour full of hydroplanes during the thirties, when the place enjoyed a brief renaissance. There were as many as eight flights a day from Paris! There are also some nineteenth-century pictures executed during a prosperous period when the seafaring families owned about three hundred three-masted schooners. A history of ups and downs if ever there was one.

Since there isn't much to do in the island except get brown and swim, it is amusing to hear the local gossips talk, after the manner of peasant-poets, about a lost treasure chest full of gold pieces, buried somewhere in the foothills around the town by pirates during the Middle Ages. There is also, according to Strabo who once visited the island, a lost city with the charming name of Cysthine, which has left no trace. Such legends, if they are legends rather than literal truth, make one keep a sharp eye out when picnicking on the bare, brown hills with their rare outbursts of vine and vegetation. If time and tide are favour-able, the local patriots will insist that you visit their famous grottoes. It takes about an hour to reach them, but the trip will not disappoint anyone energetic enough to undertake the somewhat chancy journey along the fretted coast of the island. The grottoes are finer than those of Capri, but the visit has to be carefully calculated; for, when the sea rises under wind, the entrances get blocked, and there is a risk of being trapped inside. They have several names, one of which, *Fokiali*, suggests that seals once congregated here, as in so many places in Greece. The dimensions given for this fine natural feature – 150 metres long and 80 metres broad – do not manage to convey its real splendour, which comes from the height of the ceiling (in places 35 metres). Prodigious sea shadows falter and flicker about in the blue darkness. It is worth the risk and effort. Go!

The visit will make you realize, too, that here in Castelorizo, one is halfway to Patrick Kinross's *Orphaned Isle*, Cyprus, submerged now as once Crete was in the toils of that hideous Laocoön, international politics.

The slow return to Rhodes must be faced before you are free to skirt gaunt Symi and head north into Cos, the island of Hippocrates, which has never failed to excite the visitor to eulogy. Poet and wayfarer alike have always appreciated Cos for its green abundance and quietness. It lies lapped in a fold of the Turkish mainland, which thrusts out great promontories now, one upon another, with spectacular fjords laid up between. Cos, the most sheltered of the Dodecanese Islands and deservedly the most praised. It would be downright dishonest to raise a dissenting voice against merits so self-evident in these green and smiling valleys, rich with fruit and flowers. Even its long and variegated history seems less full of bloodshed than that of its neighbours – though perhaps this is an illusion.

There are places benign and places baleful; and I seem to remember that in the treatise on *Soils, Airs, Waters* attributed to Hippocrates himself, the doctor-saint of Cos makes some attempt to describe the often fortuitous combination of the three elements necessary to create a site with natural healing properties. Such a study was an obvious undertaking for the ancient Greek priest-healers, since it was in these benign spots that the Aesculapia were erected – not always where there were mineral springs, though sometimes, as in Cos, these were present. Without being unduly imaginative, the modern visitor to such choice areas will feel, or seem to feel, some of the harmony and natural richness which in the past made these ancient sanatoria places of world pilgrimage for the sick and troubled. The gaps in our knowledge about ancient methods of healing are particularly irritating, for what we know comes largely from late Roman sources. The incubatio is an example; a room where the sick patient was made to sleep, his diagnosis being dependent on the dreams produced during his first night. The great snakes also, that lived in the pits, had a definite role to play in the process – symbolic or functional, who can say? Aesculapian lore is a hopeless tangle, and we live in hopes that one day soon the Indian elements of the caduceus will be sorted out by some competent student of comparative religion, so that we may enjoy more deeply our visits to Cos and Epidaurus. These two places seem to bask in the same choice calm and smiling peace.

The seascapes are very fine here in the approaches to Cos. Northward, in the blue haze, are the dark shapes of the Calymnos hills, while opposite is the strange wild hinterland of Turkey, with its vast empty spaces seemingly so wild and untenanted. The deep water sweeps round gradually, changing colour as it enters the noble little bay of the capital, which is crowned with a fifteenth-century fortress left behind by the knights when they abandoned these smiling regions for a grimmer and bonier Malta. Dotted around hereabouts one also sees a number of strategically placed martellos, which were used once to keep the narrow straits under observation – for this little corner was, in terms of warfare against the infidel, always a 'hot' area. Big fleets could gather in the shade of Turkey for an assault on the Venetian or Genoese forces. There were excellent yards for re-fitting at Symi and in later times in Leros. Yet despite the dangers and rigours, 'There is no pleasanter land under the Heavens than Cos', writes Pourqueville, 'and viewing its lovely scented gardens you would say it was a terrestrial paradise.'

Today this is even more true, for it remains an unspoilt backwater where the visitor will find good beaches, unsophisticated but clean little hotels, and cool breezes even in mid-summer.

The old capital was called Astipalea, but after it was sacked the Coans decided to move house, and a new city, Chora, was established on its present site in 366 BC – a very successful move, if we are to believe the eulogies of Diodorus: 'The people of Cos at that time settled themselves in the town they now enjoy, adorning it with the gardens it now has. It became extremely populous and a very costly wall was constructed right round it, and a harbour built. From this time onwards, it grew apace, both in public revenues and in private fortunes, and in general it rivalled the most celebrated cities of the world.'

There is little in modern Chora which echoes this golden period, though the green gardens are still there, and the oleanders and olives continue to flourish. Today, the little town is on the scruffy side. Among the shadows and echoes of its remoter renown, one comes upon several evocative names which are almost as celebrated as Hippocrates himself. Among them is Theocritus, who came all the way from his native Sicily to study with Philetas and who is popularly supposed to have used his Coan experience to furnish the detail in his Seventh Idyll. Whether this is true or not is a problem for profounder scholars than I, but some of the difficulty in disentangling influences may come from the similarity between the two landscapes. Sicily is, in this sense, as thoroughly Greek as Cyprus; the poet must have felt quite at home in Cos. Another echoing name is Apelles, whose world-famous statue of Aphrodite is supposed to have adorned the Aesculapion – which lies some two miles out of town on very easily negotiable roads and should not be missed at any price.

Although the site of the Aesculapion is really the thing most worth seeing, the three-terraced sanatorium lies in a beautiful position, tucked into a limestone fold of the hill. It has been in part reconstructed and perhaps retouched by the Italians, but not too fancifully I think. The original has disappeared, but we know that the Hellenistic version, on which the Italian archaeologists worked, covered the ancient site – which was revived and remodelled by a physician called Xenophon, who is said to have poisoned the poor Emperor Claudius. (History is full of surprises, and one wonders whether a man capable of reviving such a hallowed site would also be capable of dispatching his emperor.) Talking of poison reminds me that the grave and noble formulations of the healing code – the Oath of the Hippocratic doctor – do not appear in even the most detailed guide books. It is worth quoting here, since even in translation some of the magical quality of his idealism and humanity comes through and it is relevant to the spirit of Cos:

I shall look upon him who shall have taught me this art even as one of my parents. I will share my substance with him and relieve his need should he be in want. His children shall be as my own kin, and I will teach them the art, if they so wish, without fee or covenant ... The regimen I adopt shall be for the benefit of my patients according to my ability and judgment, and not for their hurt or for any wrongdoing. I will give no deadly drug to anyone, even if it be asked of me, nor will I counsel such, and most especially I will not aid a woman to procure an abortion. Whatsoever house I enter, I will go there for the benefit of the sick, refraining from all wrongdoing or corruption, and most especially from any act of seduction, of male or female, of bond or free. Whatever things I may hear concerning the life of men during my attendance on the sick, or even apart from them, which should be kept secret, I will keep my own counsel upon, deeming such things as sacred secrets.

The three restored terraces well justify their existence, for it would be difficult without them to visualize how the whole area must have looked – the lowest terrace appears to have been the hospital, and the highest one the temple area. But even at its very oldest period, the site was several times enlarged before the Romans came on to the scene, so that as usual all the inscriptions are confused and tentative. There is a strange antique architrave just south of the main Aesculapion area, in which there was a spring named Bourinna by the private physician of Nero, a certain Andromachos of Crete. It is horrible to think

that somewhere inside this sacred area there once stood statues
of Nero, who so obligingly incarnated not only Aesculapius
himself but also Hygeia and Epioni for the sculptor's chisel.
There is nothing like being a god. But let us leave these strange
fragments of information and conjecture, so laboriously gathered together in the guide books. Whatever happens, do not
miss the splendid views from the first long terrace; you can see
as far as Bodrun (ancient Halicarnassus) on the Turkish coast
and in fair weather even catch a glimpse of rugged Samos.

There are several atmospheric villages worth a visit in the
island, and some have medieval monuments or icons to show,
but there is nothing you really should not miss. Pretty Karda-
mena will not disappoint, and if you climb to Asfendiou, you
will at once consider the pleasures of buying a village house and
spending a few years helping flowers to push up in some
sheltered courtyard tiled with black-and-white sea-pebble.

But it has got something, Cos, and can already claim a number of distinguished addicts; I know several people who come
back for holidays year after year. A small story clings to the
outskirts of my memory – about dreams. I have always longed
to know more about Aesculapian healing and, in particular,
about the function of dreams in the ancient medical system. In
Epidaurus long ago, I came across a museum curator who told
me that if you slept in the healing part of the Aesculapion you
had confused and frightening dreams and nightmares. I wanted
to experiment by camping in this spot alone for a month in
summer in order to record dreams; but the war broke out and
we were chased ignominiously into Egypt. What with the post-
war difficulty of finding jobs in the Aegean, I never managed to
secure for myself a Greek posting, and so Epidaurus had to
wait. However, once when I was in Cos and visiting the
Aesculapion on a sunny day in winter, I found a couple of
soldiers camping in a bell tent among the ruins. I stopped for a

brew-up and the traditional blow and harsh word. In the course of their chatter, they said that they had started camping inside the ruins but had slept so badly that they had moved their tent higher up and into the open where there was more wind. I asked if they had any special kind of dream – but no, it was just something about the place that had made them feel uneasy.

The ladies of Cos were famous once for their beauty, and there are still handsome antelopes about today to keep the reputation of the Coan girls high in the esteem of the world.

Before leaving the island you should visit, and indeed spend an afternoon drowsing under, the so-called plane tree of Hippocrates which, like some old boa constrictor, has completely entwined a whole square in its toils. It has sprouted arms and legs in all directions, and the kindly worshippers have propped up one limb after another, with stone columns, to prevent them breaking off. The tree spreads a deep shade when in leaf, and covers an extraordinary amount of ground. It must be extremely old, though perhaps not actually old enough to have existed in Hippocrates' time. It shades a minute mosque of great charm, and indeed the enclosed place is one of the pleasantest and prettiest corners of this smiling island. I slept under the tree for two nights hoping that the spirit of the old god-physician might confer some of his healing powers upon me, but it was winter and all I achieved was a touch of rheumatism.

Calymnos and Leros are almost Siamese twins, but there could not be two more contrasting places. Calymnos is big, blowsy and razor-shaven, yet open to the sea and sky and all their humours; Leros is a gloomy shut-in sort of place, with deep fjords full of lustreless water, black as obsidian, and as cold as a polar bear's kiss. Leros means dirty or grubby in Greek, and the inhabitants of the island are regarded as something out-of-the-ordinary by the other little Dodecanese islands. They are supposed to be surly, secretive, and double-dealing, and in my limited experience I found this to be so. But it may be that uncomfortable winter journeys across the channel that separates them from their neighbours (it is a mile at its widest) result in their giving this impression, unfairly.

Hop the strait to Calymnos, and the whole atmosphere changes; even the sky seems bluer. You are in the island of sponges now, and it is on this hazardous trade that the reputation of Calymnos depends today; throughout Greece, even in the main squares of Athens, you will find her sponges being marketed by old sailors or the widowed mothers of mariners lost at sea during the sponge seasons. Ovid saw Calymnos as 'shaded with trees and rich in honey'. No longer; the hills are shaven as smooth as a turtle's back, and the bare rock with its fur of hill *garrigue* has the slightly bluish terracotta tinge of volcanic rock. There is really nothing much to see except the fine harbour – where you will at once run into the island's obsession with sponges, which will be lying out in quantities on the quays to dry, while squatting men darn their nets against the next foray. But since the turn of the century, they have had to go further and further away for their sponges, for the Aegean beds are no longer as rich as they were.

Until the turn of the century, the traditional hunting ground for sponges was in and around these islands, particularly near Astypalea, though the men who embarked on this hazardous trade came from a number of different islands. Always the business itself seemed to be centered in Calymnos, possibly because of its excellent anchorage facilities and the storage space offered along its broad quays. Calymnos has remained the centre, even though now, with the diminishing sponge beds (not to mention the competition brought about by the invention of artificial sponges), hunters have to go much further afield and work at profounder levels. The dangers of sponge-hunting have been vastly increased by the need to dive deeper, for the old skin-diving technique has had to be replaced by costume-diving – and there is little money to spend on expensive, highly-sophisticated gear. Until recently, ancient diving-suits, long since condemned as unsafe by the British and French navies, were not uncommon, there were special diving-boats with air-pumps, and a glance at the ancient equipment still in use was enough to make the blood run cold. Perhaps now there exists some insurance against the hazards of this poetic trade; and the aqualung has made things easier. I hope so. Accidents are not infrequent, and you have to be a brave and hardy young man to adopt sponge-diving as a profession. Diving at increasing depth can also be responsible for the dreadful occupational disease of nitrogen bubble-poisoning of the blood, known as 'the bends'. Calymnos town has a number of such martyrs, bent and twisted little men, old at forty, and thrown on the scrapheap of the labour market.

It is hard to believe, when it reaches the bathroom, that the sponge is really an animal – a filter-feeding animal which propels water through the network of channels which go to make up its structure, feeding on the minute organisms which find their way into its toils. Some five thousand species exist, of every colour under the sun, but the richest and commonest variety is harvested in the eastern Mediterranean, with the Calymniot fleet playing a great part in the harvesting. About two hundred feet is average for sponge depths, although in the rich, old days there were beds sufficiently shallow to be plucked from a rowboat, with the help of a boathook or a grapnel. Nowadays it is a long burning journey to the coasts of Cyprus or Libya for a whole season, with a somewhat risky return to home base when the weather breaks. The ex-votos in the little local shrines and churches tell graphic and picturesque stories through crude little paintings of the dangers encountered and escaped – with the help of the patron saint, of course.

The preparation of the captured sponges is sometimes done aboard, more often in greater comfort along the hospitable quays of the harbour. The technique is to rot away the soft tissues and gradually press them out, rinsing repeatedly in sea-water and then letting them air-dry. It is an exacting, somewhat boring operation, and quite smelly too.

It is also somewhat startling to realize that sexual reproduction is the order of the day in all – or nearly all – species; and the sponge has almost as long and eventful a history as the Mediterranean itself. Even within the time-span of our own civilization, this useful little animal was a commonplace household adjunct in Greece and Rome. The servants in the *Odyssey* swabbed tables with it, while it was in great demand with artisans, who used it to apply paint, and with soldiers who had no drinking vessels to hand. In the Middle Ages, burned sponge was reputed to cure various illnesses. Together with olive oil it has been used from time immemorial as a contraceptive pessary by the oldest professionals – who, oblivious of the fact that they figure in the pages of Athenaeos, still flourish in the Athens *Plaka* today – using roughly the same sort of slang, in which the word 'sponge' finds many a picturesque use. Another out-of-the-way use for it was as a pad worn inside classical armour – one can see why.

Venice secured such a firm monopoly over the sponge trade during the period of her ascendancy that the little object became known as a 'Venetia'. According to Ernle Bradford, the two main marketable types today are called respectively the honeycomb and the cup – which refer to their shape. Artisans still find a use for real sponges as opposed to artificial ones, and in surgery they also have a function. But the trade is, if not declining, at least becoming a tougher and tougher problem for the Calymnos sailors. They must go further afield in their small boats, which have hardly changed in styling and size since the days of the *Odyssey*.

I once saw the fleet setting out for Libya, and the sight was unforgettable, worthy of some great classical painter. We had come bumping and ballocking into harbour in the early afternoon to find everyone assembled on the quays – the wives and children all in their Sunday best. The boats had been waiting for the weather to break – there had been squalls and rain all day. The taverns were open and here and there sprouted a man with a glass in his hand, but the tension in the air, the pain of leave-taking, the heavy weight of the absence to be borne, the uncertainties and dangers to be encountered . . . everything was marked on the dark faces of the silent women. They were as still and undemonstrative as leaves, and the children holding their skirts looked up anxiously into their faces from time to time, as if to try to ascertain what their emotions might be, so that they could model their own behaviour on that of the grown-ups. A deep, instinctive sadness and concern reigned, a few jests and raucous exchanges by the men could not dispel the deep charm of sorrow which lay over the town. A church bell bonged and was silent. Oppressed by a feeling of poetic fatality – so ancient Greek in its vividness – we came ashore silently and sat on rickety chairs against the tavern wall to watch the departure. For already the signs of a lift in weather were apparent, and the dispositions of the fishing boats were such as to remind one of runners 'on their marks' waiting for the pistol. The tavern-keeper, a veteran whose diver's palsy had driven him to retire at the age of thirty, served some cold octopus with red sauce and a fiery *ouzo*. But there was none of the usual chaffing and gossip. Some last-minute touches were being put to the nearest *caique*, and I saw their heavy wooden breadbin fully stocked with the dry biscuit, hard as rock, that is called *paximadi*. (Cyprus proverb: 'The hardest biscuit always falls to the sailor with the fewest teeth.') They would suck and gnaw these things all through the voyage, occasionally varying this stony diet with whatever they found in the ports where they touched – vegetables or lamb. Apart from *paximadi*, the basic shipboard food was chunks of pig fat, which were laid up in the lockers for use. A sinister taste this food has, too. But it must do the trick, for later in Yugoslavia my driver, who had been a local field peasant, produced what he said was a typical field worker's midday meal: it consisted of a huge chunk of pork fat, a tilt of fiery *slivovic* and a brown crust of bread. In the snow it was excellent for stamina, but down in the Aegean? They live on nothing, the sponge fleets; one old man spoke of them with a rhetorical flourish as 'men who suck their living from sponges as the sponges suck theirs from the tide'.

The captains had not been wrong: a veil of dense, bluish light now fell over the harbour, the sun blazed out, and the most extraordinary calm began to fall and spread. On the horizon there were still some battle lines of sheep moving about, but the middle distance was already sighing its way back into stillness. One could smell that the night would be leaden calm, starless, humid and damp, but with only an oily swell to trouble about. Dawn would see them closing in to Crete, and with any luck they would next day sight Africa . . . There was a shout, and the leading vessel started to churn and sway, its engines started. More cries and gesticulations; the cavalcade assembled, bucking and stamping, and began to make its way towards the harbour entrance. On the quay, everyone stood quite still, like a Greek chorus, the blood quickened by the drama of this leave-taking with its burning emotions and its hazards. No bravado, though. The sailors turned back from time to time and waved, but nobody moved among the black-clad groups on the quay. Then, as the last boat rounded the ultimate spur, a tall, bearded sailor stretched out his arms and waved, immediately crossing himself, and at once in silence all our hands went up in a hieratic farewell. It was only after a hush, such as might greet the ending of some great piece of music, that one heard one or two sobs from the dark ranks of the women, and then the strident chatter of the children bubbling up irrepressibly as from some hidden spring of happiness. The sponge-fleet had put to sea. The quiet animation of relief set in now, and the taverns slowly filled up with the men left behind, mostly old seafarers or landworkers. For the women, the long wait of months had begun.

Calymnos's capital is an unprepossessing little place; the narrow streets have an untended look, and it is not surprising that it does not enjoy the suffrage of the tourists to anything like the extent of Cos in the south and Patmos in the north. The reason, I think, is that the inhabitants think of it as more a sponge-workshop than a place of residence; and their secret is that they all have little summer houses on the western flank of the island, for which, once the good weather arrives and the fleet departs, they abandon Pothia. Anyone who coasts the western shore will certainly appreciate their preference – it is full of deserted beaches and lonely bays, perfect for bathing-picnics or work on the Differential Calculus – not to speak of the Unified Field Theory. In this lambent, fine air, one feels the pulse-beat of the ancient pre-Socratic philosophers: men like Heraclitus, who first posed questions we are still trying to answer satisfactorily. It is pleasant to think of them lazing about, eating olives and spitting the pips into their hands, as they wrestled with questions which weigh down the human reason and the intuition alike. Here and there, on the firm gold sand, you will find the scribble of gulls' feet and be reminded that the first blackboard of the thinker must have been the sand. Picking up a piece of driftwood, he thoughtfully drew a sacred triangle or a Pythagorean pentacle; all this long before papyrus was discovered and the scroll born.

In this sort of island there is nothing much to do once the fleet has gone, so that you can always rent a boat or a small *caique* for a modest fee and explore the nooks and crannies of its piratical coastline. It is quite a good idea to do what Greek holidaymakers so often do, get yourself 'marooned' for a day or a weekend. Start by borrowing a sack and filling it with a couple of blocks of ice upon which to put your beer, wine, butter, and anything else which might turn with the heat. Strike a price with your boatman to carry you to the bathing beach of your choice and Crusoe you. But if you do this, *do not* forget to take an umbrella or parasol – even several of them. The stretch of heat from midday to sundown can turn a Nordic skin to roast pork and cost the unwary person a couple of days in bed with fever; it's a fine way to ruin a holiday. Your boatman will return at evening to get you, and carry you home to harbour at sundown, exhausted and happy and burning (in several senses) for a cold shower and an *ouzo* with ice, plus a slice of delicious cold octopus. There is nothing to compare with the sense of well-being after such a day – and it is all quarried out of frugality. Greece is a wonderful school for hoggish nations; you suddenly realize that you don't need all the clobber of so-called civilization to achieve happiness and physical well-being. Just to think of a Paris menu, or a Los Angeles dustbin, fills one with shame, makes one queasy. How did we get to be this way – we pigs?

One *caveat*, which you will learn from your Greek friends: don't pay the boatman the full price, all in a lump. Pay an advance on the full price and the rest when you are safely home. I say this because some boatmen are forgetful creatures, and I am reminded of an occasion in Mykonos when a kindly American paid the whole fare to be Crusoe'd on Delos, without knowing that the boatman combined alcoholism with amnesia.

He was stuck for the night; and when at last he got back, his boatman was found drunk in a tavern and asserted that he had never seen the American before in his life. Although this kind of forgetfulness is relatively rare, it is worth taking precautions.

It is worth knowing, too, that in such a case you would certainly be able to secure redress by calling on the Tourist Police. They are a unique invention, as far as I know – a civil police force whose sole job is to watch over tourists, smooth out their difficulties, keep an eye on swindling prices. They have no criminal function, being a sort of *garde champêtre*, but they are very much up to the mark; and every morning they patrol the market, checking prices and running in tradesmen who try to smart-alec the tourist. In any question of altercation, you should not hesitate to call on them. They were invented by that wonderful man Karamanlis, the present Prime Minister – certainly the greatest Greek political figure since Venizelos. He also invented the marvellous new road system and the little government hotels called the Xenias. Those of us who have done Greece on foot, muleback, and in derelict, smoking buses, always covered in flea-bites, will never cease to bless the name of the man who has made everything so easy of access. It is not his fault that vulgar speculators have tried to ruin the atmosphere with the juke-box and transistor, with the so-called First Class Hotel – factors which only alienate the poor tourist who comes from a country where these things are manufactured, and is trying to get away from them.

I shall say little – there is little to say – about the grotto of the Seven Virgins, which lies a little way outside the town. As with so many inconvenient ancient Greek Nereids, the Orthodox church tried to make a moral story out of them. Such was their purity that, when some wicked pirates came, they retired to a cave and were never heard of again. However, they work the same miracles as their ancestors the nymphs – as you will see from the wall inscriptions and the slips of petticoat attached here and there, even to bushes outside. If you wish to conceive, a slip of your petticoat and a prayer to them will usually do the trick. I know a lady who tried this with great success, and her son, like any Calymniot sponge-fisherman, actually went to sea when he grew up.

The Dodecanese (Twelve) Islands lie or trail down the whole length of frowning Turkey – a slender vertebral column, each one a mountain tip – linking the two big islands, Samos and Rhodes, head and tail, so to speak. Perhaps 'frowning' is a trifle unkind, though the Turkish mountain ranges overtop the island hills and seem free from all life that is not nomadic. Yet the fate of this group of islands has always been actively linked to the present Turkish mainland, and it is only in recent times that they have found themselves cut off. I suspect that the Asia Minor disaster, that foolish Greek campaign, was one of the causes, and that it has left a traumatic wound in the sly and secretive Turkish temperament, rather as the repeated invasions by Germany have affected the French. It is not possible to convince an ordinary Frenchman that Germany is now no longer belligerent; he won't swallow it. So I think a good deal of heady, Greek propaganda about The Great Idea of a Greater Greece overseas has made the Turks suspicious and unco-operative. Where does this Great Idea come from? Perhaps it is some absurd vestigial reaction, echoing the ancient Greek expansion into Italy and Sicily . . . No, this can't be true, because each little colony – Rhodes, Corinth, Athens, and so on – acted separately, and they were often at war with each other. It is more likely to be some relic of a Byzantine pipe-dream. But whatever its origin, its consequence was fatal to two neighbours who have need of each other. Much of ancient Greek history took place over the water – Troy, Halicarnassus, are still there to be visited; while in more recent times, one has only to read a novel like *Aeolia* by

Venezis to realize how much the Greeks felt at home in Turkey and what a wrench it was for them to find themselves 'exiled' to places like Athens or Salonika. Think of Smyrna in flames, of Ataturk ... The Greeks have always been hasty, intemperate and great chatterboxes, while the Turks by temperament are shy, secretive and literal-minded. When they lived side by side, they got on famously. Even in Byron's day not all pachas were tyrants; as a breed, they were mostly lazy and profligate, were dumb and could be bribed. The Greeks I knew from Asia Minor have a real, amused affection for the Turks. In Rhodes, one told me that when they wanted impartial and fair legal judgment on some matter under arbitration, they asked a Turkish *mufti* to pronounce on it and accepted what he said.

The Dodecanese lingered long under Turkish rule; but they were referred to as the 'Privileged Islands' since they enjoyed tax exemptions and special privileges granted in the age of Suleiman the Magnificent. These they kept right up until 1908, when the islands united against Turkish rule – egged on by you-know-who. They were liberated in 1912, and Greece was promised that they would be restored to her at the end of the war. However, at the Treaty of Sèvres, the promise simply evaporated and they were given to Italy as a reward for her war services. It was not until 1948 that they returned to Greece; yet they have always been as distinctively Greek as any other Aegean island. One wonders how the Greeks have managed to keep their affection for the British in spite of all this jobbery.

Though the word 'Dodecanese' was not officially applied to them until 1908, they must always have been thought of as a group of twelve, as they are so referred to by a Byzantine chronicler as early as 758 or thereabouts.

The most northerly, and in a queer sort of way the most anomalous, of the group is Patmos, which lies like a tortoise in a spatter of atolls, sculpturally rather fine, but not scenically outstanding. What makes it seem strange is that it is wholly a Christian island, with no whiff of ancient Greece about it. There seems to be no trace there of the usual succession of invasions, or Neolithic habitations, or whatnot. It suddenly emerges in full glory with the *Apocalypse*, that strange, transcendental poem which is worthy of an early Dylan Thomas. The mere fact that the *Apocalypse* was born in the lugubrious hole that the monks still show you with pride and awe instantly puts Patmos into the top class of poetic evocation.

The monastery on top of the island is grimly beautiful in a rather reproachful way, and it crowns perfectly the small oatcake of the island, which has practically no green, is nearly all uncompromising stone. Seven hills, seven letters, seven candlesticks, seven stars . . . The punch-drunk numerologist who gave us this magnificent doom-laden poem is said to have conceived and executed it in a cave, over which there stands now a chapel dedicated to St Anne and the *Apocalypse*. Here the resident monk will show you not only a picture of St Anne, but also the hole in the rock which was riven by the voice of God as it came upon St John. The whole extravanganza was taken down at the speed of revelation itself, presumably in shorthand, by his disciple, Prochorus, who used a protruding piece of wall as a desk. It reads magnificently in our English version – as richly as a Welsh nervous breakdown at an Eisteddfod. On the wall, a silver halo marks the spot where the Apostle laid his head to rest. The place is inconceivably gloomy in winter – my last visit was during a storm. The wind howls outside and, inside the dark rock-chamber, you hear the mountain teeming with invisible springs, the noise of water everywhere macerating pebbles, the drip, drip of rain at the entrance. The monk of that epoch was a sad rascal, who looked like a half-drowned spaniel but was clearly very superstitious, for he crossed himself ardently every time the wind moaned. I was glad to get out and back to the

port where my companion had brewed up in a tavern with no
window panes. Pencils of white light moved about the sky like
searchlights in the pitch-dark afternoon. It was only three in the
afternoon, and yet lights had to be lighted. Successive flashes of
lightning flared on the windows of the monastery high up on
the crown of the hill. I pitied poor Prochorus at his stone desk,
taking down this elaborate poem with its Asiatic images. The
site of the revelation was neglected for centuries, and it was
only in 1088 that the Emperor Alexis Comnenos granted the
place to St Christodoulos for the founding of a monastery.

When one thinks how rife piracy was in these waters at that
time, one wonders whether the emperor's gift was a polite way
of exiling an awful bore. Whether or no, it was an act of great
temerity to start off and found a monastery in so unprotected a
place. Nevertheless, the old saint set about building and the
result of his labours and that of several generations after him is
still here for us to admire. It is all painted stark white, and the
towers and steeples are patterned in cubist motifs of great
beauty, without a trace of prettiness. From the top, walking the
ramparts of this lowering castle, you can see that Patmos is
formed from three masses of metamorphic rock, all but severed
from each other. Port Scala, an excellent lie-in when there is
high wind or a brutal sea, is a deep-cut fjord which all but
sections the island into two parts. The site of the ancient town
was down here when, for a brief while, it was an Ionian settlement; later on, the Romans exiled troublesome politicians here.
The rest is anonymity and piracy until the good St Christodoulos came along; and the strength and strategic positioning
of his great castle-monastery shows to what extent the place
had to be made defensible. The body of its founder lies in a
casket in a chapel full of squirming Byzantine decoration whose
murky splendour is impressive but not very uplifting. As for St
John ... it does not seem absolutely certain that the great

document he produced was written in Patmos at all; we know only that Domitian had him exiled here about AD 95. What is curious is that the 'Acts of St John', a work of pious hagiography written by his disciple, Prochorus, deals with all the miracles he performed in the island but does not actually mention that the *Apocalypse* was written here. Anyway, the book itself was never accepted by the Orthodox and figures in the *Apocrypha*. It was just too good.

Pacing the battlements of the monastery, you can enjoy a splendid view of the whole island, and also catch a glimpse of sinister Mount Cerceteus lying to the north like a watchful hammer-head shark. It seems to attract electrical storms, and the frequent displays of fireworks have given rise to a number of legends in the island itself, where the peasants call it St John's Light. I have tried to find a concrete side to this rather odd ascription – perhaps a folk-tale or a legend which would explain what the devil (*sic*) St John might have had to do with electrical storms on the faraway mountain – but have had no success. The peasant woman I asked could not answer my question, but it certainly did not trouble her; she simply shrugged her shoulders and went on beating an octopus against the rocks of Scala, in order to soften it up for lunch. The real treasure of Patmos is the great library, and this is what makes it worthwhile to mount a mule and go wobbling up the precipitous road to the monastery; this and of course the views.

The great library is now no more than a shadow of its former self. Diligent 'collectors' across a couple of centuries have stolen or borrowed priceless things, which have later turned up in the national libraries of Germany, France and England. The same argument which is trotted out to excuse the affair of the Elgin Marbles is in order here – namely, that local ignorance and neglect constituted a greater danger to the manuscripts than their pilfering for a market which at least preserved the spoils of these forays. There would, say we, have *been* no Elgin Marbles to squabble over had Elgin not bought them – for the local Greak apathy was exceeded only by Turkish neglect. And now that the Acropolis itself is melting away, a victim of the petrol engine, what is one to think? Myself, I think I should have given them back and kept copies of them in plaster for the British Museum. For us, they are a mere possession of great historic interest. For the Greeks they are a symbol, inextricably bound up with their national struggle not only against the Turks, but also against an image of themselves as bastard descendants of foreign tribes (not Greeks at all); an image which they very successfully shattered during the Albanian campaign, thus putting modern Greece squarely on the world maps as the right true heir to the Periclean heritage. Their simple 'No' to Mussolini was as perfect as any Periclean declaration.

In the catalogue of the Patmos library, some six hundred manuscripts are recorded; but now only two hundred and forty are left to admire. The most valuable, and at the same time the most charming to the eye, is the celebrated Codex Porphyrius of the fifth century, of which the major portion is still in Russia. The Orthodox Church has always had strong links with the Balkans, though there are now only a few monasteries left which were originally populated by Russian monks for whom Mount Athos was always a place of holy pilgrimage. The absoluteness of this strange peninsula, where no female creature (neither woman nor hen) is welcome, mark it out as an uncompromising forcing-house for monks disposed to mysticism. Mind you, laymen with a religious turn of mind often arrange to take a retreat in an Athos monastery, in order to purge their souls of the material dross of everyday life. The two poets, Kazanzakis and Sikelianos, came here together and spent over a year in prayer and meditation – a period of religious striving about which Kazanzakis has left us a moving testimony.

His mind was divided between, on the one hand, the spontaneous old rogue Zorba, exulting in life, and on the other, the problems of St Paul and St Francis, which he found so tormenting. His work spans the full spectrum of the Greek soul, which is highly sceptical and irreverent, and at the same time profoundly religious, though only in the anthropological sense. I recall a diplomat telling me once that whenever he travelled with Vichinsky to the United Nations, the old Russian Communist delegate never failed to cross himself in the Byzantine style before taking a plane. It is wise to take such precautions. One never knows.

And so northward in the direction of Samos, but with a stopover at the unrewarding and rugged Icaria which has an unkempt air, as if it has never been loved by any of its inhabitants. This is understandable; it won't bear comparison with its magnetic neighbours, and moreover, it lies awkwardly abaft the channel, as if the first intention was to be a stopper of it. All that its position achieves is interference with the free-running tides from north to south, creating the sort of lee which is not sufficiently interesting for people under sail. The impression it gives of disorder and vacillating purpose is increased by a visit ashore – the road system has the air of being thought up by a drunken postman. There are some thermal springs, but they do not enjoy great renown. To write more about Icaria would be like trying to write the Lord's Prayer on a penny. Onward then to the spacious bays of Marathocampus in Samos, and the grizzled head of Mount Cerceteus.

The Northern Sporades

*

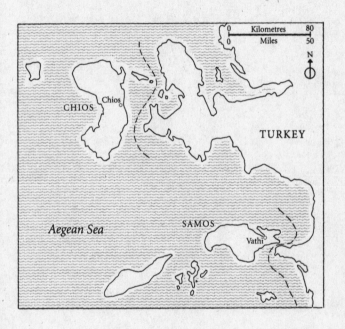

Samos and Chios

There is some justification for linking these two islands together; they are equally important historically, and both share the proximity of the Turkish mainland which in ancient times must have given them a distinct metropolitan flavour. Samos is separated from the mainland by a small gap hardly two kilometres in length. To me, the approach to this famous island is more beautiful than the island itself. You travel, by magnificent sea-roads, as if across the heart of some fine old Victorian steel-engraving by Lear or Landseer, among headlands and promontories of unstudied grandeur, which the Victorian traveller always described as 'sublime'. It is sublime. After this approach, the island itself, despite its harsh backbone of mountain, despite the grizzled head of Mount Cerceteus which lifts itself up to nearly 5000 feet (1520 m), is a little disappointing.

Chios, twenty miles away, boasts of Homer, while Samos can only put up one tyrant of genius and a mathematician called Aristarchus – who has no right to be as little known as he is, for, after all, his heliocentric notions of the heavens anticipated Copernicus by some two thousand years. Fertility was the essence of classical Samos, and provided it with even more nicknames than Rhodes. Homer alludes to the island as watery, but he was outdone by other Samiot enthusiasts, who called it *Anthemis* for its flowers, *Phylis* for its greenery, *Pityoussa* for its pines, *Dryoussa* for its oaks, and so on. Indeed people were so carried away by the greenness and abundance of Samos that Menander, the poet, announced that the fowls in this Eden produced not only eggs but milk as well. Perhaps he was parodying the extravagance of Samiot claims? I saw very few fowls (and found the food calamitous) when I spent a weekend in Vathi, the main harbour, which is a colourful enough little place but awkwardly sited for the frequent winds, that scatter spray and dust with equal abandon. The second harbour, Tigani (Frypan), is more attractive; spacious and eloquent itself, it has fine views of the Turkish mountains which hover down to Cape Kanapitza. There are several little taverns with good seafood, and here, if you wish to pander to local patriotism, you may ask for a performance of the loveliest Greek folk song of all, *Samiotissa* ('Samiot girl'), and use its stately, lilting measure to learn the finest and gravest of the Greek dances, the *Kalamatiano*.

It is singular that, in an island so famous for its sculpture, artificers in precious metals, and carvers, the names of few eminent individuals have descended to today. Polycrates the tyrant, who made Samos queen of the seas in 535 BC, has hogged the stage of history.

The reputation of Polycrates is not undeserved for, apart from his conquests on land and sea, he was also a discriminating patron of the arts, who invited many distinguished poets to visit his island court. His rise to fame was staggering in its swiftness, and at the height of his power he had a fleet of galleys of one hundred and fifty oars and an army of a thousand bowmen on call. At heart he remained a corsair, and his maraudings seem to have been unplanned and without any central object. He went to war for the fun of it; yet, magically, was always the winner. He inspired a small vignette by Herodotus, on which his fame still largely rests. In order to escape the jealousy of the gods, he threw a rich emerald ring into the sea; but after a day or two a fisherman turned up at the court with a huge fish for dinner. When it was carved, the ring was found inside. 'A sure sign', says the historian, '(for a man so lucky that even what he had thrown away came back to him) that he would die a miserable death.' Which he indeed did, for he finally allowed himself to be lured into Ionia and arrested by his enemies, who revenged themselves on his past misdeeds by flaying and crucifying him.

It was under Polycrates's rough rule that three of the greatest engineering feats of the ancient Greek world were carried out. The first was the great mole which protects the harbour; Lesbian slaves were forced to fashion this as a punishment for taking arms against the Samiots. The second was the extraordinary tunnel which exists even to this day as a water-conduit for the capital. The third was the temple of Hera which was one of the wonders of the ancient world, and of which little now remains except the site, starkly beautiful on its headland where goats browse and untiring eagles weave overhead. Cape Colonna, as the place is called, has priceless views of the mainland from every spur; but of Hera's temple only a single column marked the spot when last I was there.

The tunnel which brought the water to the ancient town is certainly a fantastic feat of engineering, for its time. About a mile long, eight feet wide and eight high, it is still negotiable for most of its length. Some sections in the middle have caved in, but I was told that, with the help of a torch, one could still get through quite easily. I went halfway along it many years ago, to where there is a tiny Byzantine chapel, in which, mysteriously enough, the oil in the lamp seemed to be freshly poured. I wondered what sort of zealot or sacristan snaked down the dark tunnel to perform this votive act. It is something I have wondered many times in Greece. There are numerous remote, deserted chapels or hermitages, either on the tops of mountains as in Crete, or on the seashore surrounded by high cliffs so that they can only be reached by sea; yet I have hardly come upon one, however remote, which had not been recently dusted, and the oil in the altar lamps replenished by invisible hands. Little pagan wayside shrines keep you heart-whole in the Greek countryside; my own pet shrine to St Arsenius in Corfu is entirely cut off from the land by high cliffs, but it is always tended – one might suppose by spirits, for I have never glimpsed the tender. However, other shrines are modest in comparison with the temple built for the prayers of the tyrant; for Polycrates, nothing but the best would do. The original temple boasted 134 Ionic columns, and when it was burned down its successor was even larger. This gorgeous monument had the merit of affording work to the best sculptors and architects of the day, and doubtless deserved its ancient reputation as the finest thing achieved in the ancient world.

Because of its richness and ambiguous position, Samos has always been a pawn in the game of international politics, from the time the Spartans landed (and were soon replaced by Athenians), onwards. As a Roman province, she enjoyed a short period of stability and happiness, since Augustus liked the place and accorded it his favours. Then, still in Roman times, Antony sacked it. This cocktail-party playboy chose Samos for one of his greatest displays, a mammoth party, at which he was ably assisted by Cleopatra, and to which the whole civilized world was bidden; the feasting and debauchery went on for months. This was Antony's way of starting a war – a kind of preliminary flourish, so to speak.

As for the famous Samian wine – find it who can, in the island of its birth. I suspect that one would have to know one of the great families of the island to taste it; the taverns do not have anything to justify its reputation. Yet it exists, that foaming cup that Byron was always 'dashing down' in a fever of petulance because Greece was not free. I have drunk it in several private houses in Athens, notably in that of the Colossus of Maroussi, who has it specially sent over the water (and from whose vinous disquisitions I have learned much of what I know about present-day Samos). There is also a Samos *mastika*, if you like anisette, which gives you the feeling of having been caught up in a combine-harvester and bundled out as trussed straw.

There is goodish upland-shooting in Samos during the winter months, and its wildness is commended by campers and walkers. You feel the wildness of Asia Minor in the air, and in the hazy distances sense the obscure, nomadic tribes on the mainland across the way, where huge and grumpy mountains lie like sofas out of work.

Chios is very different, though its size and geographical position are similar. The impression of desuetude is quite marked in the little capital town, and I think that earthquakes have been responsible for overturning its more precious architectural glories. A feeling of past luxuriance remains – smothered in dusty gardens full of oranges, lemons, pomegranates, flowering judases and cypresses; but the town has the kind of seediness that comes from business dealings. Yet it is a rich little island, which exports fruit, cheese and jams to Athens, and has made a speciality of the juice of the mastic plant which, according to the pious historians of hard liquor, was a gift from St Isidore – though what a self-respecting saint like Isidore was doing so far from his home territory in Salonika (his church is a treasure) I cannot tell.

The story of modern Chios is the story of this mastic plant. It is a plant that grows all over the Mediterranean, but only the Chiots have specialized in its cultivation, and developed it on a large scale. In addition to the drink, there is a pleasant white chewing-gum with a delicious flavour made from the plant. This has always been in great demand in the Turkish harems, since it combines the qualities of breath-sweetener and ordinary chewing-gum with helpful digestive and tranquillizing qualities. The plant is a relatively common one – *Pistacia lentiscus* – and one is surprised on looking it up in the encyclopedia to read: 'The production of the mastic has been, from the time of Dioscorides, almost exclusively confined to the island of Chios.' One suspects that the first big market for mastic was the seraglio, for at one time the whole trade passed into Turkish hands, and was re-financed. When I first reached Athens in 1935, the little tablets of mastic were in common use, but as time went on they were replaced by American chewing-gum which, though less refreshing, was considered more *chic* by the Athenians.

If the capital is somewhat depressing, one can find much to admire in the extraordinary green plain called the Campos, which is the source of the island's present-day wealth. It lies some way from the town; and here the holdings and country houses of the rich families have congregated, to form an ensemble of great charm and originality which is, as far as I know, unique among the islands, even among the greenest such as Rhodes and Corfu. It is a romantic place, of shuttered gardens defended by great wrought-iron gates half-rusted black, and with tangled groves of citrus and olive stretching away up into the sky. And, like all such places, it is apparently tenantless. Empty houses, gardens without gardeners, weathercocks which do not turn on battered towers, dogs that crouch but do not speak. You can wander for hours in search of the Sleeping Beauty – so likely does it seem that she will be drowsing somewhere here – or else of Daphnis and Chloe, though it is not their island, strictly speaking.

The prevailing odour of dust and lemons and rock-honey is what you will most probably bring with you out of Chios. A more intrepid wanderer than myself, Ernle Bradford, has noted: 'I can confirm that one can smell the citrus groves of Chios from the sea, specially if one arrives in the early morning, and there has been a dew-fall overnight. The fertile islands like

Samos, Corfu and Rhodes, to mention but three, all have a definable smell.' But you are more likely to experience this under sail during one of those lagging summer calms when your boat lolls and sways towards your landfall, hardly moving. And even before the smell the far creaking of *cicadas* will come across the water to you, like rusty keys.

The mastic villages in the south of the island are unremarkable save for their cultivated bushes of the herb, some six feet high, like the new-style French olive-trees which are cropped low, in the manner of tea-bushes. Incisions in the body of the plant bleed the mastic juice. The drink is still going strong, and you can still find the chewing-gum, though the trade in it is no longer what it was. Of the 'submarine' – that absurdity invented by the cafés to thrill its youngest customers – I have written elsewhere; it consists of a spoonful of mastic confiture plunged into a glass of cold water. The name in Greek means 'an Underwater Thing' and you see a very ancient Greek expression on children's faces as they suck the white jam from the spoon. They are obviously in Disneyland, aboard the big submarine which is one of the marvels of the American scene.

As for Homer . . . of the seven cities which have contended, in the words of the old epigram, the claims of Chios to be his birthplace are well founded if one notes the reference in the Homeric Hymns to 'the blind old man of rocky Chios'. In the north of the island, Kardamyla is supposed to be where he was born. Why not? There is a block of stone called 'The stone of Homer' outside Chios town which is more likely to be an ancient menhir or something of the kind. It reminds the visitor of the big block of Agrigento marble thrown down in a field outside the village of Chaos in Sicily: where the ashes of the great Pirandello have been scattered.

Nearby is Pashavrisi – or Pashaspring – which is rapidly becoming a summer resort of consequence. Good beaches with an eatable *taverna* to hand are not numerous in Chios unless you are adventurous and have time to cover a good distance by taxi. It is wise to use the taxi to visit the splendid monastery of Nea Moni, situated just below the crown of the mountain called Provatium. Splendour and isolation combine with a rich set of eleventh-century frescoes to make such a trip memorable. The frescoes were sadly jumbled by the great earthquake of 1881, though enough are still extant to provide a graphic notion of what they must once have been. With the new interest in Byzantine art as an aesthetic there is talk here, as elsewhere, of having them tactfully restored. The monastery has however fallen upon meagre days, and its once hundred-strong monkery is now reduced to a handful of lumbago-ridden mystics who are bored stiff with the scenery and the frescoes and are eager to have a chat with people from the outer world.

Some of the monks are ex-brigands – it is (or was) a convention in Greece that brigands, when they are getting on and have no pension, abruptly repent and become monks of great splendour. In most monasteries there is a brigand picture taken in the good old days when the ambushes and purse-slittings were good. The transformed brigand often has it framed and hung on the walls of his cell. I have seen a dozen of these pictures in various places in Greece, and the posture of the band has some of the diffident solemnity of a football eleven of adolescents. The camera has only recently been accepted in Greece; in the thirties it was widely regarded as a machine for casting the Evil Eye on people who were unwary enough to allow their souls to be snatched by the contrivance. I remember a group of monks on Mount Taygetus in Laconia running for shelter and ducking behind a rood screen as I unleashed my old Rolleiflex. After the last war, the superstition was conquered, and everywhere I was badgered by people – especially monks – to take their photographs. But some of the old fear still exists in the remote villages of Crete, where a peasant woman will shield her face, or else, having been snapped, will spit into her breast and repeat the magic formula against bewitchment. In the last century, before the daguerreotype was invented, draughtsmen who wanted human portraits ran into this problem in Greece, though it was not perhaps so ingrained here as in Moslem countries. Now you even meet people who have been photographed with Sophia Loren – which they rightly remember as a great event.

One of the great tragic events of the modern history of Chios is the massacre of 1822, which inspired some of Victor Hugo's choicest rhetoric and a magnificent picture by Delacroix, a copy of which is to be found in the museum. The little islet of Psara, which lies quite near, was similarly devastated by the Turks and inspired a lapidary poem by Solomos, who wrote the national anthem for the Greeks. The two most uplifting and noble national anthems are the Greek and the French, which embody the feelings of an entire epoch and a whole race. Other national anthems seem dead by comparison. Listen to the Greek one sung with the words. The only song in English which comparably ignites the heart and uplifts the soul is the Blake oratorio 'Jerusalem'. Even Mozart could do nothing memorable with 'God Save the King', though he meant to pay a compliment, for he admired England (because of Hume).

The history of Chios is not significantly different from that of the neighbouring islands. The same succession of piratical nations have held it, alternatively sacking it or securing for it a few years of peace and prosperity. For such a pretty island, it is odd that its image is more industrial than romantic. You feel that both Samos and Chios were always stepping-stones to the continent; even in winter, they were not blocked up by heavy seas as the central group of Cyclades are even to this day. They traded in winter; and of course once on the mainland, the islanders easily touched the tail end of the spice routes and the caravan highways to India. Hence a certain sophistication of outlook, which they shared in ancient times with Lesbos. Nowadays, the rich absentee landlords prefer Paris or London as a place of residence; but summer brings them back.

In its respect for the seasons the pattern of Greek life is constant. Families, even in ancient times, possessed a little house or a big property by the sea. Here they set up shop for the sunny weather, held court and invited all their friends and their children. I remember one holiday on an island, where I had arrived with letters of introduction to an old lady of wealth and distinction, an obscure, Venetian countess who still guarded her long-extinct title. The family was just loading up to go to the summer property which lay on the other side of the island. I was at once invited to join them – a merry band of cousins and aunts and uncles, with their children, and hampers loaded with enough food to sink a ship. The setting-off was impressive. Seven or eight *fiacres* or gharries were lined up at the door and solemnly loaded with all that might be necessary for three or four months' stay on the other side of the island. The country property was a fine, unkempt old villa with wrought-iron gates which squeaked abominably; it was pitched on a headland above a lion-coloured beach. Two mad monks were the care-takers, one deaf and one lame; they fed the pigeons and kept the hunting dogs in trim.

I set off with my hosts – the long line of *fiacres* raising a white plume of dust along the white roads. The trip took about two hours, not more. We moved like a column of infantry, with the old lady in the leading *fiacre*. We were waved goodbye by the grandmother, who had supervised the loading with great care, standing on the steps clicking the house-keys in her hand and admonishing, criticizing, or praising. (She kept the food-cupboards well locked and every morning dished out supplies for the day.) The grandmother was staying behind but would be coming over to join us and take up her family duties in the other house within a couple of days. The baggage-train contained everything necessary for the family's health and well-being in the weeks to come – toys, pets, nannies, cutlery, pots and pans, phonographs, a boat, easels and colours, and even a small upright piano, which occupied a *fiacre* to itself and jogged contentedly along behind the column uttering from time to time a plangent whimper. (On the morrow a piano-tuner would ride across the island and set it to rights in its new abode.)

By the time we arrived, the country house had been reactivated, for the servants had walked across the island during the night and warned the mad monks. The rooms had been opened up and aired, beds made, staircases dusted, gutters, swollen with winter leaves, unplugged. Even the beds were made, with fine old linen sheets which smelled of lavender, and the dusty mirrors cleaned and angled. There had also been a huge delivery of ice-blocks, which were stacked in the improvised freezer – a sort of underground room or crypt, whose walls were insulated with the pulped flesh of the prickly pear. (For ordinary daily purposes, wine and butter were simply put down the well in a hamper.) Meanwhile, way below, in the sunken garden full of delightfully bad statuary, the blue sea prowled and sighed, impatiently waiting for its children and their boat.

The form of this summer migration has varied little throughout the centuries, though of course some details are different (today, for example, there is a refrigerator, either electric or, for remoter places, paraffin-operated). When you read of Nausicaa playing ball on the beach and discovering the naked Odysseus in the bulrushes, or of Sappho going into the country with her maids, this is the sort of background to events. No piano, of course, but Sappho would have taken the harps and lutes necessary for her summer symposium, including the little one she invented.

The tradition, however modified, will continue, one feels, as long as the Greek summer remains what it has always been – hot, dry, touched by the island winds at sunset, and then cool-to-cold at night, with a sky of such clear brilliance that you can lie for hours watching it breathe, counting the shooting stars as they cross and recross the darkness, and then watching the Pleiades rise like the tiny horns of new born lambs or the first flowers opening upon the spring. On such occasions, one is aware of the big silences of the philosophers whom we have followed but never superseded, those men so deeply conscious of the slow-burning fuse of death which invisible fingers had lighted on their first birthday.

In the town, you never forget the presence of the mainland – the grim promontory of Karaburna – a name like a drumbeat – which faces you across the blue water. In ancient times, Chios must have seemed a haven of civilization and comfort lying just within the shoulders of the shaggy-bear continent of Anatolia. It is still rather like that today, and will be so until the Greeks and Turks decide to become good neighbours and indispensable friends.

In islands like these, one mentally thinks back to visitors who have already been here and left us a record of their impressions; sometimes they were not poets but business men or sedate travellers moving about for their health. All such impressions are precious, for they mark the passage of time for us. An example is that fabulous globe-trotter Lithgow who, after almost twenty years of trotting, left a monumental record of his journeys – as invaluable as it is lively, though there is not much humour in it. *The Total Discourse of the Rare Adventures of William Lithgow* is a great travel book, written with pain and conscience, and providing a graphic account of travel in the Mediterranean during the seventeenth century. Himself rather a curious bird, Lithgow had every reason to stay abroad and indulge an induced perambulatory paranoia. He was caught behaving in an undeclared, amorphous manner with a pretty village girl who unfortunately had five disapproving brothers. In their quiet, undemonstrative, Scots way they lopped his ears and drove him from the parish to bury his humiliation in foreign parts. The locals called him 'cut-lugged' because of his cropped ears. Shame drove him to travel. One always thinks of him in Chios because he has left us a description of the island, whose women, he avers, are of exceptional beauty: 'The women of the city of Scio are the most beautiful dames or rather Angelical creatures of all Greeks upon the face of the earth, and greatly given to venery. Their husbands are their panders, and when they see any stranger arrive, they would presently demand of him whether he would have a mistress; and so they make whores of their own wives.' Although this may well have been true in the seventeenth century, it is difficult to imagine in the sedate Chios of today. There are a few nightclubs here and the sort of night-life which in its modest way attracts Nordic tourists – and why not, when the nights are so fine and crystal clear, and the sky like old lace? It seems a crime to go to bed early in Greece, and even the little children are allowed up very late, so that when they turn in they really sleep a dead-beat sleep, instead of spending the night whining and sucking their thumbs as so many northern children do. All habits, of course, stem from climate which, in a subtle, unobtrusive manner, dictates everything about the way we live, and often about the way we love.

The Northern Aegean

*

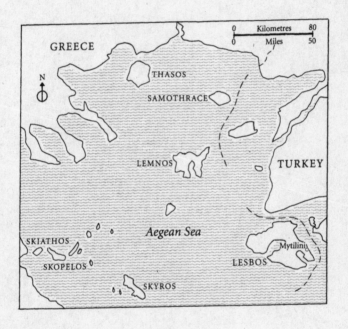

Lesbos · Lemnos · Samothrace · Thasos

Spacious and gentle is Lesbos – but how to escape from the net of ancient associations which make everything to do with the place memorable? But then, why try? Lesbos vibrates like a spiderweb with the names of high antiquity – the greatest of all being Sappho. Here, in the shadow cast by slate-grey Olympus, Sappho lived and worked, though, if Eressos is really her native hamlet, she worked with her back to the present Turkish mainland. In contrast, the modern capital of Lesbos, Mytilini, which is perched on its long irregular promontory in the eye of the wind, faces the mountains across the water. A glance at the map will show how queer its shape is – like a half-enunciated geometrical problem. Its lozenge form is abruptly carved into by two great landlocked bays, Kalloni and Iera, the former nearly ten miles long, a haven of clam water to delight the heart of a sailor. Each of these natural estuaries has a narrow entrance drilled like a sinus into the landscape. Entering them, you receive your first impression of Lesbos as a place offering tranquillity and beauty and a sort of repose which seems even to silence the *cicadas* at noon. Perhaps this impression is the result of finding such safe anchorages, where one can sleep on deck under the stars, conscious of rich glades close by, which are densely clothed in olives as hairy and untutored as those of Corfu. Lesbian fruit and olives find their way to the Athens market; so do the Lesbian *ouzo* and white wine.

Mytilini is a breezy and pleasantly animated little township without any special, awesome antiquities, and just a sufficiently mixed style of architecture to divert the traveller. It is cool in summer because of its orientation; but the whole island has a singular charm which is hard to analyse since Lesbos is not as beautiful as Rhodes or Crete or Corfu. Is one being seduced by the literary association connected with its famous name? Even if I am accused of romancing I would say 'No', and insist that Lesbos belongs to a special category of place which holds a secret magic of its own. No matter how shattered by tourism or despoiled by promoters' taste, these select places (even if they are mere holes in the ground) still echo with a sort of message that the visitor receives. 'Once a star, always a star,' says Noël Coward very rightly. There is a radiance and a throb in names like Taormina, Avignon, Delos, Tintagel, Mycenae, which will never be extinguished – or so one hopes. I would put Lesbos into this category even though it is outclassed in natural beauty by other and bigger islands to the south and east. It is hard to describe the scenery objectively when one knows that for *Daphnis and Chloe*, that delightful novel, this place was chosen as a stage for its young lovers to walk, bemused in the passionate self-discovery that first love brings and time will never repeat. The subject matter of the book is divine innocence and pure joy – for which Greece provides an appropriate backcloth; these vernal glades and combes with their fruit-blossom, oleanders and olives is the perfect setting for such a theme.

If I turn away from Sappho for the present, it is to remind myself that in the long scroll of Lesbian history her name is only one of many illustrious names. Pittacus, tyrant of the island, was among the Seven Sages of Greece and enunciated the two brief maxims which were inscribed upon the porch of the Delphic temple. Theophrastus, who lived to be 107 years old, and spent thirty-five years as the head of the Athens Academy, was a pupil of Plato and Aristotle; his long reign shows him to have been justly popular in an epoch marked by political and intellectual upheavals. Among philosophers and moralists who lived on the island were Aristotle, who taught here for two years, and the sadly neglected and traduced Epicurus, whom we are just beginning to appreciate at his true worth once more. Epicurus's philosophy exercised so widespread an influence that for a long time it was touch-and-go whether Christianity might not have to give way before it. But the poor in heart won out, don't ask me why – it is one of the great mysteries of the world. The Lesbian intellectual was held in high esteem in the ancient world. There is an anecdote about Aristotle appointing a successor to a teacher in his school. The choice lay between Menedemus of Rhodes and Theophrastus of Lesbos. The great Athenian philosopher deliberated long, and finally asked for the wines of the two islands to be served to him; he sipped them as he reflected. Then, pronouncing them both excellent, he gave the palm to the Lesbian, saying that it had more body. So Theophrastus was chosen for the post.

Plutarch has told us how famous the island already was in antiquity both for its musicians and for its poets; and the musical tradition was emphasized in mystical fashion by the fact that here the singing head of Orpheus was washed up and recovered after the Bacchantes had tossed it into the River Hebros. The famous 'dolphin-charming' Arion was a native of Methymna (now Melyves), and Terpander of Lesbos was the first to string the lyre with seven strings – an invention which for the ancient world was as decisive as the jump from clavi-chord to piano was for us. (Sappho went so far as to invent her own small version of this lyre, upon which she accompanied herself.) The opulence of Lesbos's intellectual history is matched only by the opulence of its soil, and even today you can sense this. It would be a good place to work in, and quite a number of modern writers have been sufficiently impressed to spend a year or two in the island composing their books.

Lesbos has known nothing but the best in poetry, music and philosophy – a very rich heritage for one small place!

Its geographical strangeness also plays a part, for as you enter the narrow gullet of Iera or Kalloni the fissure closes behind you, sealed by the turning mountain. You lose sight of the narrow channel by which you have entered this anguish of silence and calm; a sense of unreality supervenes and you feel panicky.

Sappho is beginning to emerge from the haze which the dark ages cast over her. For a long time she seemed almost a mythical figure, perhaps some escaped Olympian, footloose on earth. Now we know that she was a real person and are gradually finding out more about her. Even her work is slowly coming to light, though we still have only about one-twentieth of what she actually wrote. For a long time this venerated ghost of antiquity existed only by hearsay and the chance quotation of phrases from her poems which were embalmed in the work of critics and grammarians. From these crumbs it was hard to show convincing evidence of her genius, and the few biographical anecdotes were either vague or implausible. Between 1897 and 1906, however, by a stroke of luck, at a place in Egypt called Oxyrhynchus, a great find was made by the scholars of the Egypt Exploration Society.

The sand is a wonderful preserver of objects and writings, and the find consisted of a hoard of mummy-wrappings fabricated from papyrus. These writings, presumably regarded as expendable by their owners, were used as wadding for coffins, or even as stuffing for ritually embalmed animals like small crocodiles. They ranged in period from the first century BC to the tenth AD. All this workshop rubbish had been thrown on to a garbage-tip, from which the scholars managed to rescue it. Among so many ancient texts, quite a number were Sappho's poems. Our earliest papyrus is from the third century BC, some three hundred years after her death – though there is one small piece of pottery inscribed in a fourth-century hand. At the time of writing, however, not everything has been deciphered and released, so some new poems may yet emerge. Her great popularity in the lands where Greek was spoken ensured that her texts were jotted down by many different hands – which provides a fertile field for scholars of variant readings.

If we are to trust reports she was small and swart, and was compared to the nightingale, which is a particularly ugly little bird. 'Small and dark, with unshapely wings enfolding a tiny body'; this was the poetess whom Plato called the Tenth Muse. The little portrait of her – made long after her death – on the red-figured hydria by Polygnetus, which is in the National Museum of Athens, depicts a slender woman with a disproportionately big head and a long, reflective nose. She might be the sister of Virginia Woolf, so close is the resemblance.

Her poems were accessible to everyone; they were not alembicated and difficult. Moreover they were sung or danced or mimed before the general public. So great was their simple and vehement force that their author was treated almost as a goddess and statues to her were erected all over the civilized world. More than a thousand years of ancient testimony – 600 BC to AD 600 – insisted that she was the greatest poetess the world had ever known. Then a chill wave of doubt and sanctimoniousness set in and gradually her work was almost totally destroyed, while allegations as to her sexual proclivities began to be bandied about, largely under the influence of Ovid's satyrical allusions.

Born in 615 BC, Sappho was married to a rich businessman from Andros, who, however, is not mentioned in any of the fragments of her verse which we have today. That she was wealthy and from an aristocratic background there seems little doubt. She presumably played her part in the political life of Lesbos, for twice she was banished. She seems to have travelled a good deal in Greece, and to have made a great impression on the celebrated men she met; Alcaeus, her contemporary, called her 'pure and holy Sappho', which has prompted the great scholar C. M. Bowra to speculate on whether she was the prime mover in a *Thiases* or semi-religious college of women centred upon the cult of Aphrodite and the Muses. Priestess, director, and living muse, she marshalled her group of girls and organized the celebrations which marked the seasons. Looking back from today, it is hard to realize how much this old religion formed part and parcel of the Greek corpus of belief.

I suspect that Greek religion, looked at through the smoked glasses of Pauline Christianity, shows a somewhat distorted version of itself. But in a world where the gods meddled so actively in the life of men, and where men could actually celebrate a ritual marriage with a goddess, the effective life of the ordinary people must have been vastly different from our own. You never knew, when there was a knock on the door, whether it was Aphrodite herself in human form outside. Often it was; though you did not usually realize this until after she had gone. Man's soul moved easily between earth and sky, and it is not really possible for us to appreciate the sort of religious considerations which dictated the ancient Greek's order of priorities. Today, it is only the poets who have not lost the faculty of sensing the Aphrodite under the disguise of an old shepherdess or a wrinkled crone. It is likely that the Greeks had developed different faculties of awareness from our own – an immediacy of recognition of things cosmic, or even of states like death. Conversely, they would have found it impossible to read St John of the Cross without amazement and perhaps disgust; and a crucifix would have taken some understanding, even though they were cheerfully accustomed to animal-sacrifice in the name of one of their gods. One has to keep all this in mind when trying to feel one's way into the hearts and minds of ancient peoples. As for Sappho, how much was she goddess and how much poet? We shall never perhaps know. But that she was very much a woman, and a passionate one to boot, there seems little doubt from the poems we have of hers.

One senses, too, what it was in her attitude which struck such a chord in the heart of the whole civilization which bore her. The poetry was at once fine and energetic as a vision of her feelings; people found it unusual, in an epoch of classical invocation to abstract personifications, to come upon verse which was in touch with the universal as well as commonplace emotions like vexation, passion, pathos, desire. A whole personality was actualized in her work; hers was not simply a superlative but frigid technique. An original and unexpectedly touching person emerges from the supple verses, from the music. That is why old Strabo calls her 'a miracle of a young woman', and that is why the older Solon admired her. I think too that it is fair to sense behind this praise an acceptance of her moral excellence as a muse and earth representative of Aphrodite. There is, at any rate, no suggestion of lubricity or impropriety in private conduct in these early references – whatever the state of morals in Lesbos at that time. The suggestions of lesbian predispositions and illicit loves come later from Ovid; but even he goes back on them, and says that she lost her taste for girls by falling in love with a man. What does it all matter?

There is no reason to doubt the popular story of her death, though serious scholars have always treated it as intrinsically improbable. Why? She followed a lover, Phaon, through the islands and, when he refused her love and left her, jumped from the White Cliff in Lefkas to her death. She would have been about fifty, for in a fragment she mentions her wrinkles and the fact that she is past the age of child-bearing. The visitor to Lesbos will find such tales as this one of her death, and the problems they raise of truth or legend, tease his mind, whether he is travelling across the jade water of Iera at sunset with the slither of flying fish at his prow, or whether tucked against a tavern wall at Castro in Mytilini – a wall which shelters him from the wind, as he watches the shadow-play of vine-leaves upon the courtyard walls of the pink, blue and white houses of the town. There have been some digs at Eressos, her home town, but nothing really spectacular has been uncovered which might serve as a link with the forgotten epoch when Lesbos was one of the most civilized islands of the Greek archipelago.

Homosexuality in ancient Greece is an interesting subject. It is not reasonable to suppose that the Greeks were any more or less homosexual than their neighbours – the Persians, for example; but the Greeks were singular in that they institutionalized and solemnized the proclivity. It seems clear that homosexuality gradually grew up, and that during the Doric period – up to, say, Homer – the predilection, if it existed, was not yet subject to civic sanction. Aristotle explained the phenomenon by saying that Dorians found it a way of expressly limiting population; they were the first to encourage the love of boys and to try to segregate women from society. There is nothing intrinsically irrational about this. Population has always been the curse of developing civilizations. The Romans exposed girl-children in an effort to regulate it. In some South Sea islands, the amount of food available was calculated per head and surplus population was exposed to ensure the safety of the community. In our time, a high infant mortality has done something like the same job – but not, alas, in Egypt, India and elsewhere. At any rate, the boy-love of the Greeks, once adopted, took firm root and found even the holiest sanctions of religion.

Pederasty pervaded Greek culture as a necessary feature of superior citizenship; it was a form of chivalry, it sanctified virtue. Judaism, and after it Christianity, fought the habit from the outset, but had little success to begin with. Finally, in 342, it resorted to criminal punishment. Monosexualism developed with monotheism. The Bible makes no special reference to homosexuality. But for the Jews the sexual cravings had to be subordinated in the interests of the tribe, and social motives therefore dictated their attitude also – which was very different from the open and poetic Greek ideal. The Greek code of behaviour was sufficiently original to deserve a mention here; and it is not out of context in this chapter if one remarks, apropos Sappho, that no such code obtained for lesbian practices, unless somehow they were also partly institutionalized in the temples devoted to female deities such as Aphrodite. It is vexatious to know so little about the profounder feelings and attitudes of the old Greeks; the joky, sexy, bawdy incidents graven on the vases, scenes in which gods and goddesses took part, may have had some quite special cathartic significance. I mean, if one interpreted literally the blood and skulls of Tibetan temple-decoration, one would think the worshippers were bloodthirsty cannibals, rather than Buddhists. So Greek satire and smut might have made laughter figure among the cathartic canons of Aristotle, along with the pity and terror which bloodshed and horror represented on the stage was supposed to induce in the spectator.

Although some traces of the boy cult were to be found among the Ionians, the actual custom, like knighthood, only became fashionable with the Dorians. It became, for example, a privilege only permitted to the free citizen, the knight. Slaves were expressly forbidden to practise homosexuality under pain of death. There were also strict rules which admitted no deviation. In Sparta, Crete, Thebes, the training for *Arete* (virtue) among the dominant classes was based on pederasty. The Spartan lover was held accountable for his 'companion', who became attached to him at the age of twelve; he, and not his boy, was punished severely for any shameful act on the latter's part. Sparta of course was the model fascist state – it is curious how these repressive systems and their perverted concepts arise. The Nazis invented nothing, it seems. ('The battlefield at Chaeronea was covered with the bodies of lovers lying in pairs . . .')

Stranger still, from an anthropological point of view, the choice of a boy-lover in Crete assumed the form of a bridal theft, like becoming betrothed to a girl. The lover advised the family of his intention to come and abduct the boy. If the family did not like the proposed 'match' they did their best to thwart it; but the higher the social position of the lover, the greater the honour for the boy and his family. After being initiated, the chosen one was sent home bearing ritual gifts. In Thera and in Crete, such unions even enjoyed official religious sanction, the actual coupling of the knight and his boy taking place formally under the protection of some god or hero. At Thebes, the seventh-century inscriptions make the matter abundantly clear. Upon the holy promontory, about seventy metres from the temple of Apollo Kerneies, outside the city, we find chiselled in large script, upon a site consecrated to Zeus, the following: 'On this holy spot, sacred to Zeus, Krion has consummated his union with the son of Bathycles and, proclaiming it proudly to the world, dedicates to it this imperishable memorial. And many Thebans with him and after him have united themselves with their boys on this same holy spot.'

In Crete, it was considered a shame for a boy to possess no knightly lover, and a great honour for him to be desired by many. Both parties, the Cretans thought, would profit morally and spiritually from such a union. As in a code of chivalry, each was inspired to do his best in order to prove his mettle, to become an *agathos anir* (virtuous man). Early heroic tales seem to take this relationship into account, for the wondrous deeds of Heracles were carried out in honour of a male lover, Eurystheus. Repelling a wooing knight was considered a blot on one's character. Plutarch relates the story of how Aristodamos, a knight, lost patience with an obstinate boy and struck him down with his sword – by which love act the knightly lover transferred his chivalric virtue to his page.

It is difficult for us who still dwell in the shadow of Freud to realize what all this meant to the people who lived with it then. There are hints of a similar predisposition in the English public school codes of 'friendship', though such friendships were implicit, and not institutionalized, while pederasty was and is frowned upon. Moreover, since psychoanalysis raided the larder of the unconscious we have developed notions about narcissism and its effects which the old Greeks would have found bizarre in the extreme. What would they have made of these remarks by Stekel?

In each of us there lives another who is the precise counterpart of ourselves. In the other sex we love our counterpart and through the love for our own sex we endeavour to run away from that counterpart . . . The mother instinct and the hatred of motherhood are not split in the human heart. The homosexual woman always shows her hatred of motherhood . . . What does the homosexual substitute for procreation? In the first place the seeking of himself, his like, and then a purposeful sterility. He renounces the immortality implied in procreation; but many homosexual artists achieve immortality in the realm of spiritual endeavour. We have seen with what powerful hatred the homosexual encounters his own environment; whether he turns his hatred towards the other sex, his own, or even against himself, he remains the inveterate hater trying to reconcile the feelings of man's aboriginal nature with the ethical requirements of later culture . . . The truth is that he is unable to love; that is a peculiarity he shares with all artists who are also incapable of loving. Poets formulate a longing for love because they are incapable of it, and this drives them towards the love adventure which proves in vain. But the poet differs from the criminal because he is aware of his incapacity as a grave handicap, and out of hatred and scorn he fashions a love for humanity. It is the function of sexuality to conquer this basic hatred.

A Greek would have been puzzled and perhaps disdainful because we have not invented a mechanism to cope with this. Also, of course, our view still smells of Pauline repression, of Aboriginal Sin, however much it is disguised in frigid medical terms. The truth perhaps is that nature itself cures imbalances of population, blindly tipping the scales down when it proves necessary, on one side or the other; and so the customs of different peoples at different times vary.

To return to Sappho: at the moment we do not know the real truth about her, and perhaps we never will; and if we think of the waves of puritan counter-propaganda – such as the one that produced Clement of Alexandria's attacks on 'obscene' gnostics – which always follow relatively calm political periods, we should be warned that our present estimates of the lady may well have been distorted by some witch-burning group of now forgotten historians. Of course fashions in love change, just as fashions in poetry do. I knew an Italian surrealist poet who won a fitful glory by describing the transports of Zeus and Hera as 'the mating of surgical pianos'. I wonder what Sappho would have thought about that. We are also told that she was after all a married woman, and indeed had a daughter of her own. Her little group may have been as innocent as the 'finishing school' that the impoverished Duchess of X set up in Kensington, to gain a few guineas and mould the socialites of the future from the adolescent children of her friends.

The aristocratic streak in Lesbos seems to have started very early; at one time the nobility liked to trace its descent from Agamemnon, who is supposed to have conquered the island during the Trojan War. Once, the island was called Pentapolis, or the Five Cities (Mytilini, Eressos, Methymna, Antissa and Pyrrha); but her huge natural harbours made it unnecessary for the Lesbians to make the same sort of decision as the Rhodians, in founding their capital. Lesbos was always rich economically, and also, perhaps because of this, politically; it was once a prominent Aeolian settlement, with colonies in the Troad and in Thrace, and with Pergamum not far away. To some extent, one still feels her pre-eminence today, for Lesbos is far more beautiful and colourful than the little group of islands which surround it – certainly than the two northern ones, Samothrace and Lemnos. It was here, in the storming of Mytilini that Julius Caesar first made his mark as a soldier, rescuing one of his comrades under enemy fire, for which he was awarded a crown of oak leaves.

Nevertheless, this corner of the Aegean is the home of many of history's greatest fiascos, which stretch from Troy to the Dardanelles campaign. One of the more dramatic disasters occurred during the Peloponnesian War and was caused by Lesbian arrogance. The ruling oligarchy forced a revolt against Athens, which cost the island dear – a two-year siege, followed by a savage sentence upon the islanders which was only avoided because of a gorgeous bit of rhetoric by a certain Demodotus. Cleon had already whipped up the feelings of the Athenian Assembly with his demand for condign punishment – every man in Lesbos to be put to death, every woman and child to be sold into slavery; indeed, the ship bearing these instructions had already left. Then Demodotus took the floor and urged cooler reflection on this quite preposterous judgment. Now, anyone who can persuade a Greek politician to cool his temper and moderate his judgment is a remarkable person, and Demodotus well deserves the generous space which Thucydides accords the text of the speech in his account of what happened. So marked was its effect that the Athenians at once sent off a second ship to countermand the original orders, limiting judgment to the ringleaders of the plot. With every rower's muscle straining, the relief ship arrived just in time to avoid the unnecessary slaughter, which was just as well; the decision was far-sighted as well as generous, for at the time it was taken Athens was locked in a death-grip with the Spartans.

To realize the contrast between Lesbos and the rest of the group, you have only to cross the water to Lemnos, a damnably dull island, although there are one or two little items of its classical history worth recording. Here, for example, the brutish Hephaestus set up his forge and bellows. Here he consummated that disastrous marriage with Aphrodite – how did they do it? He was horned like a Medusa in less than no time – and rather surprisingly the women of Lemnos took issue with Aphrodite on his behalf. Of course, it was fatal to incur the wrath of the love-goddess; Aphrodite punished them with a spell which made them repugnant to their husbands, and finally, in despair, the sex-starved women set upon their menfolk and murdered them. There must be a moral in all this, but I confess it escapes me. Happily for the widows, the Argonauts were just passing, so the question of finding newer and abler men was solved and the island instantly re-populated. Another odd visitor was Philoctetes, he of the gangrened leg. Ernle Bradford has suggested that his legend may have got itself mixed up with that of the famous healing earth of Lemnos, which was considered so valuable that only a small portion of it, dug up by a priestess on one certain day of the year, was permitted to leave the island; Galen came to watch it being dug and states that only one cartload was allowed out. Actually this earth has had a wide sale all over Europe and you can still apparently buy portions of it; whether it has ever been analysed or not, I do not know. In classical times the earth 'cake' was impressed with the head of Aphrodite. Nowadays the sacred digging takes place under the eye of an Orthodox priest, on the feast of the Saviour, 6 August.

I do not think it is wrong to take Lesbos as an axis and consider Lemnos, Thasos and Samothrace as forming a small complex of islands, the most northerly group in Greece. Up in this corner of the map the tonality of things changes slightly, especially for the tourist; these islands are the summer play-grounds of Salonika and Kavalla, and communications with them are somewhat awkward and haphazard, involving the use of places like Volos and Alexandroupolis as springboards. The main cruises would certainly visit Lesbos, and perhaps at a pinch Thasos, but probably not Samothrace and Lemnos. What also changes is the prehistory, which here concerns remote and poorly known places like Phrygia and Persia. Before the Greek Olympians came along and orientated religion, quite rightly, towards the *Folies Bergères*, the dark hinterland of what we now know as Turkey set up puissant secret cults, dominated by gods and goddesses whom the Greeks adopted and humanized – I see it like that. A very powerful and complicated set of supersti-tions and beliefs about which we know very little today was responsible for temples and altars which stretched from here right the way across to Sicily, to Mount Erix with its strange multi-faceted Aphrodite. The Greek stamp is so firmly upon all this that we tend to forget that some of it existed before the Greeks – and that even their delicious alphabet was borrowed.

In a sense, Samothrace, which remains so obstinately difficult to land on for lack of a harbour, is the most mysterious of the northern group. Its great fang, Mount Fengari (Mount Moon), rides the sky in a manner worthy of its name – rising out of a lunar landscape of white marble. How to get ashore and how to get away again are the sole preoccupations of the people who travel to this surly and ungiving place. Fengari, over 5000 feet (1520 m) high, is the highest mountain hereabouts, and only

equalled by the ragged heights and promontories of secret
Athos, which bounds the Thracian Sea on the western arm.
Apart from its physical inaccessibility and its impression of
withdrawn taciturnity, the place is rendered all the more mysterious by the obscure cult of the Cabeiri which once flour-
ished here, and about which we know hardly anything except
that its provenance was Phrygian or Phoenician. Their name
(they were a group of interlinked deities, a family) is presumed
to come from Phoenician and to mean 'The Mighty Ones'.
They were fertility gods, their chief symbol being the phallus,
and their rites of initiation kept strictly secret. On account of
these gods, the island has always had a reputation for secrecy
and mysterious rites which might have involved human sacrifice (as in Rhodes and in Sicily). I have never managed to get
ashore, but even from the sea Samothrace gives an impression
of hulking, sulky indifference to visitors. It's gloomy, it's barbaric; I didn't like it one little bit; I felt the cannibals warming
up the cooking pots, and opted to stay aboard.

My choice was a wise one, for the wind changed abruptly in
the night and there was that wild scramble to get aboard again
which characterizes negligent yachtsmen. No one had a chance
to get a sample of the marble and reflect on whether it was
exportable – the concern of my companions – or to brood on
the secret rites of the Cabeiri. Among the more celebrated historical initiates of the so-called 'Samothracian gods' were Philip
of Macedon and Olympias his consort. Arsinoe, sister and wife
to a Ptolemy, took refuge here as well. The word 'refuge' is
relevant for, owing to its damnable, harbourless condition, the
island remained always separate (and therefore free) during the
long inter-island struggles which decimated whole populations,
razed the richest towns and spread death and slavery in every
corner of the Mediterranean. Physical and geographical factors
joined hands with psychological to keep the island in peace

through the centuries. But people came in pilgrimage to the shrines of the gods, and retired with purple amulets round their necks which denoted successful initiation into the cult. The Cabeiri were particularly fond of seafarers, if I remember rightly, and their shrines must have been hung with ex-votos almost as profuse in their graphic gratitude as those which modern Greek island churches enjoy – in honour of some patron saint.

The actual sanctuary of the Cabeiric gods has been found and excavated in a narrow ravine, stony and grim – so I was told – near the township called Palaeopolis. It was in a rock niche somewhere thereabouts that the French discovered the famous Winged Victory of Samothrace which now graces the Louvre. I would like to know how they got it off the island – for this was before the age of helicopters. Incidentally, here once more we come upon our fine-feathered friend Demetrius Poly-orcetes (who caused the Colossus of Rhodes) for it was he who, in fine feckless style, had the Winged Victory commissioned and set up to celebrate his victory over Ptolemy II in 305 BC. I wonder that there is not a popular biography of this uncouth but endearing fellow, for his sieges were on a Cecil B. De Mille scale, his defeats were resounding, and he always celebrated a defeat by setting up, or causing to be set up, a masterpiece.

The Cabeiri were adopted by the ancient Greeks and rebaptized as Castor and Polydeuces; the Romans followed suit, changing the name once more, but leaving the functions of the gods undisturbed. Pilgrimages continued. I am told that there is nothing very much to see – the shattered remains of a theatre and a fine, solitary Genoese castle; but it is on the eminence of Mount Fengari that Poseidon sat to watch the progress of the Trojan War. If there are no harbours, there are plenty of white marble beaches for the curious. But the sea is lonely hereabouts.

None of this is true of Thasos, which is one of those delights among islands, reserved for travellers who are not afraid to make an effort to seek out the calm green places – so rare in the Aegean – where one can hear the splash of fresh springs on every hand. Thasos is a handsome, romantic little island, named after a grandson of Poseidon, with an atmosphere of calm beatitude which makes one's sleep most deep and refreshing, the nights being blanket-cool, and the days, though windless, not too hot. In ancient times the wines and nuts were known, and even today they exist in a world which has outstripped the good but modest table-reds of the place; there are two. What one inhales here with dilated nostrils and heart is the scent of pine and lilac. The richness and shadow are balm after you have shed a dozen skins in Delos or Rhodes. In these lowland strips of forest, you can walk on coarse grass and see cattle pastured.

You can get here from Kavalla – the usual route – but it is a long pull. The island is almost attached to the mainland. What we used to do in the old days, and there is no reason why one should not do the same today, is push up to Keramoti by car. Thence there is a steamer (or *caique*) run of only about an hour and a half, depending on the mood Poseidon happens to be in. One feels he might be more indulgent to those who wish to visit an island named after his grandson – but he isn't always. All I can say is that I had no trouble. Of course you would have a more impressive journey if you shipped from Salonika, because the bigger vessels make a wider sweep and usually carry you along the Athos peninsula, which has a weird array of monasteries – so thin and tapering that you are reminded of pictures of the Potala in Lhasa, and are surprised not to see their canted roofs covered with snow. But it is a good deal longer. The direct trip is more intimate because more amateurish, and you will make the acquaintance of village folk coming back from mainland trips to visit relatives, suitably loaded with wine, eggs and various other comestibles which they will not be able to resist opening on board. Burned in my memory is the vision of a fat elderly man with a razor in one hand handing round slices of cold pork to a group of pallid, shivering, village women holding slices of lemon to their noses. He said, in the most definite tone: 'If anyone is sick I shall cut his or her legs off above the waist and throw him or her into the sea, so help me.' And this threat had a miraculous effect for, retch as we might, nobody was sick until the little *Stavros* sailed into the harbour, and delivered us to the tender mercies of the local grog-shop and restaurant – where all inequalities of balance and temper were restored by short swift touches of a marvellous *mastika* which I found nowhere else.

If the little capital charms, it is not because it has any very striking antiquities to show, but because the general arrangement is homogeneous – all epochs are simultaneously represented. While the town goes by the official name of Limena, or Limin Panaghias (Virgin's Harbour) I met nobody who did not refer to it as Theases. It is pitched square upon the site of the ancient town, facing the narrow strait, and profits from what wind the sullen mainland sends it – in summer not enough perhaps. The remains of the Heracleion and the triumphal arch of Caracalla are set a little back from the waterfront. The old walls girdle the ensemble of buildings. There are different layers of its cultures co-existing happily with its horrid modern barns and rabbit hutches – what *has* happened to Greek taste? It is a pleasant place to stroll about in, despite the ferocity of the modern buildings; but it is regrettable that, in an island of marble, only reinforced concrete seems to be used for building. There is enough marble in Thasos to pave all the capitals of Europe – yet the harbour is paved with cement blocks. The only use I saw of the local product was the crushed marble chips that were mixed with clay to surface village roads.

Never mind. For keen bathers, there are fine beaches like Makri Ammos (Long Sands), while walkers use the efficient local bus system to visit some of the pretty inland villages – which form good take-off points for serious walking, as opposed to just mooching and brooding. The latter can best be done in a town with well-distributed cafés and enough relics of the past to please the more discerning. The Acropolis is pleasant, but in such a state of smithereens that a *Guide Bleu* will have to be used. Alternatively there is a highly bibulous local guide, whom we christened the *Guide Rose*, and who was vague, rhapsodic and threw his arms about, speaking what he took to be French. There is a pleasant satyr sculptured over the gate of Silenus – hats should be tipped to him. The guide (*Rose*) insisted that if you winked at it it winked back – not always, but mostly. We all tried winks of different shapes and sizes, and some even tried a leer or two; but the thing did not stir, and we were forced to abandon this promising ESP experience, persuading the guide back to the tavern, where already a dance to celebrate a wedding was in progress. Before leaving this somewhat immodest relief, the guide pointed out that Silenus's enormous organs of generation had been hammered away by puritans, whereas, on a postcard of 1935, which he produced, they were in full flower. What to us is obscene was probably holy for the Greeks, as it was for the Indians. St Paul passed Thasos with those three gloomy dicks Timothy, Silas and Luke. Looking at the poor Silenus on the gate, one reflects on the power of paranoiacs and the sadness of monotheism.

In the calm vernal glades of Thasos you feel that the ancients had a simpler, better way of living than we have. But perhaps this is romancing.

Skiathos · Skopelos · Skyros

The next three islands are not only similar geographically but give the impression of being a mini-group of scallywags (they all begin with the letters SK), lolling along the coast of Euboea, loitering with intent, so to speak. Three maiden aunts turned pirates. A lack of notable antiquities has shielded them from the worst indignities to be suffered from people; they lack, for the most part, the amenities which tourists are persuaded they need. However, they are perfect places to build that secluded island house, in order that you may live the good life which is always somehow connected in your mind with beauty and solitude.

The recent history of these three places has been somewhat mixed up and thrown about by the extensive Greco-Turkish exchange of populations in the twenties; but if there is little that is ancient for you to see, you can admire the beauty and style of the Greek island face and form – specially among the old people, calm as sea-shells, sitting in church porches gossiping, or upon pavements made of black-and-white sea-pebbles. But a sense of remoteness and estrangement is theirs. They are off the main track of tourism, which is the only summer life for these Aegean Islands. Remember, too, that the Greek ferries close down in October and, if you live on an island, you only get mail once or twice a week in winter, not more. If you want to motor back to Europe you must make the long haul via Yugoslavia with its snowy mountains. But in these moments, with their long sunny siesta silences, broken only by the drunken braying of mules in the olive glades, you can muse upon the island face of the modern Greek, with all its classical qualities still intact. Faces honed by privation to a beauty which only the austerity of death will qualify, by adding immobility, and by freezing them.

The islands themselves seem somewhat like orphans – say the orphans of Byronic corsairs; but well-nourished and well-to-do orphans, for they are surprisingly green, all three of them. Clearly their geological history is different from that of the marble islands we have just left. A geologist's diagnosis would be: metamorphic, laminated rock, with quite extensive pockets of limestone, and lots of fresh springs.

Even if the tourists don't flock here, the islanders know them. They receive many visitors from the mainland, who take ship at Volos to come here for the summer, to spend a modest *villegiature*. It is easy to forget that the average Greek today, even a highly placed functionary, is poorer than the average tourist who visits Greece. The doctor, dentist, professor tend to steer clear of fashionable islands because of the inflated prices. They do quite as well in places like Skopelos, lunching on a piece of fish with a glimpse of salad, followed by a smidgeon of cheese and a bowl of peaches. They also pay one-third of what we are charged for the same meal.

Tourists, despite the vigilance of the Tourist Police, are regarded by the island villagers as fair game, because it is understood that they are all millionaires with extensive steel factories in Pittsburgh. The remoter the island, of course, the firmer this conviction is, and the harder it is to correct, unless one speaks Greek and reacts forcibly.

The coast along which the three corsairs skulk is a thankless and profitless one, the coast of Euboea; there are few harbours and fewer lighthouses, and the channel is as full of wind as a big drum. You will not meet too many sailors pleasure-cruising among the three; the currents and winds are somewhat tricky. But occasionally you will see some great foreigner – an ocean-going yacht from far away, spreading its white canvas wings like palms as it tests the pulse of the wind's eye, and probes softly north, whispering; taking its passengers to where they can glimpse the steep, star-crowned cliffs of the Holy Mountain, womanless Athos.

Skopelos means 'reef' or 'rock' – I looked it up once in a dictionary. But I think the 'skop' part of the word (like that in our own 'telescope') tends to mean vantage-point, perhaps something like the Italian 'belvedere'. This is the middle island of the group and thus best calculated to keep its eye on what happens in the spacious channels between. I make no mention of Alonnessus, which spoils the euphony of my theme, without adding anything at all in the way of grace or history. As for Skiathos and Skyros, I would like to derive them from echoes of the word for shade – 'skia'; both are green, something almost beyond belief for a mariner who has just left the central Cyclades, where the wind crackles in the dry grasses of Delos as if it travelled across some ancient parchment. Here water and cypresses and shade give one back a sense of plentitude and peace – particularly on Skiathos, the beauty of the group, whose perched capital neatly divides a harbour like a *mons veneris*; its dazzling white houses built as if from lump sugar, its labyrinth of quizzical churches.

The Greek motto must be: 'If time hangs heavy, why not build a church?' The size doesn't matter; it can be tiny, and adapted from a hole in a rock, or as big and barn-like as a ship's chandler's religious aspirations. All these Greek islands are riddled with tiny churches – some of them quite bizarre in their wriggly contorted Byzantinism. Moreover, the locals have also done their own thing, making their interiors celebrated in terms of old furniture and wall panels and decorative sideboards. A Sicilian exuberance reigns, and it is customary to leave the courtyard door ajar so that strangers can peek in and admire what they see. This is also a way of getting into a free chat and gossip, which is so very dear to the Greek heart, particularly on the remoter islands.

The capitals of Skyros and Skiathos are the most populous of the group – some four thousand souls – which gives an indication of their intellectual magnitude; if one lived here, one would live a little like a beachcomber, waiting for the next boat, depending on the radio. Most people are no longer equipped for a life of real solitude; the city with its stresses has conditioned them. Once I went for two years without reading a newspaper or listening to a radio, and I was surprised on emerging from this long abstinence to find that nothing seemed to have happened in the interval. There was, it seemed, no really new news. The headlines in the newspapers had the same deadly banality, and described identical situations to those which had existed on the day I gave up reading them. It was rather a jolt. Is there, then, no such thing as real news – is the whole idea of news an illusion? On small remote islands one is apt to think so.

You experience something similar, but more deeply, if you go on a long fishing expedition where you do not have occasion to speak for as much as ten days. You can feel your thoughts rusting quietly away, until they drop into that blessed limbo of nescience which is the very beginning of another kind of wisdom – a wisdom which people must secretly seek without always being conscious of the fact. Here, sitting under a tree, staring at the thick oily meniscus of a hazy midday sea with Euboea etched upon it, you hover between sleep and waking and feel rather like Crusoe. On this deceptively beautiful coast, the winds and waters did for Xerxes and his gigantic fleet of four hundred vessels. They were grounded by gales and munched to pieces by the jagged cliffs of Euboea – a fitting end to the hubristic Persian expedition. When Athens received the news, great was the rejoicing, and a temple to the north-east wind was erected on the banks of the Illysos. What cads!

For my money, Skiathos, with its sweet geometry and homogeneous layout, is the best looker of the three capitals. But I may have been influenced by the fact that the beach of Koukounaries is by common consent the finest in Greece, and that really does mean something in a country with so many wonderful beaches. 'Pinecones', it is called, and I had the luck to see it before someone gave the show away. Nowadays it has a small hotel pitched on it. In old times, during the sunny season, little temporary shelters, roughly arranged as taverns or eating-houses, came into being and provided music and *mastika* of a delightful village kind – innocent and unsophisticated. Whoever wished could tread a measure in the evenings, to the jerk of a drum and violin, while the moon rose over the still waters. Obviously, there have been changes – though I was delighted to hear this wonderful place praised by some young visitors who had recently spent a summer in the island. So perhaps all is not yet lost.

It was in Skiathos, too, that I had one of many long and instructive conversations with a lunatic; this one swept out the church. It made me realize how humane the Greek islanders are in the face of such afflictions – much more so than we are, for Greece has retained a bit of the reverence and superstition which used to be attached to the idea of madness, treating it as a privileged state. This reverence probably dates back to ancient times, when the soothsayer or sage was not quite the best-balanced member of the community – he saw visions, heard voices. Harmless lunatics in Greece are regarded today as lucky people to have around, and there is always plenty of work for such mascots. Instead of being locked away from the community they play an active and valuable role in its affairs. Every business tries to co-opt a nut if possible, for he brings good luck. When I first reached Greece ten thousand light-years ago, every garage had one, and he was so terribly helpful – I am thinking specially of one named Kostas in Corfu – that there were sometimes dire results – even an accident.

Kostas, after a long career of usefulness, made one bad slip while investigating a car whose petrol-gauge had broken. He hit upon the ingenious idea of ascertaining the petrol level in the tank with the help of a lighted candle. Mercifully the tank was almost empty, but the ensuing explosion was enough to send Kostas flying into the surrounding décor. He was badly burned and spent a long time in hospital – so long that he quite disappeared from circulation. When he emerged, he had changed his job. The newly born Greek dictatorship of Metaxas had decreed that all the youth of Greece must join the National Youth – a paramilitary organization – for training. It was modelled upon Italian and German equivalents. Judge the amazed delight of everyone when Kostas, clad in uniform, led the first parade, bearing a banner aloft, and goose-stepping fit to kill. All felt that the incident illustrated the mental level of the dictatorship.

In Skiathos, the patient, pale young man was a failed priest, who had remained as a sort of honorary sacristan to the church of St Michael. My Greek was bad, and his hardly better, since he stammered. After a bit of relentless intellectual sparring, a sort of despair seized him and, mounting his broomstick like a hobby horse, he galloped off into the sky – or so at first it seemed. Actually he had fallen over the terrace into a flower bed. It seemed useless to prolong such an inconsequential relationship, so I merely observed that in my country only witches rode broomsticks, and left it at that. I remember walks with him in the blazing heat, among the vines. Someone claimed that the plums of the island were world-renowned, but I could find none either on trees or on tavern menus, so I concluded that they had all been exported to Athens. On the other hand, there were fine olives and marvellous almonds in quantity. There is no ancient history worth recording, and the odd monastery or two lie empty and mouldering among the cypresses. They had once been rich dependencies of Athos, I was told, and I repeat this piece of possible misinformation for what it may be worth. I know that the monasteries do own a lot of secular land in the nearest islands.

In Skyros, two unlikely shadows frequent the plane-shaded glades and whispering springs – Theseus and Rupert Brooke. Just what the former is doing here would be difficult to divine; he retired here in old age, sad and disabused by life, and worn down by all the adventures he had lived through. King Lycomedes agreed to put him up, but was manifestly jealous of his guest's celebrity. After all, apart from the exploit with the Minotaur, and the disgraceful abandonment of the loving Ariadne in Naxos, the hero had been pretty steadily in action throughout a long life, abducting one pretty female after another. There were no bounds to his cupidity – Helen herself was one of his victims; he also organized the abduction of Persephone and actually managed to get into the Underworld with this praiseworthy object in view; he was always accompanied by his faithful friend Pirithous on these expeditions. Although they got into the Underworld, they could not get out again, and had to invoke the help of a fellow-hero – Heracles, no less. Theseus's great succession of love-adventures would be enough to make anyone jealous, and Lycomedes grew so tired of listening to the hero's reminiscences that he finally set upon him and had him thrown into the sea. His remains were buried in Skyros, whence the pious general Cimon had them brought back to Athens and placed in the sacred enclosure of the Theseum.

My favourite among the abductions of Theseus has always been the rape of Antiope – for he did not hesitate to attack even the feared Amazons and carry one off. She later bore him a son, Hippolytus. Being utterly fickle, he repudiated her and took up with Phaedra. This so enraged the Amazons that they invaded Greece and, after a series of smashing victories, found themselves actually contesting the Acropolis with the armed forces of Attica. Theseus had carried off the sister of the Amazon Queen, Hippolyta, and this base desertion of Antiope caused such anger among the Amazons that they planned this avenging expedition against the Greeks. Amazon forces landed even in Attica. Nothing could stop this army of tall ash-blonde warriors, whose origins are supposed to have been Caucasian. They had settled centuries before in Cappadocia and their capital, which was ruled over by a queen, was called Themiscyra. On all their frontiers there was a 'No Men Allowed' sign; but these blonde terrors were no lesbians, they simply did not want to be subject to the masculine whim. They were keen on hunting, shooting and fishing, like the British Royal Family today, and took a slightly dazed view of art. But they were a good deal more honest than a lot of our own liberated ladies, for they acknowledged the basic need for union with men, and every year at mating time – or 'lilac time' as Ivor Novello used to call it – they gathered on the frontiers which they shared with the nervous Gargarensians and sought a temporary union with a man. When this bore fruit, they handed back the boys but kept the girls to swell their numbers, and these were trained in war and in the chase. Artemis was their patron saint.

Those who have ever met an Amazon in the flesh will be able to testify that the missing right breast (in order to free the right arm for the long bow) is a complete myth. It is a relief to be reassured on this point by competent scholars, who say that the word *a-mazos* or 'breastless' could equally mean 'heavy-breasted'. In fact, in none of the reliefs or sculptures that we have of Amazons locked in mortal combat is there any suggestion of a removed right breast. Amazon troops were taken with deadly seriousness, and the graves of those who fell in the attack on Athens were long pointed out and even offerings made to the shades of these fallen warriors. Many towns were proud to claim that they had been founded by Amazons – Smyrna, Ephesus, and Paphos among them.

Scholars of comparative mythology have provided us with a portrait of Artemis, which suggests that she was the toughest and most merciless of the goddesses – a bit of a bitch in fact; any defection, even accidental, was punished immediately. When consulted about a plague she had caused to descend upon Attica, she announced that it would only end if and when all the girl children of the capital were dedicated to her; thus a huge procession of children every year wound its way up the Acropolis to her shrine in order to preserve Athens from the pestilence. This is only one example of her harshness; she was a goddess who never hesitated to order floggings or fill a bridal chamber full of snakes – as the luckless Admetus, who had accidentally annoyed her, could testify.

There was perhaps a bit of the Artemis touch about the Amazons in battle, for they gave no quarter; their forces engaged Bellerophon in Lycia, and indeed attacked Heracles as well who, as chance would have it, slew Hippolyta, their queen, in battle. During the Trojan War, they came to the aid of Troy when their young Queen Penthesilea was killed by Achilles. I myself believe – though there is not an atom of truth in it – that the shadowy descendants today of the vanished Amazons are those blonde beauties known in Turkey as Circassians, and made famous by their high reputation as the supreme ladies of the seraglio. You see them sometimes in Greece; they are ash-blonde with very fine silken hair, moon faces, and sweet round chins. They are the essence of feminity and often appear in Turkish travel-posters and on boxes of *Rahat Loucoum* (Turkish Delight). They have very slightly bowed legs like sugar-tongs and marvellous thighs.

I will not go any further into the press book of Artemis, but leave the rest to the readers of the big Larousse. She was a strangely vindictive creature, and quite unpredictable. After all, she is supposed to have been very keen on Orion, but one day the luckless man happened by accident to touch her, while they were both hunting in Chios. It jangled her nerves and set her on edge so that she summoned a great scorpion up from the earth which stung him viciously in the heel. I ask you! And he a fellow-hunter with whom she had been on close terms of mutual admiration and, some said, even of love.

Skiathos used to have a prosperous naval yard which turned out a number of small craft each year, but I am told the trade is in decline thanks to the development of the Piraeus shipbuilding industry. Skiathans, however, still make the traditional type of *caique* known as *trechandiri*, from the word *trecho* meaning 'to run'. These are elegant little *caiques*, with a peculiar kind of pouting prow, and are really much speedier than the broad-bottomed, run-of-the-mill *caique*, which tends to wallow and yaw when full of cargo. I heard an owner ordering one and talking about the slips at Skiathos where it would be assembled. Apparently it was cheaper to have the job done in Skiathos than in Athens.

Skopelos, such an odd shape on the map, is no favourite of mine; but it deserves a note because its little town, which whorls its way up round an amphitheatre shaped like a helix, is a pleasant place to pass an afternoon. If you are in a restless mood you will be soothed by the information that there are apparently 360 churches on the island, and at least 120 in the capital. When the inhabitants suffer from insomnia they count, not sheep (for there are none on the island) but churches. The sailing hereabouts is windy and capricious, and the pleasantest place for an excursion is a little fishing village over the hills called Agnonda. But on the whole it is a pleasure to take to the wind-swept sea once more, and hammer down the forty-odd miles to the south-east from Skopelos, until one heaves-to in Tris Boukes of Skyros – or Trebuki Bay – a good anchorage in a sound almost sealed by little islets. Here died Rupert Brooke during World War I, aboard a French hospital ship, of typhoid fever.

The poetic Brooke legend has become modified and diluted by time, but something tangible remains. As an adolescent, like everyone else I idolized him, but even now, though the blind idolatry has waned, I still respect and admire much of his work. It was good work for his time, and considering the influences he underwent; and we should beware of fashion, that fickle jade. (Remember that for seventy years after his death Shakespeare was almost forgotten.) Brooke is buried in an olive grove about a mile from the shore – a picturesque enough spot; but it is a devil of a walk in the heat, part of the way leading up a stony wadi that is more reminiscent of the Cairo desert than a Greek isle. April 1915 was the date of the burial, and for some time little attention was paid to the grave, which became pleasantly overgrown and mossed up. Then, in 1960, the Navy obtained permission to tidy up the precinct and enclose it in railings, all newly whitewashed and painted and shipshape. This was all to the good. Ernle Bradford was shocked to find that Greek trippers had scribbled their names over the tomb when last he was there; but he reflects reasonably enough: 'My first reaction was one of indignation, but then I remembered Byron's name carved in the marble of Sunion – if Byron on Sunion why not

Anagnos and others on Brooke's tomb in Skyros?' Why not indeed?

Tourists never change; sometimes, though not often, their inordinate desire to share the immortality of a great personage turns out to be useful – though not often. I am thinking of tourist scribbles of this kind upon the ancient monuments in Egypt. I have forgotten the exact context, but there is a famous monument (Karnac?) which proves the presence of Greeks in a certain place at a certain period; Kilroy had left his moniker scratched in the ancient stone. In Byron's case, it seems obvious that he did not groove his name himself at Sunion, for it is not his hand and nothing like his signature. What happened was this: after a heavy dinner, washed down with a fine red *Naoussa*, his host, overcome with emotion at having the great poet at his table, called for a mason and ordered him to engrave a memento on one of the pillars of Sunion. It takes some finding today, and it is fair to suppose that Byron would not have indulged in such sacrilege by himself; but as a guest what was he to do? However, the unfortunate result is that Smith and Jones have rushed in with uninhibited zeal to claim their own slice of immortality, and the whole of the Sunion temple is a mass of graffiti today, thick as lace.

Brooke's more modest tomb is now spruced up in fair naval fashion, and the railings will prevent graffiti accumulating. In town, one can inspect the epicene sculpture erected to his memory, and note that during the troubles in the 1950s in Cyprus the people of Skyros were sufficiently stirred up with patriotism to rename the little square where it stands, 'Cyprus Square' – something of a backhander for the British. I was also told that the nude youth in the sculpture caused a certain amount of middle-class distaste among the nicer sort of people in the capital. Well, it is epicene, but to feel shocked by a nude is surely rather out of date. What remains is the presence, in this finely classical island, of an English poet who somehow managed to symbolize the sentiments of a nation as it embarked on a world war; and the presence still echoes on in the memories of the old – though by now the palimpsest has been overlaid with images from a more recent war on a more terrible scale. The olives hereabouts are very silent about the matter – trees are not moralists. Their shade heals and forgives human folly; besides, the trees of Skyros have seen other heroes from older civilizations.

Did I mention only *two* shades? I lied, for there are three, and I kept the most important up my sleeve, because he is the only one who offers me an anecdote with which to close the chapter on this little group of islands. Achilles!

The sombre shade of the young warrior hangs over the tale of Troy, all because of a prophecy that he would conquer it but be prematurely killed. At nine years old, he was handed over to the centaur Chiron – a rum sort of tutor to have. He was nourished with the entrails of bears and the marrow bones of lions and other animals. A poetic gloom seems to lie over his character, and one hesitates to ascribe it to sustained indigestion. Like Luther. But the vein of poetry and sadness is real. His mother, Thetis, knew of the prophecy and could not bear the thought of an early death for him. She disguised him as a girl and sent him to the court of Lycomedes, hoping in this way that he would escape the fate decreed for him. It was the wrong way to try to meddle with his karma, and can only have increased his sense of inadequacy. Achilles is a brooding figure and even his great exploits in the field have a tragic flavour. At any rate, whatever his feelings were while he was disguised as a girl, Odysseus guessed at the truth and, by an ingenious trick, forced him to reveal himself. Arriving at the palace with a gift of trinkets and baubles for the women of the household, Odysseus placed a sword and shield among them. Then he ordered an alarm to be sounded without. The women rushed for their presents but Achilles, by a conditioned reflex of which Chiron would have approved, seized sword and shield and put himself in a posture of defence. The discovery proved to him that one cannot cheat destiny; he quietly gave in and joined forces with Odysseus. Skyros saw him no more, and from henceforth he belongs to poetry. His valour outside the walls of Ilion is on public record now – the combat with Hector is one of the great hand-to-hand battles of the world. But his fatal heel . . . Before Troy fell, he was pierced in this vulnerable member by an arrow, fired either by Paris or by Apollo, which caused his downfall and death. He made this as costly and spectacular as befitted a superstar – even facing the invulnerable warrior Cycnus, whom he strangled with the strap which secured his helmet; though, when Achilles tried to despoil him of his armour, the defeated Cycnus suddenly got himself turned into a swan.

The tomb of Achilles in Sigaeum, according to Pliny, was one over which no bird ever flew, so strange and ominous was the atmosphere which brooded over it.

The present Acropolis of Skyros is the most probable site for the palace of the legendary Lycomedes, who arranged the death of Theseus. There is some suggestion that the murdered man had some ancestral land in the island, but this is not certain. At any rate, after Marathon when the ghost of Theseus appeared in the ranks of the Athenian forces, the omens were read, and an embassy was sent to bring back his remains for burial in Attic earth. His festival, the Theseia, was thenceforward celebrated on 21 October. One wonders if this could be the actual day on which his murder took place?

These three, then, are the somewhat inconclusive shades which haunt the silences of the olive glades on Skyros. It would not, however, be an island to retire to, like Corfu or Rhodes, but one could sleep away (and swim away) a memorable summer or two here, and the lack of tourist amenities even to this day would secure your solitude – if that is what you came here to look for.

The Cyclades

*

Aegean Sea

ANDROS

KEA

TINOS

MYKONOS

SYROS   RHENIA

KYTHNOS

DELOS

SERIPHOS

PAROS

NAXOS

SIPHNOS

KIMOLOS

AMORGOS

SIKINOS   IOS

MILOS

PHOLEGANDROS

Kilometres   80

Miles   50

N

Naxos and Paros

This is not the first time that Naxos and Paros have been presented together, nor will it be the last. They seem to coexist in the mind as being of comparable charm and magnitude. But there are several radical differences. Naxos is a bit of a slut, while Paros is all gold and white like her once famous marbles. If Naxos is a vivid parrot, then Paros is a white dove. You wake earlier in Naxos, but you sleep deeper in Paros.

'The Cyclades is one corner of the map where the word "seduction" applies with more appositeness than anywhere else on earth. Yet so many of them could with justice be called just sterile rocks; but in the heart of the Grecian sea, where the gods have scattered them, these humble rocks glimmer like precious stones.' Thus Gobineau, who wrote a fine novel about the islands called *Akrivie Phragopoulo*, which gives an admirable portrait of the Greece of a century ago. 'The islands coming up – there lies Paros with its sister Antiparos; a bit further on, in the haze, Santorin; and then, straight ahead, Naxos – lovely Naxos with its hills and valleys and gorges appearing slowly out of the smoke.' With all his French lust for colour, he notes the dawn light shifting from nacre to saffron, from lilac to rose . . . but it would be several hours yet before they reached her, as the wind was slack and the sails drooped. The two islands are separated by only five miles of water – but here you are travelling across the prismatic heart of the Greek sea. If a dolphin does not rise and wink at you, or a quiver full of flying fish swirl across your bows, you can ask for your money back.

Particularly in the late spring. And the presence of so many famous islands so near to you, softly girdling the confines of the seen world, has a cradling effect – your imagination feels rocked and cherished by the present and the past alike. The very names of the islands are like a melody.

Naxos is the largest and most fertile of the whole Cyclades group, and this despite earthquakes and new islands emerging, as near Santorin, seems to have happened pretty constantly since that wayward god Dionysus adopted the island, and fell in love with the sleeping Ariadne on one of Naxos's remoter beaches. Here, once more, we lift a curtain upon a corner of the perplexing Cretan Minotaur theme – for Ariadne, the daughter of Minos and of Pasiphae, was the girl whom Theseus married after she had helped him fulfil his bull-slaying mission in the depths of the labyrinth. Aphrodite perhaps had something to do with the matter, for Theseus was under her protection, and it was she who arranged for Ariadne to love the youth, and finally to succour him, thanks to the magic ball of twine which Daedalus had given her before he left the island. With this slender marker Theseus managed to enter the darkness and navigate surely in the corridors of the labyrinth, so that when at last he emerged, having killed her monstrous half-brother, the girl Ariadne, by now hopelessly in love, fled with him in all haste from the Cretan capital.

On the way back to Athens their ship touched at Naxos – which incidentally was not on the direct route at all – and it was here that Theseus, so mysteriously, abandoned his bride and left the island alone. One wonders about his state of mind – had the terrible experience of the Minotaur disturbed its balance? Why should he leave poor Ariadne so abruptly? The fact that he forgot to hoist the appropriate flag on arrival in Athens, and thus caused the death of his father, is proof positive that all was not right with him. There are several explanations, though none seems conclusive. Some authorities say that he had become lovestruck by another maiden, called Aigle, others that he had decided it would be unwise to return to Athens married to the daughter of their ancient enemy Minos.

At any rate, while his ship laboured north upon Sunion, and while sad Ariadne slept, another ship from another direction approached Naxos with an unknown god aboard – the youthful Dionysus. This ship was a pirate craft whose crew, blissfully unaware that their captive was a god – far less that he was the wine-god of antiquity – were hoping to sell him off in a slave-market hereabouts. They did not stand a chance for, when the young Dionysus got wind of their intentions, he – here comes the famous picture which has captured everyone's youthful imagination – caused a vine to sprout out of the hull and clamber up the mast to immobilize the sails. Ivy snaked out and looped itself in the rigging. The oars began to writhe and turned into huge serpents. As if this was not enough for the poor pirates, he then transformed himself into a lion and roared so loudly that everyone jumped overboard in terror. Laughing, Dionysus resumed his human form, summoned a fair wind, and had himself wafted towards this strange green gem of an island which rose out of the waters to meet him. Henceforward, this was to become more or less the adoptive headquarters of the wine-trade, a trade half-material and half-mystical, half-orgiastic and half-sacramental.

As for Dionysus, one must presume that this young sprig, who found the sleeping Ariadne and married her, was a fairly late reincarnation of a much more ancient god – as old as the vine itself – whose magic origins stretch way back into prehistory.

Be that as it may, the green abundance of Naxos is even today a fitting place for such an apotheosis, and, though the Naxian wine does not match up to that of many of its neighbours, it is still drinkable, while the island has a fine, polished presence which still bespeaks richness and plenty in fruit, flowers and nuts. Approaching it across the water, you feel you understand how Ariadne could have been so happy here. She bore the young god many a child, and he, in his 'tree-god' incarnation – one among his many passports – saw to it that the whole of nature burst into bloom to share their happiness. Moreover, he hung a necklace of stars in the sky for his bride which we still know as the *Corona Borealis*.

A glance at the Larousse *Encyclopedia of Mythology* will indicate the bewildering tangle of attributes which make up the portrait of this most important god. They are so many and so various that the subject becomes daunting. One thing that is clear is that he was not made for a quiet home life. The almost unimaginable antiquity of the vine itself may be partly responsible for the complexity of his nature; it seems to have a pedigree as long as that of *Homo sapiens* himself. Scholars speak of fossilized leaves and seeds found in Miocene and Tertiary deposits; it has been traced in early lake-dwellings in the Swiss Alps, as well as in the mummy-cases of dead Egyptians. Details of wine-trading figure in hieroglyphics in the fourth century BC, and by the time of Homer and also of Noah wine was an article of common consumption. Much later, the precise Pliny describes ninety-one varieties of grape and fifty different wines known to the Romans.

In early times there seems to have been some indecision about how to treat it – for the vine is a climber and will simply crawl about on the ground if left to itself. Nor will it bear properly, unless pruned. Here and there, in Naxos, you will see it trained up a fig tree, and be reminded of references in the Bible to this custom. Its need to be pruned must have been one of the great discoveries of antiquity. My own theory, for what it is worth, is that the rite of circumcision is a ritual based on vine-culture and on the ancient observation that, to bear fully, vines must be pruned. Circumcision was an act of sympathetic magic to enable men also to 'bear' well – presumably males?

In early times, the island of Naxos was known as Dionysia because of the density of its green orchards and vineyards. But the modern town bears few traces of a classical past, except that the many finds of the later archaeologists suggest the medieval town was situated plumb on the Mycenean site. The little white town you see today is an appendix to Rhodes, though the scale is miniature, and its Venetian heritage has not been retouched and jazzed up as it has in Rhodes. There was indeed a long Venetian occupation, and the knights once held a large *commanderie* in the island as well as an arsenal, in about the fifteenth century. As you enter harbour, your eye will catch sight of the little islet sometimes called Bacchus in demotic Greek, where a scrabble of ruins attests the existence of an ancient temple, supposedly dedicated to Apollo though often called the Temple of Dionysus. There is not much else older than the knights, but the little white town rises elegantly and harmoniously on to the crown of the hill, where the citadel stands (once more on the obvious site of an ancient acropolis). Once more, too, there is a warren of narrow, dazzling streets and chapels washed whiter than white by successive coats of limewash. The cathedral is not memorable, but the town has all the tumbledown atmosphere which comes from Venetian palazzi allowed to go to rack and ruin – and this may have occasioned the passion that Byron seems to have nourished for Naxos. In his earlier days, Byron flirted with the idea of buying Ithaca; but when he saw Naxos, he turned traitor and expressed the wish to return one day to settle there. It is a bolder, more resolutely Aegean version of Corfu – which would, by the way, have been perfect for Byron: but the British were there, and that gave him the cold shudders, whence Naxos . . .

As may be imagined, the Christian Church had a good deal of trouble with Dionysus, and was finally obliged to do what Governments do to troublesome opponents – ennoble them. As St Dionysios, he was pressed into service on the side of law and order, and he exists to this day very thinly disguised as this medieval equivalent of a king. The modern, approved version of his arrival in Naxos is worth quoting, for it shows that while his name has been changed by an iota, his character has not been changed by a jot. The modern peasant story goes like this:

St Dionysios on his way to Naxos saw a small plant which excited his wonder. He dug it up, and because the sun was hot sought shelter for it. Looking about he saw the bone of a bird's leg and he placed the plant in it to keep it safe, but the plant grew and grew, and looking about for a larger covering he came upon the leg-bone of a lion. Unable to detach the bird's bone he placed the whole inside the lion's bone. But again it grew and grew and, as he looked about, he came upon the leg-bone of an ass and placed the whole thing in that. So he came to Naxos and, when he planted the first vine, for this little plant was the first vine, he could not detach it from its coverings, so he buried the whole lot together. Then the vine grew grapes and men made wine, and drank of it for the first time! At first when they drank they sang like birds; then, continuing, they grew strong like lions; but continuing thus, they last of all became as foolish as asses.

The story was recounted to Lawson about sixty years ago by a peasant from Euboea, who was illiterate and presumably had it from a long oral tradition.

The deep valleys and groves of the Naxian hinterland are largely unexplored; there are many ruined citadels and crumbling monasteries with battered frescoes, but few treasures of importance. The real treasure is the landscape itself. Some of the fig-trees are so old that they have burst open, and in one which borders the main road out of the town, the great fissure has been turned into a tiny wayside shrine with a small pictured

Virgin in it. A bottle of olive oil and a dried fig have been laid before the little icon, obviously the first fruits of some religious landholder. The lushness, the scent of lemons and the deep dust are reminiscent of Chios, though Naxos is even more heavily endowed with greenery and has a better water distribution.

The town, for all its faded elegance, is somewhat dusty and desiccated in summer; because for ages it did not figure on any tourist itinerary, it has an aura of neglect and abandon, which meant that when I was there the taverns were slatternly and the *ouzo* of poor quality. In such cases you have to be a bit high-handed and risk opprobrium as an awful snob from Athens; but of what avail all the ducal escutcheons if the *ouzo* is newt's blood? Once too there seemed nothing to eat in the two taverns except bread; we walked about the town, in the quaint phrase of Shakespeare, 'crammed with distressful bread'.

When a Naxiot wants to tell you to go to hell, he will tell you to go to Apollona. This turns out to be rather good advice, for the village of that name lies at the further end of the island and is extremely handsome; it has the best walks, and the most impressive scenery. In fact Apollona is the only excursion worth making, unless you are a fanatic for ruined fortresses and abandoned nunneries of which there are many, several in picturesque situations. Apollona is for real – and the girdle of cliff-shapes gives it real atmosphere. There used also to be a drinkable tavern there owned by a profuse and somewhat risky widow, who was obviously kept very much on the run by the village gad – a fragrant brute with huge canines.

The site is ancient, and historically speaking the old town is supposed to have had a temple of Apollo in it, whence the name it still has today. All over the Cyclades you come across this Dionysus–Apollo duet; it isn't clear whether they were rivals or partners when Olympus was a going concern. From modern Apollona the views are superb and, if you have a turn for walking, it would make a pleasant base. About a quarter of an hour from the town there is a quarry containing a giant sculpture sketch – unliberated as yet from the rock – which is almost ten metres long and suggests that it might have become something like a Sicilian telamon. But where now is the temple which such an animal might bear on his shoulders or head? It has vanished. Or was the sculpture simply a freak – a rough sketch for a giant figure? There is supposed to be a grotto named after Zeus somewhere on Mount Ozia but, apart from the scenery and fine gold air, the long walk to it is not really worth the candle. Besides who would want to displace Mount Ida as the site of the birth? It would not take more than a long weekend to get to know Naxos thoroughly; perhaps greater familiarity would enable you to override the small deficiencies I have recorded. The flavour of the place is pleasant and alert and, as you gaze over the rail to watch its lights fade into the night, you may have a Byronic twinge of nostalgia and decide that one day you might return to settle among those mazy streets and silent dusty squares.

The jump from Naxos to Paros is also a jump from one poet to another, one age to another; for Paros is the *lieu d'élection* of the poet Seferis, who used to claim with smiling diffidence that it was the loveliest of all the Cyclades and that the organization of its streets and squares aspired to the condition of music. Here he liked to spend his summers, walking among the brilliantly variegated colour schemes of the little town, worrying at his verses like a hound. In truth it is much prettier than Naxos and has some of that indefinable beatitude which comes from a truly perfect siting of its capital in relation to the prevailing winds. Both Aphrodite and the Delian Apollo had shrines here and, while there is no magic, healing icon, the feast of the Assumption on 15 August is celebrated here with as much fervour as it is in Tinos.

What is the secret of its charm – the feeling of zestful ease it gives you while you navigate those dazzling white streets punctuated with whole balconies and bowers of flowers in bloom? The two long, main streets are more or less parallel, and they have been criss-crossed and stitched with interconnecting lanes of pure whiteness, which give the impression of being simply felicitous afterthoughts. The town, once symmetrically laid out, has been scribbled over by an absent-minded god. I think that is what Seferis liked about it, its unexpectedness. Every day, when you awake, it seems quite fresh, as though finished in the night and opened to the public just this morning. The standard Venetian castle rides the traditional acropolis crown of the ancient city. The ancient stone has been run into the old walls in a most flagrant way, and here and there you will find rows of drums and columns seized from a now vanished temple to Hera. So one age wolfs the glories of its predecessor. But any architect will tell you how wonderful it is to find one's building material already on site. Given the Naxian's disrespectful attitude towards antiquity, it is lucky that the famous Parian marble remains (though half of it is in Oxford) – which, among other things, gives us a possible date for the birth of Homer (regarded as apocryphal by the scholars).

The famous Parian marble, with its sweet, almost translucent blond colour, is not being mined any more – or it was not when last I was there. They told me that the seam had been a slender one and was exhausted. However, a visit to the old quarry, where all those choice cuts came from, suggests otherwise: indeed I think it would be possible even today to have a large block for a statue cut from this fine stone. The light sinks deep into its surface and reflects back from way inside – giving an impression of lightness and transparency. Later sculptors such as Michelangelo and Canova became enamoured of white Carrara, but in my opinion this famous Greek stone is superior.

The quarries, which lie some way off the main road to Naoussa, were deserted when I was there. A few tumbledown buildings marked a fleeting attempt by a French company to re-open the seams and market the marble. But the project failed.

Walking about the cuttings in the blazing heat – there is a delightful little wall-relief to the nymphs, obviously carved by a sculptor who was waiting for his block to be cut and trimmed – my thoughts turned to my first lesson in ancient Greek in far-away London around 1925. I went to a small Elizabethan grammar school in Southwark for a couple of terms, where Mr Gammon, who always seemed a trifle drunk, and articulated somewhat thickly, showed me what a devil the Attic grammar is: 'Inflected languages *are* hell.' More than this he introduced his pupils to the Greek aesthetic by holding up a battered picture of the Venus de Milo and saying: 'What do you think they were up to? Were they just trying to make us tingle with lust? Certainly not!' And he banged his desk violently. Then he lowered his voice and said in a grave tone: 'They were asking themselves what beauty was, and whether it lay in proportion.' He swept us with his gin-swept glance and sighed. It was a memorable remark in spite of its depravity and, for me, it went deep; long afterwards, reading Longus, and thinking about the proportions of the Acropolis with the help of Vitruvius, I remembered Gammon gratefully. The point he made is worth making again today.

I also owe to him the story of the acanthus pattern which crowns the Corinthian column. A young and beautiful Corinthian girl became ill and died. After she was buried, her nurse placed all her treasures in a basket and, lest she should feel lonely without them, placed the basket upon the tomb, over the roots of an acanthus plant. She covered the basket against the weather with a tile. When spring came the acanthus grew its leaves around the basket. The tile bent them back. The keen eye of Callimachus, who was passing, fell upon this striking combination of forms and he adopted the motif for the Corinthian column which he was just designing. So the head of this column – the most perfect of the Greek style – became a monument to a young girl who died some 2500 years ago. It is an attractive story.

Gammon also had much to tell us about the Greek temple, which he insisted was not merely a house, or even a church, but a sort of mathematical declaration of the male and female principle raised to its highest power. In their search for the Golden Mean, they were haunted by the Ideal of Perfection. Where did it reside? The admirable Vitruvius has left us some rich and thoughtful observations on the architectural problems the Greeks faced. The passage is so useful to remember when you confront ancient Greek sculpture, that I make no excuse for copying it out in full, since Vitruvius is not easy to get hold of today.

When Ion had founded thirteen colonies in Caria – among them Ephesus and Miletus – the immigrants began to build temples to the immortals, such as they had seen in Achaia, and first of all to Apollo Panionic. When they were about to set up the columns in this temple they could no longer recall the measurements. While they were considering how to make them at once trustworthy and graceful it occurred to them to measure a man's foot and compare it with his height. Finding that the foot measured a sixth part of the height they applied this to the column by laying off its lowest diameter six times along the length of the column, inclusive of the capital. Thus did the Doric column begin to represent the compressed beauty of the male body in building.

The Roman goes on to explain that for Diana's Temple a female slenderness was the architect's model.

At the bottom they laid a foot like a sole; into the capital they introduced snails, which hung down right and left like artificially curled locks; on the forehead they put rolls and bunches of fruit for hair, and down the whole shaft they made grooves to resemble the folds in female attire. Thus in the two styles of column they invented, the one was copied from the naked and unadorned body of the man, the other from the dainty figure of an adorned woman. But those who came later, with a more critical and finer taste, preferred less massiveness and accordingly fixed the height of the Doric column at seven and of the Ionian at nine times the diameter.

He goes on to add that the Corinthian column emulates the slenderness of a virgin. If some scholars doubt the authenticity of all this, it is at least highly suggestive, and useful to bear in mind when looking at Greek work.

If you straggle back to the road from the blazing quarries, and go on to Naoussa, you will find a delightful little fishing village with the usual Venetian fort cresting it. Among these ruins, when trying to pick flowers, I alerted a couple of large reddish scorpions and was happy to escape their stings. A scorpion sting is very painful and there seems to be no treatment for it. The swimming, in a cove nearby, was fine, and I was sorry to get on the road again.

I recall other *dicta* by Mr Gammon – *dicta* full of fungus, you might say, for that low voice was furry with drink. 'What is the message of the caryatids, my boy, tell me that? What, you don't know? I will tell you.' Leaning forward on his desk he said: 'Every girl has a duty to look ever so slightly pregnant.' This was when we were alone – I had been kept in to write a hundred lines while he invigilated; he would never have dared to say anything so improper to the whole class. I have often wondered if Gammon managed a trip to the Greece he so much adored – where his queer Erasmic pronunciation would have seemed laughable, as I realized when I heard live Greeks talk. And it takes time to adjust from school Greek of the

'What Ho on The Rialto' kind to the five diphthongs of the modern tongue.

It may seem a bit odd to be thinking of Mr Gammon in far-away smoky London while wandering about the quarries of Paros; but it is thanks to enthusiasts like him that one culture secures a foothold in another. Gammon planted in me so many observations, like barbs, that I early had a feeling of familiarity with the Greek thing. And I was not surprised to discover when I got there that Greece was almost exactly as he had taught me that it might be. Watching Paros slowly fading into the trembling amethyst dusk of the summer night, I could hear Gammon's voice in my ear again. He was talking about 480 BC, in the heart of Cockney London, not far from Tooley Street with its roaring and howling drays racing beer barrels down to the wharf at Tower Bridge. (The oxen of the sun, Gammon might have called them for his mind was full of Homer.)

You will say the Persians were utter rotters and I agree. But here and there there was a spark. Even Xerxes, my boy. Would you believe it, he had never seen a plane tree in all its majesty? It was the symbol of genius to the Athenians, for their philosophers sat in the shade of the tree when they were in spouting mood. But Xerxes! When he crossed the Hellespont he saw one for the first time. It stopped him dead in his tracks. It must have been like seeing your first Gothic cathedral, or Mount Everest. He fell hopelessly in love with it. The whole damn army of a million odd men came to a dead stop while he paid tribute to this tremendous object. He adorned the tree with all the jewels of his court, taken from the lords and ladies and concubines, loading the branches until they sagged. He declared the tree his wife and mistress, and even said that it was a goddess. It was highly embarrassing for the General Staff. It looked for a while as if the whole campaign would be called off while he sat drooling over this tree. Disaster was, however, very narrowly averted, and he was persuaded to resume the march.

Mykonos · Delos · Rhenia · Tinos · Andros

At first sight it may seem somewhat arbitrary to treat the rest of the Cyclades as a central double constellation, and divide them into a northern and a southern group. Anyone who knows them, however, will think the decision justified on the grounds that Tinos, the Lourdes of modern Greece, lies almost cheek to cheek with Delos, the Lourdes of the ancient. The rings of association (pebbles dropped into the well of Greek history) widen according to contrasting yet strictly complementary magnetic fields; one speaks for Apollo and ancient Greece, the other for Byzance and the post-1828 era which brought modern Greece to birth. The result is a truthful and balanced presentation of a Greece with several profiles, of an etching in successive stages. If I put the point of my compasses upon the famous monastery of Tinos and describe a circle, I would separate off a group composed of Andros, Mykonos, Delos; and then Syros, Kythnos and Kea – a group sufficiently rich in beauty and historical associations to strike the visitor as being the very heart of Greece – the island Greece: the heart of the Greek experience. He will not be wrong. It is here in the brown, wave-washed Cyclades, here or never, that you can absorb and digest this fervent landscape and appreciate the continual intellectual ferment of the people who inhabit it.

The mercuric prototypes made familiar by the old Greek dramatists are still here, in the modern *agora*; they have not stirred in their frames – merchant-bankers, adventurers, seamen, shipowners, *négociants* in wine and oil and fruit, peasants, priests, poets, paupers – the whole *dramatis personae* of the Aristophanic scene. Moreover, each of the islands with its characteristic accent and garb is pictured in the modern Greek shadow-play, which is showing signs of a new revival. This great cycle, devoted to the adventures of Karaghiosis, the modern epic hero, is something more than a Punch and Judy show, being full of topicality and political allusion. The new Odysseus, the much diminished hero of the modern world, is a figure rather like the Chaplin tramp, who triumphs over the Turkish overlords by superior cunning. His satyrical turn of speech, however, and his repertoire of jokes are pure Aristophanes in their riskiness and tang. You will surely find this little shadow-play in one of the islands, for it tours there every summer, with a large cast of hand-operated marionettes – Corfiots, Zantiots, Cretans, Viziers, Agas, each presenting a highly accentuated local style – a medallion of place.

Among so many imperatives – for here in the Cyclades the traveller cannot afford to be lazy, for fear of missing a vital experience – it is perhaps best to begin with Mykonos, the most likely tourist landfall, the island which has perhaps suffered the most from its recent over-popularity and the wrong kind of tourist. ('Pray, what is the "right" kind of tourist?' I don't know.)

They will tell you on all sides, and with some justification, that Mykonos is finished, crowded out, crushed flat by the feet of the faithful. These people are disgorged in passive droves by the great cruise liners *en route* for Delos, which lies just across the strait, half-an-hour distant. Painfully plodding in Germanic crocodiles, often led by a stout member of a tourist club holding aloft a banner, they march off round Delos, like a human sacrifice to a culture which has ceased to identify with its own roots in the past. These pale, muffin faces are hunting eagerly in the past for the lost clues to their present. So much flesh roasted in this torrid sun, their devoutness is as touching as it is exasperating. Mykonos and Delos reel under their presence, but usually only for a month or two, and not every day.

Whatever tourism has done to the island, Mykonos *must* be seen, cannot be missed out or scamped. It would be like missing out Venice because of the tourists or Fez because of the smell in the *souks*. Of course scale makes nonsense of such a comparison; nevertheless, there is nothing quite like this extraordinary cubist village, with its flittering, dancing shadows, and its flaring nightmare of whiteness, which haunts its noons and hence your siestas. Its colonnades and curling streets, with their kennel-like houses, sprouting extravagant balconies of tottering painted wood, lead on and on, turning slowly inward upon themselves to form labyrinths, hazing-in all sense of direction until one surrenders to the knowledge that one is irremediably lost in a village hardly bigger than Hampstead.

Everywhere the white arcades and chapels repeat themselves in an obsessive rhythm of originality and congruence; and what is marvellous is that in Mykonos there are no foreign echoes from Venice, Genoa and the rest. Everything is as newly minted as a new-laid Easter egg, and just as beautiful. You can walk for hours in what is an imitation *souk* hung with carpets, brocades, island blankets, donkey bags, shawls in all their bewildering variety. Relentless perspectives of light and shade marry the voluptuous shapes of breasts translated into cupolas and apses, into squinches and dovecots. Take Picasso, Brancusi and Gaudi, knock their heads together, and you might get something like Mykonos by evening light, foundering into violet whiteness against a blue-black sea. You forget the Germans, you forget the ladies burned purple, you forget everything and just feast your eyes and mind upon this extravagant bazaar of candescent loveliness. And at the end of every gyre or whorl (you are inside a seashell) you suddenly plunge out upon the harbour with its welcoming lines of cafés and chop-houses, set out under brilliant awnings or in some places shaded by tall mulberries. Nightfall is the time, *ouzo*-time, after an exhausting day of doing nothing purposefully (the opposite of killing time), when you feel the need of these cafés. The violets, pinks, rose, and grey, of the sinking sun on the walls – just before the wink of the green ray which says goodnight – are all the more haunting for being reproduced in little in the cloudy glass of *ouzo* before you on the table. It is like inhabiting a rainbow.

When darkness comes, the little town becomes even more mysterious and beguiling, whether by electric light or by fizzing gaslight or by the serene yellow glow-worm light of paraffin-lamps; the shadows leap and caper on the dancing walls The wind presses on your lips, on your shutters, on your sleeping eyelids; it can rise to a shriek, or sink to a moan like a woman in labour, but it never lets up – always pressing and letting go, pressing and letting go, pressing and releasing your ear-drums. You sleep in a cocoon of wind, and on Delos you hear it whistle like a snake in the burned grass. Its continually changing pressure and eternal whispering give you vertigo. Never will you go to sleep so soundly as you will in Mykonos – and it is the deep sleep of early infancy. In the morning, when you push back your shutters, the whiteness comes up to meet you again like the caress of wet eyelashes.

The architecture is of no special time or merit; the Greek islander has built himself a home, that is all, and like a sea-animal the shell he constructs prefigures the contours of his nature with its extremes of mysticism and rationalism, asceticism and voluptuousness. Walking about this village, which echoes no age or style, you feel that only paradise could be composed like this, so haphazardly and yet so harmoniously. Here plane geometry takes wing and becomes curved of surface. The little square boxes of houses are pure, unplanned expressions of the islanders' inner metric. Everywhere the tiny chapels bud and proliferate like some crazy illustration of genetic fission; self-multiplying breasts, fused one upon the other, joined like the separate cloves which go to make a garlic-head or an orange; compartmented upon the same mathematical principle as the pomegranate-fruit which nods its toy crown at you over many a walled garden gate. No, however many tourists come with their chatter and their litter, little Mykonos will not let the stranger down. Its exemplary purity of tone and line will hush them, its island wind alarm their sleep, its black seascape nudge their nerves with the premonition of things as yet unformed and unformulated in their inner natures; perhaps the very things they have come here to experience . . . It is not cosy, it does not try to charm. It brands you like a hot iron.

I say this advisedly, for as late as October 1976 I visited it with a couple of French friends who had never seen it. I was pale with terror, lest its glamour had been defaced, lest its purity had departed. They were just the people to enjoy and evaluate the momentous experience it had to offer. But then, what the devil? Was I romancing about this place, which I first knew in 1940 when there was not a single hotel there? I am given to rhapsody and exaggeration. Perhaps Mykonos would be a terrible experience? I was afraid. But *nothing* had changed and the island was virtually empty. On the cool sea-front at evening we counted half a dozen other tourists like ourselves. It was a miracle. And the new *tavernas* were marvellous, the seafood they served being in the best Athens style, which is saying something when you recall the sea-front *tavernas* below the yacht club in Turkolimano, Piraeus.

Mykonos has so little history to intimidate one that it is a pleasure to get to know that little. Always overshadowed by famous Delos, it is the Cinderella of the islands, even today. There is nothing much to see except the granitic earth, lightly covered by parched grass which is stirred by the harsh unslaked wind. Apparently the island was used by Poseidon once to batter in the skulls of some giants he found irritating. More interesting than this was the invasion of the Ionians, for they brought with them the cult of Dionysus, and thenceforth the coinage of the island wore the god's head on one face and a bunch of grapes on the reverse. There is not much more to know, and anyway I supplied my potted biography of this aggravating god of wine in the section on Naxos, where he was rightly regarded as the most interesting man of the season.

As for the three hundred and forty little Orthodox chapels in the capital, they all seem to be private property, belonging to the various families who, at one time or another, had estates in the island. They are all tiny, and seemingly decorated *con furioso* by unbalanced monks with Sicilian backgrounds.

In the violet whiteness of the falling dusk, if you go astray and tumble into one of these chapels you can say a prayer for the goddess of labyrinths who managed to inspire it; and at dawn, when you throw back the shutters to emerge on the balcony of the doll's house you have rented for a night, you will be all the more overcome by the confused yet marvellously homogeneous composition of interpenetrating staircases which rise up at you – some broken off and eclipsed, only to restart again at another level, higher up; some candidly broken off, like the stems of plants. You will delight in the live trees growing right up through the centre of houses which politely give them room, built round them so that washing can be hung out to dry in the branches. (What else is a tree for?) To crown it all is a fantastic display of variegated chimney-pots and weather vanes spinning in the wind, which opens and shuts the palms with a clicking sound as if they were Chinese fans.

Mykonos offers you a sort of prototype of the eye-caressing beauties which will charm you in less selective places – in Poros, in Paros, or in vine-wreathed Naxos. Everywhere else, history has created a sort of jumble sale of styles which are jolted together and made pleasing simply by paint and whitewash and blue sea; disjunct forms – Venetian mouldings, modern balconies, medieval windows, concrete pavements ... Not so Mykonos. Here is a true primitive form with its cyclopean eggplant style, its bulb chapels; a form decorated not only by rhapsodic Hellenistic statues of the classical epoch, but by those primitive ladies with faraway smiles who inhabit the tiny museum on the Acropolis, the wicked Cycladean queens in exile.

If you are a painter or a poet, you will feel, when you walk here at early morning, or late at night, by a full moon, part of the extraordinary natural forces which have shaped a peach, have ensured the exact calibration of a starfish or an orange or an octopus. It seems as if you divine intuitively the function of this vast, desolate, hungry machine we call nature. This is no less true in the terrible but more famous desolation of Delos, where you may stand on a deserted threshing floor with the jackstraw blowing about your ankles and wonder at the effort that human beings have made to try to stamp a reminder of their little significance upon places like these – these nude islands brindled like sand-lions, ravaged now only by wind which moves across the embers of past civilizations, stirring here and there the pathos of an historical echo. There are no *cicadas* here, or few, for *cicadas* like shade and the violin accompaniment of running water if possible. But there are occasional wild hares in the hills, brown as their brown soil and big in size, which are good eating, if you can hit one.

Perhaps my somewhat proprietary feelings about Mykonos are due to the fact that I first saw it about 1940, just as the war was really beginning. For a long time we had lived in the penumbra of a war declared on all sides but not implemented;

almost a whole year, with the Maginot Line frozen and Greece technically a neutral. But the whole of Europe was breaking up under us, like the raft of Odysseus, and we knew it. It was a matter of time before we would have to swim for it. Already leave-takings were sharper and more poignant because they foreshadowed the more definitive leave-takings the true war would bring. Nobody dared to hope he would survive. It was popularly supposed that German bombing would obliterate in a couple of hours all the capitals of Europe. Thus it was in the twilight of European history that I said goodbye to Henry Miller, who was ordered back to the States by his Consul. I posted off the letter which was afterwards to make a postscript to his *Colossus of Maroussi*, and took ship at night for Mykonos, where I hoped to spend a fortnight of quiet with my wife. At that time, I had begun to understand Greece through the friendships I had made with the young people of Athens, a remarkable body of spirits – some of fortune, some poor – but all endowed with the riches of the buoyant Greek nature. Moreover they were all raised in four languages, and consequently the whole of Europe was theirs. Of exceptional personal beauty and style, the type to which they belonged was always recognizable on Greek coins or sculptures in the museum. Rich or poor, they could live like nabobs or like tramps without ever losing their taste for life, without ever yielding before adversity. These young men were an education in themselves. It is a pleasure to put down their names – each had something personal to teach me through his attitude to life and his intrinsic Greekness. I think of Andre Nomikos, painter; Stephan Syriotis, high functionary; Matsas, diplomat; Seferis, poet; Elytis, poet; Alexis Ladas, Peter Payne, among so many others. Stephan Syriotis spent his summer hidden in Mykonos with his small boat, living in seclusion almost, and coming back to the little hamlet of Mykonos only for provisions of lentils and rice and wine. For the rest, he led the life of a seabird, swimming on faraway beaches, reading and sleeping away the days until he needs must return to Athens and his job.

I admire solitariness and realized then that in the heart of every Greek there is a buried monk, waiting to emerge when fortune fails and when youth is spent; it is not only the bandits who dream of retirement in some distant monastery. It is to Stephan that I owe my first visit to Mykonos and, by the same token, to Delos, where he made me free of two tiny beaches which are still there, still untenanted. They are hardly bigger than a concert-grand, it is true, but there is some undercut rock, where you can hide provisions in the coolness of wet sand; and the little shelving beach slopes quickly into deep water where, while you paddle, you can watch the island of Hecate glowering at you across the way.

I re-discovered this tiny corner in 1966, using the same technique that Stephan had shown me in 1939. I think it would work even today. Get hold of Janko or Pavlo or any of his descendants and strike a price for a boat – quite a small *benzina* will do. Ask him to borrow a sack and place therein twenty bottles of beer, some ham, a tin of butter, a chunk of bread and some fruit, all separately wrapped. Bid him take you to the bay of Phourni and decant you below the old site of the abandoned Aesculapion. It is technically forbidden to camp on Delos, but Apollo made an exception for my wife, who was recovering from a grave operation, and even welcomed her with an evening calm and a special sunset. I practised a slight deception, knowing that the guardians retire early (there is nothing to steal on Delos; everything is either smashed or too big to lift). Janko came back in the evening, ostensibly to take us back to Mykonos, but in fact to bring us some welcome Thermos flasks of hot coffee and soup. Then he returned to base, and the guardians presumably thought we had gone with him; but no, we unpacked sleeping bags and waited for the moon to rise. How silent and ominous Delos is at night, with the slither of snakes and huge green lizards among the stones.

We swam by the rising moon, the old Apollo therapy, and came back dripping and shivery to our warm soup, bully beef and coffee. At about midnight, the moon was so flaring white that we both awoke with a start, thinking we had heard a cry, perhaps from some wild seabird. We took a prowl among the ruins. There was a hole in the barbed wire which gave access to some proconsular villa, built by some long dead Roman magistrate. The tessellated floor had a fish or dolphin design, I don't remember which now; but the salt and dust had dried over it and obliterated it. At any rate (we did not need the torches we had brought; you could have read a Greek newspaper by the moon's light), I filled a pail with seawater and swished it over the floor and suddenly the whole design printed itself like a photograph does in a developing-tray. I still remember the way the eyes emerged, even though I do not recall if they were dolphin's or fish's. Fish, I think.

Mykonos at that time was little frequented because of faulty and haphazard communications with Athens; but it was a choice and secret place which Athenians loved, and which they kept very much to themselves. It was a compliment to be made free of this little club of Mykoniots *d'élection*, and I have never ceased to be grateful to Stephan Syriotis for tipping me off about it.

It is strange to remember how shaky the communications were in those days – now one can telephone for a room! Because of the lack of a safe anchorage and the tremendous bustle of the wind, one was pushed ashore in a bumboat, and, in default of any hotel whatsoever, one had to lodge *chez l'habitant* as the French guides have it. This led at once to spirited wrangling and enjoyable encounters. In my case, I was adopted by a huge wall-eyed goddess called, strangely enough, Poppeia, who looked like a Sicilian mama fresh from the crater of Etna. But first I was processed and beaten to my knees by her husband Janko, who stood me an *ouzo* to steady my nerves before leading the way to his little house. After all that flurry and argument I found later that, in an excess of cleverness, he had cheated himself, and I made up the difference. Actually, I lodged among his scrawny chickens in a clean comfortable cot, eating at the tavern under a spreading mulberry tree. It was his boat I used, and his complicity I enjoyed in the Delos connection.

This huge couple lived in harmony and happiness, shouting and yelling at each other the livelong day. When their paths crossed as they went about their various tasks, which was often for the house was small, they never failed to smack each other resoundingly on the behind with a calloused palm. So Zeus must have lived with Hera in ages past. Their laughter and exultation was infectious; the whole neighbourhood resounded with their chuckles and chortles. It was what Shakespeare has so justly called the 'marriage of true mounds'. This marvellous couple has alas vanished, and nobody knows what became of them. After the war their house fell down and they never came back. I hunted for them in '66 but had to make do with a younger and more agile Janko for my illegal Delos run. The spreading mulberry tree was still there, and the tavern had blossomed into quite a big establishment with excellent fare, though under new ownership.

Of Delos itself, it is hard to write because it is more than one island. Half bank and half shrine, it corresponds to the inimitable Greek spirit, which manages to combine enlightened self-interest with fire-insurance. Moreover, it seems different at different times of the day; when the bankers go home, so to speak, the ancient gods come out to enjoy the moonlight. Delos was the Wall Street of the ancient world, and the first thought a visitor has is one of marvel that there exists no real harbour for such a great maritime *entrepôt*, such a critical staging-post between Europe and Asia. I must confess that none of the explanations I have heard concerning the preeminence of Delos as a maritime centre really holds water; the absence of a good harbour really is a great mystery. The French have been picking away at the island since before the turn of the century and, with their diligence, have unearthed and almost completely identified the separate buildings and temples of this great harbourless complex of trading houses. Of its commercial importance there is no doubt; but how could such a volume of merchandise be brought ashore, stored, re-freighted and re-dispatched?

Here is the explanation offered by the sailor-scholar, Ernle Bradford:

Delos, the hub around which the Cyclades (Kukloi-rings) radiate, was formed by nature to be the focal point of a seaman's world. If one is tempted to ask why so small an island, without any natural resources, ever became what it did, then the answer can be given by any sailor. Delos is the last and best anchorage between Europe and Asia. To the east it is shielded by Mykonos, to the north by Tinos, and to the west by Rhenia. Looking at a chart it is easy to see how the direct sea-route between the Gulf of Nauplia (with Argos at his head) flows straight across the latitude of 37° 10′ north of Patmos and Samos. Exactly in the centre of the trading route between the Dardanelles and Crete. Religious centres may sometimes, as at Rome or Lourdes, attract trade and commerce. But more often one will find that where trade is, there are also temples. Merchants, then as now, are eager to purchase security in both worlds.

This is fairly spoken, but when you are actually anchored in the tiny harbour of Delos, alongside the ancient mole, whether in a *caique* or cruise ship, you realize that you could not funnel a quantity of merchandise ashore with any regularity or safety –

at least not a quantity which might correspond to the extensive and elaborate storage complex of the ancient town. The whole strait between Rhenia and Delos is a chancy affair, and one constantly looks for the huge harbour which alone could accommodate such a volume of trade, store and re-expedite it. It is all the more mysterious when one thinks of the marvellous harbours available in the surrounding islands – almost anywhere would be surer than Delos. People who have wintered in Greece and snaked about on island craft will also wonder what used to happen to Delos port in winter, when Boreas hurtled down the Rhenia channel and curdled the sea into a mass of white-caps? Even in summer one can be held up for a day by wind in Mykonos.

Also bewildering is the mythology connected with the island; in particular the birth of Apollo whose mother, Leto, flying from the wrath of Hera, finally took refuge here – or, if not here, in Rhenia hard-by which, like Delos, has been identified with Ortygia (Quail Island) – a name that keeps turning up in Greece and Sicily. 'Then Leto clasped a palm tree in her arms' (thus the Homeric hymn) 'pressed the soft ground with her knees, and the earth beneath her smiled and the child leaped into the light. All the goddesses cried out with joy. Then, O Phoebus, the goddesses washed thee in sweet water, limpid and pure, and they gave thee for swaddling clothes a white veil of tissue, light and fresh, which they tied with a golden girdle.'

It is unsatisfactory really, for the attributes of Apollo proliferate to such a degree that you can hardly feel proprietary about him in Delos, however much you may sympathize with poor Leto. He was an all-purpose god. One connects him with the powers of divination, and therefore, usually with Delphi; yet he *was* also the god of light *par excellence*, and when Delos was chosen (it means 'the Brilliant') as a name to replace Ortygia, it was to suggest that the god's burning ray had fallen upon the island. Then, as if to irritate us, the scholars say that there was a sacred grove called Ortygia near Ephesus, and in some versions of the legend his birth occurred there ... At any rate he was a sun-god, though he was not actually the sun himself – that was Helios. Phoebus = brilliant, Xanthus = fair, Chrysosomes = golden-locked – these epithets justify his marvellous youthful looks in all sculptures connected with his name. There was perhaps a vein of introspection and sadness in him too for 'he delighted in high places, the frowning peaks of high mountains, wave-lapped beetling promontories'. This was part of the prophetic side of his protean nature – after all, he was a love-child.

His light ripened the fruits of the earth, and in Delos the first crops used to be dedicated to him; they are still dedicated, though nowadays to the Virgin or the village saint. (You will find offerings of first fruits, and of oil for the lamp, at every tiny wayside shrine in Greece today.) But Apollo was as good as any modern saint – he destroyed both mice and locusts when they endangered the crops. Strangely enough, even today incursions of locusts are blown over from the African deserts, though not on any great scale. I have seen two such small invasions, one in Rhodes, which cost several acres of burned grass to control and caused some alarm. Just how Apollo went about their destruction in default of kerosene oil is not recorded in the Larousse *Encyclopedia of Mythology*, that indispensable work of reference, in which the enumeration of his gifts takes up several pages of close print.

Little Mount Cynthus, so charming by the light of the moon, seems artificial by daylight – as if it had been fashioned by man for some mysterious purpose as yet unknown.

As for the lake, the less said the better, for it has dried up; though the guardian once told me that after the rare winter rain, one can hear the croak of green tree frogs in the ancient cisterns. The lizards are huge, and vivid emerald, and strut and scuttle about the stones as if they owned them. The sacred birth took place on the north side of Cynthus under a spreading date palm; immediately, the barren land burst forth in springs, flowers and fruit, and the sacred swans wheeled across the sacred lake. Was a date palm such a rarity in ancient Greece, one wonders when one reads that after this episode the palm became sacred to Apollo? It is true that Odysseus compares the beauty of Nausicaa to 'a young palm tree which I saw when I was in Delos, growing close to the altar of Apollo'. The sacred geese have also departed today.

The usual landing for the Mykonos visitor is the sacred port. This is a trifle to the north of what is known as the ancient commercial harbour, whose amenities are picked out in clear detail by the ruins of warehouses, granaries and quays. The old site of the Apollo Temple lies two hundred yards inland from the little jetty, and shoulders the old *agora* of the *Competaliastes* which is nearer to the old port. The layout of the square is authoritative, and it must have had great atmosphere when all the statues were upright. Among these was the giant statue of Apollo which was of Naxian provenance, and must have been accounted a technological wonder, for the inscription on its base announced: 'I am of the same marble, both statue and base.' Has one a right to feel there is something a little *nouveau riche* about the sentiment? Was the statue offered by the Bankers' Guild of Naxos? At any rate, ruin has overtaken it, along with everything else. It has been hacked to pieces; one chunk lies near the temple of Artemis, a foot is in London, a hand in the Museum of Delos. 'It needs an effort of the imagination to reconstruct the sanctuary as it once was,' says a modern writer; it does indeed, especially the soaring bronze palm tree which overshadowed the huge figure of the god.

If you find something unsatisfactory about the relics and

associations of the principal hero-god of the place, your sense of wonder and delight will come back if you go directly north from the site of the sacred lake to the little group of lean Mycenean lions, which pose themselves for a leap in the harsh glare of the sun. They have an archaic style that suggests they have been crossed with a Persian cheetah, and though their numbers have been depleted by time and vandalism (there were once nine), five of them still remain in a row, poised and silently snarling, to greet the approaching visitor. At once the poetry and the harmony of the place seem restored, and you forget the guilds of bankers that perhaps commissioned them to be carved – for they are made of Naxian marble, like the statue of the god.

A vague unrest haunts one during the daylight hours in Delos – you will notice that I exempt the night. Its source is the endless search for a clue which will illuminate the intimate connection that obviously existed between treasure and worship in the ancient world – between the counting house and the sacred temple in whose shadow it operated. Perhaps somewhere there is a treatise on ancient Greek banking and its theory of values, which throws some light upon this superstitious linking of the material with the supernatural. Even modern cultures show traces of the same link, and I suppose that the hoarding instinct is as old as history, flowing through all the ancient epochs – Stone, Bronze, Iron – up to the Middle Ages, when it crystallized into the sacerdotal banking houses of the Templars and thence on to John Company and Chase Manhattan, so to speak. It is not invidious to see the temple enclosure of a sacred town like Delphi or Delos as a sort of spiritual dynamo, generating forces to ward off evil influence, bad luck, even the ever-present thieving hands which waited to pounce upon unguarded treasure.

Perhaps, for cyclopean man, the protecting gods were trees,

the sacred groves and enclosures which held a magic to ward off evil spirits. But what could his treasure have been; what was he afraid would be stolen – the secret of fire perhaps? To push imagination further, I think the trees were followed by the *herms*, those sculptured heads on tall columns which watched over crossroads of the cities and the private courtyards of families, sharing their duties with the *lares* and *penates*. After that, magic expressed itself in the statue primarily as a representation of the deity, and then its cocoon, the temple.

In any case, there must have been a very active belief that the temple gods were well disposed to material gain; they brought good luck and a following wind to one's enterprises, on condition that they had their cut in precious stones, statuary, or plate. In this sense, the modern Americans, with their frank avowal that material gain is holy, are very like the ancient Greeks – who must, like the modern peasant in Greece, have promised the local saint (then it was Apollo) a gold or bronze palm-tree if he would kindly help the fleet arrive safely back from Syria. The ancient, direct superstition is more disguised in modern times, but still there. It is not true, however, that the annual reports of the bigger banks in the USA begin: 'In the name of God the Father, Son and Holy Ghost, Amen. Gentlemen, as the poet Keats has written: "Beauty is loot, loot Beauty . . . "' There is not a word of truth in this.

In Delos at midday, the dry, island wind parches lips and heart, shivers the brown grass, and whispers among the ruins. Outside the sacred port, the Meltemi has started to stir up the channel until it boils white like milk. You will have to wait in patience for it to falter and fall, as it will with the early dusk, before taking your ship for Mykonos. And when evening comes, the strange Pharaonic bronze and green lights seem to play about the site of the ancient Serapeion, reminding one, not of Cycladean blue and white, but of the exhausted colours of the

Nile valley. There is hardly a god who did not plant himself here, introduced by the traders and mariners of the whole Middle Orient. They were encouraged to make themselves feel entirely at home – it was good for trade; and a puissant, magical city with its 'free port' facilities encouraged the establishment of more permanent citizens – those who polished and set jewels or worked metals or carved stone. There was plenty of work for all. Only that little question of the inadequate harbour still troubles me.

When you walk here at dusk, waiting for the first blush of the rosy-bronze moon across the water, what a vast melancholy is distilled by this great ossuary, the broken whiteness of all this bundled and smashed stone! Everywhere the eye turns there is desolation; nothing whole, nothing erect, nothing complete. The curses of genius and of history have joined forces here to wreak their vengeance on everything to do with historical man – that is to say, man the predator, commercial man! For the disposition which the archaeologists have accredited to the various deities and their precincts suggests the same sort of haphazard muddle that Pausanias describes in the Acropolis – an ignoble jumble of superstitious objects, dirty wax, smashed bibelots, dusty feathers, rusty armour, broken arrows – everything overlooked, thrown about, forgotten, almost forfeiting any claim to historical significance. I am sure that had he 'done' Delos in the same way, Pausanias would have produced something like his account of the Acropolis of Athens. Yet . . . I am sorry that in Delos there is not a plaster model, made by an architect, to guide one's steps; for, thanks to the patient work of the French over so many years, almost everything about the huge site and its history is known, and its location pin-pointed.

But the melancholy remains. A whole brief civilization was swallowed up here, battered to pieces. Only the lean archaic lions and the Dionysian nook with its frieze and phalluses remain, to remind one that in spite of everything the island was once full of primal echoes and the astounding phosphorescence of Apollonian light.

There is a further mystery – at least for me – in the fact that twice the natural magic of the island was reinforced by a formal act of lustration, and a removal of anything which might connect it with death (the sepulchres, for example) and, by the same token, with life. Birth and death were officially banished from the place, and Rhenia across the water absorbed both the dead and those about to give birth. There must have been some profound reason for endowing Delos with this sort of immortality out of time. I have not been able to come upon a satisfactory explanation. Was it merely a commercial decision – to reinforce the magic of the site? The two lustrations are historically separated by more than a century. There must have been, surely, some more fundamental reason behind it. Perhaps the decision was made, for example, because of some great sin committed there. It could have been intended to be expiatory or generative of renewed power. The guide books announce this sort of thing without a tremor – yet the mere fact is obviously momentous. What does it really mean? We do not know.

It was the sage Peisistratus, when he was tyrant in Athens, who first decided to purify the holy birth-spot of Apollo. This was in 543 BC. The second time the lustration was repeated and the magic intensified was in 426 BC. At the same time a new law was promulgated forbidding all births and all deaths on the island – a weird kind of immortality indeed! It is impossible to believe that the reason was purely commercial, though there is no doubt of the tremendous economic power of this small harbourless hole of a place. The whole Levant traded here and presumably banked here, under the tutelary protection of the sacred shrines. One must, I suppose, imagine the situation was something like that of the power of the modern Swiss banking system, which depends on money transferred under guarantee of secrecy from outside. All those immense fortunes of which we read must exist entirely on trust; they cannot be acknowledged on paper because they technically do not exist. If tomorrow a Swiss bank decided to pinch the entire fortune of – name any millionaire – there would be no legal redress for him. Yet the banks have never done such a thing and never will . . . The whole fragile system rests upon a simple say-so. Delos must have had something of this commercial magic about it in antiquity.

However, there is no denying history; time erodes everything. Delos went downhill, its magic wilted and waned. We see it now very much as Pausanias would have done; in his day it was quite uninhabited, save for the guardians of the sacred temple. But the temple itself was no longer in business; the god was dead, along with all the others, and the world had moved off along a new vector. Nothing could reverse this drift. Most humiliating of all – it is Philostratus who records the fact – when Athens decided to sell off the place in a job lot, she could not find a buyer!

Salute the headless Isis on your way up the holy hillock; every faith and every creed was welcomed here. Apparently there are even traces of a small late synagogue among the other ruins. You will have the queerest feeling of sadness as your boat levels off and begins to cross the two or three sea miles which separate it from Mykonos – where all is shining calm and silence, and where the quiet windmills with their grey sails turn all the time; for never for a second does the wind let up. There on the harbour front, drinking or eating, your thoughts shift from time to time to that smudge against the sky – Delos. A mystery remains, a disquieting echo. In the tiny museum, I saw a Christian stele commemorating the death of a girl. The inscription read 'Ego dormio sed cor meum vigilat'.

This is perhaps the place to mention the name of an old man, much revered in his time, who has now disappeared from the island scene. He was an old peasant, George Polykandriotis, whom I encountered on the sea-front and who informed me that he had started work with the French Institute, aiding them in their earliest digs on Delos. Later he became familiar with the pottery and vase forms, and then discovered in himself the gift of restoring pottery. 'There is hardly a vase here or in Delos which I have not reassembled myself,' he told me. He had worked right into his old age, and now his sight had failed, which caused him great sadness. His old hands seemed still to have traces of the clay dust which had come from years of handling these precious shards and piecing them back together – as if they had gathered some of the soft, chalky bloom which is such a feature of the vases themselves. It is to this old helper that the Athens Archaeological Institute dedicated its twenty-first volume on the Delos finds – a fitting tribute.

In the central cluster of the Cyclades, the distance between the islands is so short that you navigate more by the eyes than by the stars. You are seldom without a visible landfall, except in winter; you move from smudge to smudge on a sea forever brushed by harmonious winds, which can make wires sing out and cordage groan, or treat a large passenger ship as a wind-tunnel, but which usually have the grace to die with the sun during the Etesian season. After hot days, travel by night is delicious under the canopy of stars of every size. The hush of the prow crunching its way through the lazy water makes you think of the night as a great Aeolian harp of the intuition, plucked by these sleep-echoing sounds. Then, suddenly, a signal goes forth; the ship booms and roars like a bull when it rounds some dark point, and a frail network of lights tells you that you are nearing a new harbour. This grave maroon shakes the heart as if it were the voice of Judgment itself.

It is time to discuss the Virgin of Tinos and her native island, for they form an imaginative link with Delos, today serving as the great Lourdes of modern Greece. The wonder-working Panaghia is modern, in the sense that she dates from the revolution of 1822, but – attesting once more the perenniality of things Greek – the spring over which her chapel was built had been famous for its cures centuries before. Her two great festivals are, if anything, rather more impressive than the one at Lourdes because of their exotic island setting, and because of the strange mixture of races and clans who bring their sick here to be healed. Even Central European gypsies manage somehow to come – so widely spread throughout the Balkans is the belief in the Virgin.

I had intended, after a stay in Mykonos, to return to Athens by the lazy little island steamer of the time, but it was nearly the Festival of the Tiniotissa and I decided to spend a night on the island during the celebrations. A Greek ceremony of this nature has an inevitable cheerfulness which breaks through the gloom and anxiety generated by so many sick people gathered together in one place – some *in extremis*, one would suppose. It has a solemnity that never becomes anxiety-sodden and depressing. The event, of course, brings great trade, prosperity and tourism to the island and hordes of hucksters, jugglers and camp followers during this brief period swarm into the capital, eager to make a little money. They sell everything, from sweets and straw hats to lucky charms and live pigeons. Probably the ancient Aesculapia also honoured this secular side of things, and outside the sacred precincts, where the priests performed their work of consecration, a whole short-lived city sprang up with flags, coloured bunting, and more practical things, for which exhausted travellers would give money readily – pure drinking water, lemon juice against flies and sea-sickness, and so on.

My festival happened to be that of 15 August 1940, that fatal day when an Italian submarine sank the cruiser *Elli* as it lay at anchor in the harbour, all dressed from top to toe with flags, in honour of the Virgin. Had my own steamer not been dawdling, we should have arrived in time to eyewitness the explosion. Mercifully, we arrived an hour afterwards, when the poor *Elli* had vanished leaving only a great puddle of dark oil on the calm sea. Flags and lifebelts floated everywhere and the survivors battled with the shock-waves of indignation which had swept over the whole city.

The actual declaration of war was a month or two off; but nobody watching the scene in Tinos had any further doubt about its imminence, nor indeed about its outcome. (Nothing that subsequently happened to the Italian army was in any way surprising.) It would be impossible to overstress the ignobleness and tactlessness of this base attack; if you wanted to drive the whole Greek nation fighting-mad, you could not do better than level such an insult at Tiniotissa on her great day, when the sick had come from so far to seek her help. Coming ashore, I saw a new expression on the Greek countenance – a silent, enraged, resolution which boded ill for the enemy. The whole town had been stirred like a beehive, and it buzzed with indignant life. In the harbour, the divers were busy about the patch of oil, and a corvette had appeared to help. Strangely, there was no weeping, no public lamentation, as there is so often. The uncanny silence showed me that the weight of this mortal insult went right to the depths of the Greek heart and could only be expunged now by war. As night fell, things settled down a bit; a seaplane came and more small craft. But the sense of shock expanded; roundabouts and swings were hushed, and radios were turned down reverently in the lounge of the ship, which had now decided to spend the night in harbour and return to Athens on the morrow.

It was prudent to wait, for nobody could be sure that this incident did not herald an out-and-out attack on the rest of the fleet in Piraeus. Conflicting messages flew everywhere, the frail telephone and telegraph system on the island became strained with anxious dignitaries asking for solid information. The sick, too, wondered if, in the case of a general outbreak of war, they would find themselves marooned. But underneath these surface anxieties there stirred an overwhelming sense of determination, rooted in anger at an act of desecration. It was as if the insult struck back beyond the civil war into ancient times – for here in Tinos there had been one of the most famous wonder-working sanctuaries of antiquity, dedicated to Poseidon and Amphitrite. I was sure the old sea-god would take such an insult to his shrine very ill, and from then on I knew that the *Elli* would be revenged, with his wholehearted aid and approval.

That night, walking about the buzzing town, I had my first glimpse of the famous shrine. It is not very distinguished as architecture, though the approach to the main *bastide* is rather splendid – a slow-flowing staircase of stone which led up to where the bays with their arches opened. I walked between a double row of recumbent figures, some sleeping in twisted positions, some moaning, some quietly talking to the friends who had accompanied them here. The deep surf-like boom of a service was beginning. The long lines of the recumbent forms, wrapped in their rags and shawls, propped on pillows, or laid on stretchers, had their presence indicated by tiny night-lights, wicks afloat in saucers of olive oil, which cast a dramatic pallor over the scene. I was reminded of the contoured hells invented by Brueghel; and then as I advanced through the bays with the arches, I seemed to see a Victorian steel-engraving of the laza-retto at Scutari. Miss Nightingale was making her first scandal-ized visit. The crowd was so great that I did not trouble with Tiniotissa herself that night; I just stood for a while, hardly able to draw breath, feeling like one of a clutch of sardines sunk deep in oil. The smell of wax and garlic was overpowering. I realized only afterwards that that evening I had been present at one of those historic moments when the fate of a nation hangs on a simple yes or no. It was like the time in the Persian Wars when, after terrible tergiversations, cowardices and every kind of dirty trick, a lot of people who cordially detested each other, suddenly decided to join forces for an afternoon and unstitch the Persian Fleet (Poseidon willing); or it was like the arrival of the Spanish Armada, which suffered much the same fate of hubris at the hands of a group of gentlemen who could not bear the sight of each other. That night Greece knew she must say 'No' and win her war.

By rushlight and moonlight all was enchanting, and I walked the streets of the little town for an hour, wrapped in the pleasure and sadness of my thoughts. Even in the dark, the town was dazzling white, giving off light like a distant star; and everywhere the smell of frankincense descended from the church, eddy after eddy, pushed by the night wind into the narrow alleys and squares of the town.

Upon the dark escarpments of the Venetian castle I thought I detected some darker brush-strokes – cypresses? This tree, which runs wild in Greece and can be seen rising in groves from bare rock-faces over the blue sea, is really an exotic; I mean that it came originally from the Himalayas with the Phoenicians, and was planted in Cyprus – that orphan among Greek islands – about, I think, 1000 BC, whence it worked its way into the Greek décor. Once adopted as a symbol of the immortal soul and equally of eternal death, the Greeks pressed it into more practical service. Perhaps the impulse came from Egypt, where it was used for mummy-cases because it was so long-lasting and relatively impervious to termites. Its durability also made it a desirable coffin-wood for Greek heroes, and perfect for the masts of their war-craft. It is curious that something which, to the peoples of the east expressed only joy and beauty should, in coming west, become associated with death and the after-life. The island of Cyprus probably took its name from the tree. I have seen it also used extensively in the interiors of Greek houses, where it has a characteristic smell, deliciously astringent, and is waxed or oiled or varnished.

I went on board to sleep that night, but preferred a deck-chair on the boat deck to a bunk in the stifling cabin. An uneasy slumber seized the town, though the light in the cabin of the radio-operator burned all night, and one could hear the relentless clawing and scratching of the ship's radio and the land telephone. At dawn, I cadged an *ouzo* and a Turkish coffee from the sleepy steward and was informed that we would be staying all day in harbour and not leaving before midnight, 'if then'. Everyone everywhere was waiting for the war to burst like a swollen boil. While this indecision continued, I decided to have a look at the island – or as much of it as I could with the help of the local bus system.

By daylight you notice sharply the straggling and inchoate forms of the town, and the frankly inadequate architecture of the Tiniotissa's church. The church is disappointing, considering that many a chunk from Apollo's Delos shrine has been run into the walls! But the night had yielded one miracle; a deaf girl had suddenly had her hearing restored, which was heartening news for the sufferers who still awaited their turn. It was a confirmation, too, that it would take more than an Italian submarine to perturb the Virgin in her work of healing. Yellow and cavernous with fatigue, the faces of the sick were worth seeing again for a moment. I realized why, when a great dignitary of the King was dying in Athens, a summons had been sent for the famous icon, which was transported to the bedside of the dying person to intercede with Charon on his behalf. This also happened at the death of King Paul, and many of my friends were confident that the Tiniotissa would obtain his recovery through intercession.

Tinos is only some twenty-seven kilometres long, and not too difficult to explore, though the general impression it conveys is disparate. Perhaps this is because it is not only the home of the Orthodox saint but also one of the strongest Catholic corners of the Cyclades; and while all is peace and apparent harmony between the faiths there is a lack of intellectual harmony among the people. The Catholics tend, without reason, to behave snobbishly, which irritates their fellow Greeks. In addition, Tinos, being so central, has had more to do with corsairs and other marauders than neighbouring islands, and been repeatedly attacked and ravaged by them; the pirate Barbarossa is one of the most picturesque corsairs (1537) who laid waste the island, though the Catalans (1292) had already passed this way. The slight disharmony between the two faiths may be caused by the Catholics having taken little part in the movement of liberation during the insurrection of 1822. They contented themselves with retiring inland to a mount called Xynara, where they built themselves a stronghold of churches and convents and schools, waiting for everything to blow over, which it eventually did. Whatever the reason, there are two currents of feeling flowing through the island, and this makes its character unclear.

The prettiest part is the interior, which contains a bewildering number of villages, sites and Venetian citadels, which are worth a visit if you have the time, and can find the bus. The bus that carried me was full of livestock and covered with drooping flags in honour of the Tiniotissa – drooping from the heat, that is, which proved to be intense. The razzle-dazzle of the whitewashed villages with their coloured washing floating in the breeze was eye-catching enough; but in those pre-war days one knew the café would be full of stray cats and fleas, and that sleeping in the church on a camp bed would mean being bitten to death by bed bugs which had come over from Turkestan with Genghis Khan.

The one fine anchorage, Panormus, is on the Andros side, where the capital town might have been wise enough to pitch its tents. Panormus is so close to Andros that this would have conferred a sense of joint identity to them both. They are separated only by a small strait, but the tides tend to swirl and swell mightily in these seas, and even quite experienced sailors are sometimes surprised by a turn in the weather and forced to run for cover.

I came back to town in somewhat erratic fashion, having accepted a lift on the back of a motorbike driven by a young farmer who was anxious to try out his English – which as far as I could judge was a form of dialect Swedish in which only one phrase, 'Very good', stood out.

On the way back I saw several more pleasant villages, some in dusty rock-country without much shade; and my friend's much-vaunted wine was not up to much. In one place called, I think, Asproti, I saw a frieze of girls with heavy antique-style water pitchers going to the fountain. Those ascending with an empty pitcher carried it on the hip, these descending with a full one bore it on a small coiled headcloth on the head. Backbreaking work, but they were as gay and as talkative as jays, and their pleasantries had lots of edge. There were also snakes on the road. We rested for a while in the heat of the day and did not reach the town until dusk. I was relieved to find that my ship had not as yet left, and invited my host to drink and dine with me. He was tremendously impressed by all the stories he was told about the sinking of the *Elli*, and dragged me from kiosk to kiosk in order to get more and more first-hand, even eyewitness, accounts to take back to his village on the morrow.

Among his other purchases I noticed a wilted chap-book of

divination from dreams, which would doubtless see him through the winter; I did not make fun of him about it, and now I am glad because I was informed long afterwards that the peasants of Greece believe that dreams provide clues which will lead them to a buried treasure. In default of treasure, a man (and, especially, a church which is low in funds and poor in congregation) can perform much with a wonder-working icon. The Tiniotissa was miraculously discovered on the very day when the Greek standard was lifted against the Turks, thus giving religious sanction to the battles. I took a last look at the church with my friend before going aboard that night. He proved most knowledgeable about the wonderful thank offerings which constituted the treasure-store of the church – bibles galore with jewel-studded covers, gold and silver plate in quantity, embroideries of oriental silk in fabulous design and ancient workmanship. He explained too the shreds of infected clothing gummed to the pillars with wax – either ex-votos for services desired or thanks for services received. As for the silver-foil trinkets hawked outside the great doors, the poorest peasant could afford at least one, and so, according to my friend, the whole mass of whorled and worked candelabra which lighted the Virgin's church came from such humble peasant offerings. Much later, in Athens, I came upon a book which confirmed almost everything he had told me. That night we parted, never to meet again. I did not get a chance to see Tinos for many a year, as by April '41 Greece was invaded. But nothing that I have so briefly recorded here needs to be changed or amended. The Tiniotissa is even more wonder-making today than ever, and many are the cures she performs every year. Power to her arm, and Poseidon be with her!

If Tinos gives you an impression of irregularity Andros will do little to dispel it, for this is another handsome, rugged island with its harbours built on the hither side. The town of Andros is picturesque enough but, once you have crossed the ample plain of Messaria (preferably in early spring when Mount Kovari is snow-capped and the fields are full of flowers) and come upon the ancient site of Palaeopolis, you will recognize yet another of those champion harbours of the ancient world, which seem to speak of epochs before the pirates came and forced the island people to move further and further inland. There is little to see but a few shattered sea-marks, a straggle of walls; an outline in X-ray of the ancient site and the modern village is still relatively undisturbed, probably due to rather irregular form. But the site!

Its story is hardly any different from Naxos and Tinos; and with Naxos it shared an ancient cult for that enigmatic and capricious composite god Dionysus. In Andros the approved version of the god suggests that he spent his whole time travelling about with a dozen false passports; he appears to have come from Boeotia. In this corner of Greece, the festivals of which we have any record sound like grim, orgiastic affairs, where the Bacchantes sacrificed, perhaps young boys. The god's influence spread down into the Cyclades and, at Lesbos and Chios, just across the way, human sacrifices also took place, which were later replaced by ritual flagellation . . .

There is something a little sinister about the deep valleys of Andros in the mid-afternoon, when the sizzle of the *cicadas* drives one to sleep, where the vegetation is deep and often one cannot see the sea, so that the island seems much bigger than in fact it is. Andros is about the same size as Tinos, but its aspect is more rugged and less variegated. It has much the same historic pattern also – Ionian, Cretan, Phoenician – but so far no wonder-working Virgin has been dug up. Its lack of antiquities will always protect it from the more strident forms of tourism, but it already has good hotels, whose cuisine is no worse than anywhere else. The star turn is Paleopolis and perhaps the island is more to be commended to sailors and campers than visitors requiring sophisticated comforts. The famous Hermes of Andros is no longer here, but in Athens; and the medieval celebrity of the place, which flowered with the sudden discovery of mulberry silk and made the Andros weave celebrated as far as Avignon, has dwindled away to nothing. The Andriots now turn their eyes to New York and Sydney where they hope to make a decent living, though it is sometimes difficult to persuade them that they will have to pay a high price for such a standard of life. But after overflowing Tinos, a weekend in Andros could well prove a delight, because the bathing and underwater-fishing are extremely good.

Syros · Kythnos · Kea

I have placed these three together because they are less interesting, further off the track, and historically less well endowed than their more beautiful neighbours; they won't compare with Naxos and Paros. They vary in importance, however, and Syros must be put squarely on the record because, though on the decline, it is still a centre of radiation for sea-traffic. In the 1870s, before steam came, it was very important as a marshalling yard for all sea movements, and almost all notable travellers began their Cycladian tour by touching here. All Victorian travel memoirs mention it, and one could make up an amusing anthology of comments about the island in the days when the harbour thronged with costumed visitors, Turkish and Greek. It was from here that one tried to find a passage for Smyrna or Alexandria. And while the island is bald and graceless in comparison with many others, it has its own dignity.

Some eight thousand Catholics live here, so the island has the same flavour of dispersed intentions as Tinos; but the harbour is fine. Today travellers are well looked after, but it is difficult to forget that the frock-coat of Gerard De Nerval caused roars of laughter; that he was dubbed 'Catholikos', snubbed as a Frank, and then nearly raped in a windmill by an old crone. However, he was only one of many travellers bound for somewhere else who had to wait for a ship here. Since the last war, Syros's importance has once more started to decline, though it is the administrative *chef-lieu* of its group, and has a big role to play in radio and telephone communications, being a staging-post for this type of traffic. Once ashore, there is not much to see and even less to know historically. Yes, the compass was invented here by the philosopher who taught Pythagoras mathematics. But De Nerval and the frock-coat . . . that is more fun. Then Byron, Chateaubriand, and other seasick geniuses have left us descriptions; and after them came Curzon and Newton and that breed of curious, highly educated statue-snatchers and essence-squeezers. Melville wrote a fine poem on the harbour . . . It is in their shadow that modern Syros lives. And its position still enables it to be an octopus so far as maritime traffic goes.

From here to Kythnos. 'Nobody ever comes to Kythnos,' said the first man I met on the island, a disgruntled old priest on a mule, sporting a taffeta sunshade. 'Why should you?' It was a fair question, for there is nothing to see except the village, nothing to eat, and nothing much to write home about. If it were not surrounded by such glorious islands it might manage to insinuate some of its charm (it has real charm) into the minds of those travellers who would compare it with Naxos or Santorin, which form part of the same little constellation. It is unfair but that is the way the world wags.

Little Kea is also off the beaten track, though the actual distance from Piraeus is only some forty sea miles; it, too, has no great splendours to offer, but ardent campers and walkers would find the abandoned convent of St Marina a tempting spot to spend a weekend. Fly-blown villages, flea-tormented and silent; dogs and cats scratching themselves to death in the dust. And the terrible *ennui* that comes with such blazing isolation in the noonday sun. Yet the windmills turn and turn throughout these islands and their message is one of silent content.

Seriphos · Siphnos · Kimolos · Milos · Sikinos
Amorgos · Pholegandros · Ios

I do not think I shall be accused of taking my islands too lightly, if I now attempt to deal with a job lot of pretty, but very similar islands, which have considerably less to commend them in terms of monuments, though their charm is undeniable. Seriphos and Siphnos sound like the Heavenly Twins, and are very similar in size and scope. Kimolos and Sikinos are hard to visit, and harder to escape from, owing to their position off the beaten track; frankly it is not worth the trouble to do so, unless you are as determined and thorough about your Aegean as old Theodore Bent – who wrote the real classic on the area.

Iron-stained Seriphos speaks of poverty and silence, and its drear reaches of rock induce a mood very different from the heart-lifting ones induced by Rhodes or Mykonos. Livadhia is a trim little port to lie in for a summer, if you have a private yacht; if not the place is more likely to suit novelists, or suicides of other kinds. Siphnos lies hard by, and this again is a pretty place, but today has no trace of the riches for which it was celebrated in antiquity. The seams have run out, the times have changed. Milos (where the 'Venus de' came from) is a damnably dull hole of a place, with a magnificent bay so large that it could welcome the whole Allied Fleet, both during the Crimean War and the war of 1914–18.

Sikinos and Amorgos are rather sinister islands with little to commend them, though the villages are pretty and the inhabitants kindly; the anchorages are poor and, if you managed to get stuck there, you would wilt with boredom like an unwatered geranium. Pholegandros is another which would appeal only to solitaries. I knew a painter once called Chloe Peploe who spent her summers there alone in the little village, painting. Political exiles used once to be sent here to cool their minds.

The exception among all these is little Ios, the most poetical and beautiful island of its size in this part of the Aegean. Homer, they say, came here to die – an inspired choice. So many cities claim to be his birthplace; only Ios claims to be where he died. His so-called tomb – why 'so-called'? – lies on the northern flank of Mount Pirgos, a marvellous site where the wild grass rustles in the north wind and the weary climber, unpacking his lunch, turns his eye towards the East, towards Asia and the distant plains of Troy.

Everything about Ios is full of the calm poetry of its quiet green glens and vineyards, its tiny spotless town, its safe and beautiful small harbour. One should make an effort to step ashore here and taste the felicity of its silences, fractured only by some distant church bell or the braying of a mule. Even the wind seems lulled, and in Ios one sleeps the full sleep of early childhood. Happily nowadays the main island boats make a call here twice a week, so that you can stay ashore for a few days and pick up the boat on its return journey. You will have no regrets.

The Home Group

*

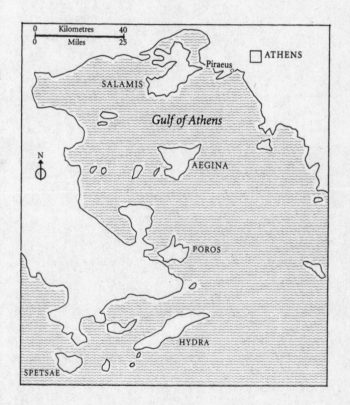

0 Kilometres 40
0 Miles 25

ATHENS

Piraeus

SALAMIS

Gulf of Athens

N

AEGINA

POROS

HYDRA

SPETSAE

Salamis · Aegina · Poros · Hydra · Spetsae

Though many travellers coming from the north begin with these islands, I have reserved them for the last section of my book, because increasingly they resemble the outer suburbs of the Attic capital. In winter, of course, when the sea rises and the storms break, they are once more cut off and retire into their primeval grimness. But, even so, they are very near Piraeus, and the Greeks think of them as weekend islands. In summer they become deservedly pleasure resorts – which may be deplored, but cannot now be discouraged. The cinema has made them known, and the world of 'juke' and 'hash' has paid them the compliment of adopting them; hence the level of sophistication, in the worst sense of the word, has risen, and the qualities of peacefulness and remoteness have diminished. No matter: they cannot be scamped, they must be seen; and the pleasure and beauty they afford outweighs all the disappointments provided by bars and rowdy discothèques, and the presence of the cinema rag-tag-and-bobtail in the juky cafés. There is no doubt that Greece within the next decade will become the Florida of Europe, and one only hopes that good taste and good sense will prevent the atmosphere and the amenities from becoming totally unworthy of such a history and such a landscape. It is a matter of keeping one's fingers crossed.

August is the cruellest month, and not only for Greece; it turns most of the fine European capitals into infernos – making taxis unbreathable, pavements almost too hot to walk on, café tables too hot to touch ... And everyone goes away, the best restaurants close up like flowers, telephones go dead. Athens is as bad as any but it is saved by its proximity to the sea. One can, after all, swim twenty minutes away from the Acropolis, and dine in the tiny Tourkolimano harbour at Phaleron, jam-packed with choice fish restaurants and millionaires' yachts. Night is cool to cold, sleep possible.

But best of all is to head for an island, and the nearer the better; Aegina, Spetsae, Poros, Hydra . . . they lie hard by, and a diligent businessman finds nowadays that he can commute from these nearby islands several times a week during the summer; hence their popularity. There is a hydrofoil link with Hydra which gets you back to Athens in a flash. And it is pos-sible to make a day excursion to Aegina, which will let you visit the wonderful temple of Artemis Aphaia and return to Athens in the evening. However, this is a barbaric way to go about things, for Aegina, brown and dusty and touchingly elegant, deserves a more respectful approach by sea – riding out of Piraeus on the deck of a ship, watching the forms of the land revolve slowly around you on the blue turntable of water – the white, dice-like Parthenon receding, Hymettus turning pearl to molten violet, lilac to watered grey. The bare, shaven skulls of the surrounding hills slowly absorbing themselves into the night sky.

The ante-room to the islands is always Salamis, which is so clearly visible from the deck of a ship that you can follow with your eyes the momentous events of September 480 BC as if on a relief map. With binoculars, you can trace every crease and curl of the little inner harbour, from which the desperate Greeks made their winning sortie and toppled the Persian line of bat-tle. You can get a bus or a cab in Piraeus that will clank you down to the old Venetian tower – the Devil's Tower – which stands on the spot where once Xerxes set up his throne of gold to watch the apparently certain destruction of the Greeks and distribute honours to his Persian commanders. Everything is so small and local that the whole of this dramatic action is easy to visualize. But you need to realize to what extent the Greeks were already scattered in disarray if you are to see just how extraordinary was this victory of despair – which determined the fate of the whole Mediterranean life-style for some time to come.

The sombre facts were these: the Greeks of the north had given in and joined the Persians. Attica was lost. There was nothing left except the tiny fleet, the Peloponnesus, a few islands, and Athens itself. Also indecision had gripped the Greeks. The land forces had retreated to the Isthmus and were busy fortifying it, for most of the sea-captains were in favour of a strategic withdrawal there – which would have been a fatal decision, since there the Persian Armada would have had room to manoeuvre, while in the narrows of Salamis they would have to be winkled out. Themistocles balanced the pros and cons, and decided that if action must be engaged in it should be at Salamis. The Persians had two thousand ships and the Greek confederation four hundred. However, the lumbering mass of muscle-bound Persian ships floundered and flapped around in the shallows of Salamis and were picked off piecemeal by the Greeks. They drove the Persian line in confusion upon the very cliffs where the egregious Xerxes sat in his golden chair, waiting for the victory which was never to be. The action was decisive – only 300 Persian ships escaped and hobbled back to Phaleron. Xerxes fled. Greece was saved.

From Piraeus to Aegina is only about fifteen sea miles and the voyage is a marvellous introduction to Greek scenery; you can glimpse whole sections of Attica, the Bay of Salamis, and the blue waters of the Saronic Gulf, at the end of which the island lies, a stepping stone for a summer holiday. You leave behind the pearly smoke of Athens out of which Hymettus rises as if from some stricken city of dream. Approaching Aegina, you round at last the long blank spit of Cape Plakakia and catch a glimpse of the remains of a once magnificent temple to Aphrodite. Then the town comes into view, with its pleasantly coloured forms set against the madder-brown patched land and the green groves of olives.

An attractive little town with a fine church, over which St Nicholas, patron saint of sailors, presides, thus reminding us that once this little island rivalled Athens in wealth and sea-power. Indeed she was so famous in war that she held her own against the mainland for decades, only being finally reduced in 458 BC – so thoroughly that she was never to recover. The battle was long and gruelling, and the destruction of Aegina and deportation of all its inhabitants was the only way the Athenians managed to secure their victory over this fierce little sea-power.

For the traveller of today, the main thing is the great temple of Aphaia, and this can be reached direct by car or bus from the port. An alternative way, by boat and mule, may be quicker but is harder on the legs. Either way, you will not regret the trip, for the temple is pitched on a high wooded knoll, facing one of the finest views you could imagine. It is an inspired site which makes you want to linger on and watch the sunset as it wheels across the gulf. On a clear day you can pick out the Parthenon from here with the naked eye, and see behind it the craggy violet snout of Lycabettos. Way down below, the sea is full of tiny, crawling ships streaking the blue with their white wakes. The temple itself – what moon goddess ever had a temple on such a site? – is still relatively present, unlike that of Aphrodite in the plain below which has been reduced to one bashed column and a scrabble of foundations. The temple of Aphaia still has over twenty Doric columns to boast of, as well as part of an architrave, and it reposes upon an artificial terrace which itself covers the filled-in foundations of an earlier building. In this sixth-century slice, they discovered an inscription which told them that the building was sacred to Artemis Aphaia. Apparently Aphaia means 'the not dark one', which points the contrast to Hecate who is 'the all dark one'. At one time the Minoans came up as far as here and the island was subjected to them, which has suggested to some scholars that the goddess may be affiliated or related to the Cretan moon goddess Dictynna. Be that as it may, there is no gainsaying the marvellous poetry of these ruins, and if this would be your first glimpse of ancient Greece you would not easily forget it.

On the other hand, Paleochori, the ancient capital, is a sad place, full of deserted gardens, tumbledown mansions, disintegrating forts, cracked churches. Once it was prosperous – one forgets that the island was occupied by Venice until as late as 1718. With the coming of the War of Independence Aegina regained much of her lost glory and became the temporary seat of the provisional Government and an active leader in the war. It is from this small corner of Greece, with such strangely dissimilar islands as Poros, Hydra and Spetsae, that the first great naval actions were mounted and financed.

In their holiday guise these islands have been so successful with tourists that transport to and from Athens is easy and various today. You can either do each one separately in a day, or do the four at once – throwing in a trip on the landward side to the site of Epidaurus (and by implication Argos, Mycenae, Nauplion), or simply getting off the boat for a night and picking up its successor the following day. From Aegina you begin to scout the mainland, and your boat will almost certainly put in at Methana, a stinking little place, baptized Dirtyport by the Greeks themselves. It smells like the entrance to Hell, though apparently it is a spa which cures skin troubles; the water whiffles with some sort of sulphuric stench. Nor is the land very enticing. But from here on the atmosphere becomes light, gay, whimsical, as if you had strayed into the fringes of some crazy water carnival. For the channel is full of boats, containing fishermen and tourists alike, and being so narrow, everything in it passes backward and forward with a few cables' length each to each; and, being so Greek, it is not possible to pass too close without waving, drinking toasts, falling overboard and whatnot. People undress and wave all their clothing in a paroxysm of *bonhomie*. Here and there in this channel, you may see the ominous back fin of a shark cut the surface, but everything is so suffused with innocent gaiety that you will feel the poor thing is only trying to wave too.

Poros is a most enchanting arrangement, obviously designed by demented Japanese children with the aid of Paul Klee and Raoul Dufy. A child's box of bricks that has been rapidly and fluently set up against a small shoulder of headland which holds the winds in thrall, it extends against the magical blue skyline its long herbaceous border of brilliant colours, hardly quite dry as yet; the moisture trembles with the cloud-light on the wet paint of the houses, and the changing light dapples it with butterflies' wings. As the harbour curves round, everything seems to move on a turntable hardly bigger than the hurdy-gurdy of a funfair, and you have the illusion that without getting off the ship you can lean over the rail and order an *ouzo*. And this sense of proximity is increased so that you seem to be sailing down the main street with the inhabitants walking in leisurely fashion alongside the ship. You feel that finally they will lay friendly hands upon the ropes and bring it slowly to a halt. The best description of entering Poros is that of Henry Miller, who captured the port in masterly fashion in his Greek travel book. It is not possible to exaggerate the charm of this little Aegean nook and the sense of elation it conveys.

Moreover, Poros does not ever *seem* so encumbered with

tourists as Hydra; though this is an illusion, because it is so justly famous that there are always visitors as well as quite a number of residents. It is the happiest place I have ever known.

Just opposite Poros, on the mainland, lies Galata, another pretty and euphoric little village, with some of the same charms but fewer amenities. They are linked by convenient ferries and, if you wish to make excursions into the Peloponnesus, this is a good stepping-off point. Walking in Poros is highly recommended, because of its shady groves with pine-needle floors. Joined to its 'mother' by a narrow isthmus, there is a romantic little island called Calavria, where once an ancient and famous sanctuary to Poseidon was erected. There is not much left of the temple today, though the remains stand on yet another superb site. It was here, however, that Demosthenes took refuge, hoping that the Macedonian barbarians would not dare to desecrate so ancient and venerable a spot. When his hopes proved vain, he poisoned himself at the altar, or at least that is the story that Plutarch tells. It may well be the pines which make Poros so memorable. The woods seem resin-drenched, everything smells like a new ship; and riding into harbour in summer, you are enveloped by gusts of sharp pine scent wafted on the still water of the harbour. The whole island smells and shines like a newly varnished canvas – the green of olives and yellow of lemons; and stealing softly across the waters, come the steady drizzle of *bouzouki* music and the higher, more febrile drizzle of sun-drunk *cicadas*.

From here, you can also easily visit the ancient harbour of Troezene. In doing so you will realize that Poros is only just an island; once one could reach it from the mainland simply by wading.

After this carnival atmosphere, what a sudden contrast it is to hit Hydra! A barren rock, nude as a skull and waterless, it crouches there in the austere splendour of its nudity, glowering at you. It is as silent and watchful as a Mycenaean lion – though perhaps that is not the right choice of image to convey its sphinxine immobility and sense of indestructibility. A battle-ship perhaps? A great horned toad? We should really ask the painter Ghika to choose a suitable image, for he is the real poet of the island and in his painting has gone as far as one man can to render Greek light and Greek stone. All the convolutions and curves of this labyrinth of walls and dazzling staircases coil and uncoil in his canvases, so that one finds oneself retracing the labyrinths of the inner ear as the eye slides down among the forms and drinks the bony colours of the glowing stone.

Hydra is only thirty-five sea miles from Athens; the time the journey takes being dependent on the number of visits the ship decides to make on the way. It is also very close to the coast – some four miles only – and, with its newly found film-fame, has become the Saint Tropez of this little group.

It is inevitable that after several successful films made here, people on the waterfront constantly hope for a glimpse of Sophia Loren – or of that other paragon of beauty and intelli-gence, Lambetti, whose portrait was framed so wonderfully by Michael Cacoyannis in *The Girl in Black*. But more funda-mental to Hydra are the seamen it has bred and the fighting record of its ships, for the main thrust against the Turks during the War of Independence was given its impetus by the corsairs of this piratical lair. With wonderful conservatism and patriot-ism, these once-great seafaring families have hung on to their mansions and almost turned them into museums, which house not only remarkable furniture of the time but also every pos-sible memento of the history of Hydra. It is as if, around the bowling-green at Plymouth Hoe, there still stood the manors of every Elizabethan mariner of renown – Drake, Raleigh, Frobisher, Grenville, and others – and as if these manors still contained unparalleled private collections of souvenirs of the battle of 1588 against the Spanish Armada . . . which would be treasure trove indeed for the visitor interested in English history. This is precisely what has happened in Hydra – the tiny harbour is backed by the solid, dumpy, private manors of those heroes who did more than anyone to set the stamp of victory on the Turkish war.

Some of them are in fact small museums, but nearly all are strictly private and permission to visit must be wangled – though the patriotic Hydriots are always delighted to welcome an interested visitor. A word with the mayor or the schoolmaster is usually enough to obtain access to this little history of the Greek Navy. To a Greek the great names of the captains are like a roll of drums, and it is an emotional business looking upon the relics of this exciting period, stored so reverently in the little chain of houses – of the Bulgaris, Tombazis, Votzis, Boudouris and Coundouriotis. One of these is now a small school taken over by the *Beaux Arts* of Athens, where visiting painters and other artists are always welcome. The prettiest and most evocative corner is perhaps the secret chapel and garden of the Boudouris house.

From 1770, when the war with the Turkish overlords was declared, Hydra was swamped with refugees from the northern sections of the Morea. With a surplus population of some 20,000 souls as against a native one of only 4000, they were almost forced into trade, with a touch of piracy on the side; and it is said that the British blockade of Europe during the Napoleonic period was a piece of luck of which they rapidly took advantage. Their ships went everywhere carrying anything, and within the space of a generation or two this huge burst of energy led to a number of Hydriots becoming fabulously wealthy. When at last the real War of Independence was declared in 1821, these patriotic corsairs ploughed all their gains back into the Greek Marine.

There are one or two excursions to be made in the island, but frankly the heat of the burning rock makes one think twice before doing anything active in high summer. The beauty and singularity of the capital are something that never wears off, even after many visits; and there are pleasant bars to loiter in, dawdling away a long hot morning which is punctuated by the old cathedral bell clearing its throat and going off with such a bang that one thinks there is a fault in the machinery. However, since the town has been tucked into a natural amphitheatre, with its shoulder and back to the Meltemi, it becomes extremely hot in August, much hotter than the other islands of the group. Not everybody likes it, in the fierce, airless heat of midsummer, and there is also a water problem; once it was supposed – even as late as the time of Turkish rule – to be well watered, for its Greek name meant just that. But it is a volcanic island, and frequent underground thrusts play havoc with water levels and bury freshwater springs. Water is now caught here in catchments as in so many other volcanic islands. Sometimes a huge floating water-tank looking like a whale is towed incongruously into port by a corvette to bring much-needed water, without which the *ouzo* would taste only half as good.

For the young and sprightly, there is a really worthwhile excursion to Mount Elias, called after the battered white convent which clings to the crest of the hill. Here savage old Kolokotrones, one of the most celebrated Klephtic leaders of the revolution, was imprisoned, and there is still a pine under which he is supposed to have passed the long siesta hours. But beware of the mid-morning heat and get early on the road, so that you reach the place before the Aegean is as yet quite awake. You can walk, or travel precipitously by donkey, as on Santorin (there are no cars or buses on Hydra as yet); enquire from Miltiades on the quayside. From the top, your horizon will have a great transparent bowl of holy light, and the old guide, if he is still extant, will show you the fragile cloudlike stains marking the outlines of Seriphos and then of Siphnos. Northward is an island masking delectable Poros; westward is the great, curdled bay of Hydra and its watchful partner, breaker of winds and currents, Dhokos, just out of sight. The two little mountains, burned white by the sun, jut up with a Sicilian extravagance. Then, if you turn towards the south, the sea is empty all the way to sombre Crete, and beyond it to Africa.

Having listed the disadvantages of Hydra I must emphasize that it is a real gem of colour and variety; and there is nothing quite like going to sleep on deck in its little funnel of a harbour, to be woken at dawn with the first arrival of fish and vegetables – when the whole waterfront turns suddenly into a coloured flower-bed. With the sun, the island opens like a dark rose, and you forget any of these small annoyances which can dog a traveller in these waters. Just lying on deck and watching the rigging sway softly against the pure white light will make you glad that you have lived long enough to realize the experience of Hydra.

. The rocky confines of the inland glens and hills remind one that the Greeks of old did not see the base and brutal landscape which we do today. Most of the fruit and vegetables now in the country came to it comparatively late. Citrus fruit, tomatoes, eucalyptus, loquat, palm, cactus, flourish here nowadays because they were imported from other lands by such industrious and curious races as the Arabs. It is even said that the olive is not native to Greece – which would be strange, for the olive is now a prime symbol of the Mediterranean. On the other hand, the rich anthology of aromatic plants, held in check today by the depredations of goat and charcoal-burner, is something which the Greek of classical times would recognize at once, as he would the indestructible upsurge of spring wild flowers which take advantage of every scrap of terrain to exploit the first rains of the year – iris, asphodel, anemone, cyclamen. The culinary herbs, too, are still those that existed in early times – garlic, lavender, rosemary, sage, and others which echo their way into all later literatures, and are part of the memories of every Aegean traveller. The traveller's feet bruise them as he walks the stony hillsides, and he will always remember their flavours in the simple food of those islands so rich in fish, so poor in beef, so full of succulent lamb and pig for the tavern spits – which still send their pleasant clouds of incense up to Olympus to tickle the imaginations of the Greek gods, if there are any left today.

To go from rocky Hydra to Spetsae is to jolt the kaleidoscope again; Spetsae is very different in form and atmosphere. Moreover, while there is no doubt about the beauty and force of Hydra, opinions are divided about Spetsae. Some find it appealing and some appalling. The truth of course is not extreme, and this cool, well-wooded, little holiday-place is perhaps the favourite of those Athenians who like life easy. Its critics assert that it is un-Greek, and more like an Italian or French island, but not so good as either Ischia or Corsica. Let pedants bicker. It was known to the ancients as Pitouissa, 'the pine-clad one', and has from earliest times been a noted health-resort, which may have been the reason for its relatively rapid modernization. Its sinuous corniche-like meandering coast road does suggest the country round Forio d'Ischia, and its sophistication is on about the same level. A few old-fashioned hotels and some delightful shady cafés are here to welcome you. But it is a most unstrenuous place, and its great extollers (among them the *Colossus of Maroussi*) find the ideal way to drink it in is to sway round it in a *fiacre*. You can tour the whole island like this, nearly always in shade, calling a halt for a meal or a drink or a bathe whenever you need. It is a good idea, for during your leisurely jog you come upon a great variety of scenery in little space; everything – coves and bays and headlands – seeming like diminished samples of some great original. There are also patches of desolation, an intruding chunk of plain karst that has strayed down from the rock-strewn watersheds – which you must cross to reach Dalmatia.

Among modern folklore attractions of Spetsae you can catch a glimpse of Spetsoupoula, the tiny islet belonging to the ship-owner Niarchos, and perhaps visit the famous college of Anargyros which is a mock-up for a British public school on the lines of Victoria College in Alexandria. The best families send their sons there, to train them up as statesmen; the result always seems to be much the same – instead of statesmen, they become politicians, a very different sort of animal. It is a pleasant act of piety to spend a few moments in the local museum, locally called the *mexis*, and ponder upon the bones of the illustrious Bouboulina which lie in a modest yellow casket enshrining all the poetry and energy of the Revolution. For this indomitable lady is a whole folklore unto herself. She did everything but grow a moustache. She captained a ship which played a central part in the battles against the Turks, and has become so much a legendary figure that one can no longer separate true from false in her story. She was supposed to indulge in a bit of piracy on the side, and even to carry off unprotesting husbands in the style of Catherine the Great. Her name and her portrait smell of gunpowder, but no one has ever been more in need of a critical biography which sifted fact from legend. A latter-day Amazon, she is remembered with appropriate affection, and some amusement.

I am surprised that the Orthodox Church has not, in its easygoing way, seen fit to sponsor her as a local saint, but maybe it has something to do with the numerous husbands she is reputed to have acquired at pistol point. The portrait of her, the only one I ever saw, depicted a swarthy, rather shy-looking lady drawn up manfully against a flag, scimitar in hand. She looked too nice to be the terrible personage the legends suggest; perhaps she saved that other side of herself for the Turks. Spetsae has little to show beyond the bones of Bouboulina despite the active and glorious role she played in the Greek Revolution. Wandering round her pretty beaches and pleasant pine glades, one somehow feels that she just escapes being a modern suburb of Athens. But I think the impression of near-suburbia must always have been there because of the real proximity of the capital. Even in ancient times the place was famed for its cool and salubrious summer climate, and even in days of sail it was so close that one could run down in with a following *boreas* in very little time. Today it is joined to Athens by swift hydrofoil as well as less speedy island craft, so that it seems that much less remote, more urban, more sophisticated. Poor Bouboulina herself strikes a raffish note more in keeping with people who might be going north to dine in the Athens *Plaka* . . .

Modern communications being what they are Spetsae is also a travel nexus for people bound in different directions – west for Epidaurus, north for Athens, east for the lonelier and lovelier cloud-cuckoo groups which I think of as the Central Cyclades, and which form a perfect contrast to her civilized and contented grace.

You journey back from the Greek islands to the mainland less with regret than with a feeling that you have touched the fringe of a mystery. We shall never know, presumably, who the Greeks really were or really are; and any brief history of the ancient world only deepens the mystery. Neither the country nor the scope of the Greek imagination seems ever to have had boundaries. Politically, they tried every kind of system, from aristo-Spartan fascism to the democracy invented by Athens and so beautifully enunciated in the speech which Thucydides attributes to Pericles. Kings, chieftains, parliaments. But they were not content to try out systems of social government in which political man might exist in equity and harmony with his fellows; they were also mad keen to discover man's place in nature, and equally anxious to learn what, ultimately, nature itself was all about. Rationalists, mystagogues, poets, philosophers – there were so many of them in Greece, with such various convictions. This variety and their appetite for abstractions were mixed with a strict irony and tenderness about what things a man can do to be happy, to be just, to be good, to drain the cup of life to the full. Among other things, they were the first to express doubts about the justice of slavery, and the role of woman in the social world. Their variety of belief was accompanied by an equivalent variety of gods, tyrants, Amazons, lawgivers, poets, princes . . . Their story is an astonishing demonstration of human curiosity and human daring. The question is not so much 'What did they have that we haven't got?'; it is rather 'What did they start that we have still been unable to finish?' They did not get to the moon, of course; but the basis of atomic physics which gave us this more-than-doubtful blessing was the work of Greek speculative thinkers.

This small country, so repeatedly raped and shattered and ground to powder, and then reduced to the bare calc of its desolate capes and headlands, never had any fixed geographical borders. It was a state of mind. And the traveller will not be wrong if he detects even today, after so many centuries of so-called decline, a pulse-beat at the heart of Greek light, which still thuds with the old anxious curiosities and concerns. Greece may be all ashes, but the phoenix is still there, waiting for its hour.

Flowers and Festivals of the Greek Islands

The Greek islands are rocky and mountainous; the mountain regions are mostly of a limestone nature, but sandstones and clays prevail in the valleys. All the geological periods are represented from the Neotriassic to the Pleistocene, including modern alluviums. In Corfu, where this subject has been more thoroughly studied, Dr Sordina's recent excavations show that the island has been inhabited from upper Palaeolithic times, some 35,000 years ago. No human skeletons have so far been found, but numerous stone tools of the Levallois-Moustier type evince that those early settlers belonged to the Neanderthal race.

The climate of the islands is warm-temperate. In Corfu, the yearly mean is about 17.5°C. Rainfall differs considerably from one island to another. Corfu has the highest rainfall in Greece (with the exception, some years, of the Jannina mainland area), with a total of about 1300 mm per year. Zante, too, has an abundant rainfall, but the other islands, and especially those in the Aegean Sea, have a much drier climate. For this reason, the Ionian Islands are mostly well wooded, while some of the smaller Aegean Islands are little more than bare rocks. The rainy season is from winter to spring, and this is followed by a three-to-five-month summer drought. Snow falls are rare, except on the higher mountains, especially those of Crete.

Flora

It should not be forgotten that the terrain of the Greek islands varies considerably in height, from sea-level to the White Mountains (2450 m) of Crete. The flora, in consequence, varies from the semi-tropical to alpine. The account below largely confines itself to providing a much-condensed list of flowers growing around sea-level – which are the ones most likely to be met with by the casual visitor.

The flora and fauna of mainland Greece and the islands are mostly that of the north-east Mediterranean basin and, owing to the mild climate, many semi-tropical plants have become acclimatized; among these are Dracaena, Yucca and Aloe. The date-palm grows freely; but, in most of the islands the fruit drops off the tree before it is ripe enough to be eaten. In the south of Crete, however, dates can reach maturity, as can bananas.

As far as the native flora is concerned, Corfu and Zante strike the casual beholder as being one vast olive grove. The reason for this is that during the long Venetian occupation (1386–1797), the peasants were encouraged by the authorities to plant olive trees and could pay their taxes in olive oil. A census taken in the 1960s gave their number as 3,100,000 for Corfu alone. The variety mostly cultivated is the Lianolia (*Olea europaea cranio-morpha*) which produces a small black olive that is very rich in oil. The Corfu trees have never been pruned and many have reached a great size and age; some of them are reputed to be six hundred years old and more. The crop is most abundant every other year, and is sometimes heavily damaged by a small fly (*Dacus oleae*) whose grubs attack the immature olives and cause them to fall to the ground. The culture of the olive on the Greek islands (and mainland) goes very far back in antiquity; and deciphering of the Cretan (Minoan) scripts on many clay tablets originating in Crete have shown from the detailed accounts kept in the Cretan palaces that taxes were paid in olive oil, and this oil was stored in the huge and often beautifully decorated storage jars kept in the magazines still to be seen at Knossos and other Minoan sites on Crete. It is clear that the culture of the olive was a very large and important part of agriculture on Crete, and almost certainly in the many other Aegean Islands where the Minoan civilization was supreme between 2500–1200 BC.

In Cephalonia, Mt Ainos (1628 m) is famous for its forest of Cephalonian Fir (*Abies cephalonica Loudon*). Chios has large numbers of Mastic Trees (*Pistacia terebinthus L.*) from which a kind of chewing-gum is made.

One of the commonest trees on the islands is the Mediterranean Cypress (*Cupressus sempervirens*), of which two varieties are seen: the slender var. *stricta* and the spreading var. *horizontalis*. The peasants call the first the male and the second the female tree; but the Cypress is in reality *monoecious* with the male and female flowers on the same tree. The Aleppo pine (*Pinus halepensis*) is also abundant. It is often attacked by the Processionary caterpillar, the larva of the moth *Thaumetopoea pityocampa*, whose untidy web-like nests can be seen hanging among the branches. The hairs of this caterpillar are highly irritating to the skin and can even cause blindness should they reach the eyes. In Crete and the south-east islands of the Dodecanese, *Pinus halepensis* is replaced by *Pinus brutia*, a species generally resembling *P. halepensis* but differing in the straight trunk and branches, its thicker leaves, and the very short and not recurved stems of the cones. Other trees are White Poplar (*Populus alba*), Elm (*Ulmus campestris*) and Eastern Plane (*Platanus orientalis*). The White Poplar seems, unfortunately, to be succumbing to various fungoid diseases and is being replaced by the more resistant Canadian Poplar (*Populus canadensis*).

Curious to say, a very common tree is the 'Tree of Heaven' (*Ailanthus altissima*) which is not indigenous to Europe at all. It was imported to France from North China as a garden tree about 1751 and has become perfectly naturalized all round the Mediterranean area; it grows rapidly and seeds itself everywhere by means of its winged seeds. It is a fine tree which can reach a height of 20 metres and more, and is a beautiful sight in June and July when it appears to be covered with huge crimson flowers. The actual flowers are, however, small and inconspicuous, greenish white in colour; it is the leaves immediately surrounding them which turn bright red and orange during florescence. The peasants dislike this tree, whose seedlings often invade their fields and vineyards, and call it *Vromodendro* (Stinking Tree) because of the disagreeable smell of its flowers and of its leaves when rubbed. But, owing to its quick growth and spreading root system, the Ailanthus is an excellent erosion-arresting tree that should be actively encouraged.

In classical times, Corfu and the opposite mainland of Epirus were famous for their oak trees – Dodona is only eighty kilometres east of Corfu – but these are rare nowadays; the uplands of both sides of the straits are bare and rocky. On the Corfu side this was due to a great extent to the Venetian shipyards whose ruins can still be seen near Govino Bay; on the Epirote hills the damage was mostly due to the Napoleonic Wars. Both the British and the French governments brought great quantities of timber from Ali Pacha, the semi-independent Turkish ruler of Jannina, for the construction of their fleets. When it is remembered that at least two thousand oaks not counting other trees – were needed to build a single ship of the line, the wholesale disappearance of entire forests can be understood.

On most of the islands Orange, Lemon, Almond and other fruit trees, together with vines, are cultivated. In many of them a dense native *maquis* can be found. This is principally composed of Myrtle (*Myrtus communis*); Laurel (*Laurus nobilis*); Lentisk (*Pistacia lentiscus*); Christ's Thorn (*Paliurus spina-christi*); Judas Tree (*Cercis sili-quastrum*); Chaste Tree (*l'itex agnus-castus*); Holm Oak (*Quercus ilex*); Kermes Oak (*Q. coccifera*); Greek Heath (*Erica verticillata*); Tree Heather (*E. arborea*); Strawberry Tree (*Arbutus unedo*); Spanish Broom (*Spartium junceum*); Thorny Broom (*Calycotome villosa*) and Bracken (*Pteridium aquilinum*). The Strawberry Tree is of interest, as its orange-red globular fruit, which ripen in autumn, can produce a kind of delirious intoxication if eaten on an empty stomach. Their flavour resembles that of the garden strawberry and a delicious jelly can be made from them.

Many of the species listed above are long-lived and would grow into large trees if allowed. Unfortunately, they are not allowed to do this owing to the depredations of goats and the fuel demands of local brick-kilns and potteries.

Calendar of Flowers and Festivals

JANUARY

In some parts of Greece January is called 'The Pruner' because now the husbandman trims vines and trees. An omen is drawn from the observation of the weather at Epiphany. The following saying illustrates this:

> Dry Epiphany and pouring Easter weather
> Bring us happiness and plenty both together.

The woods are starred with Anemones, mostly *Anemone coronaria*. They can be found in several colours: mauve, scarlet and, more rarely, white. The mauve and purple varieties of *Anemone coronaria* are very frequent not only in the Ionian Islands but in Crete, and some of the Aegean Islands, and so is the scarlet variety in Rhodes. In the south-eastern Dodecanese Islands and in Crete, *Ranunculus asiaticus*, an indication of the proximity of Asia, flowers with the Anemones, being often confused with them in colour in varieties from white to pink, scarlet and yellow.

The pink or white flowers of the cultivated and wild Almond Tree (*Amygdalus communis*) are in full bloom. Flowering often begins as early as mid-December.

The Winter Crocus (*Crocus sieberi*) shows its lavender flowers.

The Japanese Loquat (*Eriobotrya japonica*) is still in bloom – begins in December – and its delicious scent is strongest just after sunset.

The Wisteria (*Wisteria fructescens*) blooms before its leaves have appeared.

New Year's Day This day belongs to St Basil; a cake with a silver coin in it is made and cut, and luck belongs to whoever finds the coin. After supper the family plays games of divination. A slice of New Year cake under a girl's pillow will do for a Greek girl what a slice of wedding-cake does for an English girl.

Twelfth Day The curious ceremony of diving for the Cross, thrown into the sea by a priest, can be seen both in the islands and on the Greek mainland. A dozen or so shivering lads contend for the prize, and duck the winner of the reward.

The feast of St John the Baptist is on 7 January and there is mumming in the streets by children in masks.

The January weather is often fine, dry and cold (the Halcyon days).

FEBRUARY

On the 2nd falls the Feast of the Purification of the Virgin (our Candlemas), and the prevailing weather on this day is popularly supposed to last forty days.

Anemones still at their best.

The large purple Periwinkle (*Vinca major*) begins to flower.

The purple-blue Cretan Iris (*Iris unguicularis ssp. cretensis*) appears.

The deliciously scented Narcissus (*Narcissus tazetta*) thrives in damp places.

Wisteria still in bloom.

MARCH

The first cuckoo and the early spring winds. Now, in the more southern islands, the first cicadas begin to welcome the sunlight, and swallows start building under the house-eaves. (Destroy their nests and you'll get freckles, says popular legend. According to another superstition, there will be a death in the house.) On the 1st of the month the boys fashion a wooden swallow, adorn it with flowers and travel from house to house collecting pennies and singing a little song which varies from place to place in Greece. This custom is of the remotest antiquity and is mentioned by ancient Greek authors.

In some of the Aegean Islands, peasants think it unlucky to wash or plant vegetables during the first three days of March. Trees planted now will wither. The March sun burns the skin; and a red-and-white thread on the wrist will prevent your children from getting sunburn.

Some of the Orchids begin to flower, including the purple Lax-flowered Orchid (*Orchis laxiflora*) which grows in swampy areas. Also various Pyramid, Bee, and Fly Orchids.

Other Irises (*Iris attica* and *I. florentina*) appear.

The bright yellow Bog Iris (*Iris pseudacorus*) brightens the dykes and other swampy places with its quarantine-like flags.

Narcissi still found; Anemones dying off; Periwinkles still seen.

Orange and Lemon Trees in full bloom.

The Aborescent Heath (*Erica arborea*) shows its masses of white flowers. It is from the roots of this plant that 'briar' (from the French *bruyère*) pipes are made.

Easter, which sometimes falls in March, has been grafted on to what was probably the Lesser Eleusinia in ancient times – the return of Persephone. It is the period of red eggs and roasted lamb on the spit today and is ushered in by the great forty-days fast of Lent. The two Sundays before Lent are known respectively as 'Meat Sunday' and 'Cheese Sunday'. The week between them answers to our Western carnival week, and is so celebrated in the cities of Greece with masquerades, black dominoes, etc. Scholars hint at pre-Christian survivals saying that these antics suggest the Old Cronia festivals of ancient times, while Lent itself suggests a connection with the Eleusinian mysteries – commemorating Demeter's long abstinence from food during her search for her lost daughter.

The midnight Mass of Easter Saturday is the high-spot of the year's festivals and no traveller should miss the impressive ceremony. In villages the gospel is read out in the churchyard under a tree. At the end the news that 'Christ is risen' is announced to the banging of gongs and the explosion of crackers. In the dark church the priest holds up his consecrated candle and calls out to the congregation: 'Come and receive the light'; each one lights a taper from his candle and passes the light back into the dark body of the church to the rest of the congregation. If you are lucky enough to get your candle home without it going out you'll have good luck the coming year.

APRIL

In the uplands, sheep are shorn and the air is full of the plain-tive cry of lambs unable to recognize their shorn dams; about the 23rd of the month (St George's Day, the patron saint of Brigands and Englishmen) the shepherds return to the mountains with their flocks.

Orchids at their best. Irises still going strong. Narcissi ending.

The Spring Asphodel (*Asphodelus microcarpus*) shows its branched spikes of white flowers, especially in the olive woods.

The rare Snake Wort (*Dracunculus vulgaris*) shows its huge green, brown and purple blossoms – rather like an outsize Arum Lily – and can often be located from a distance by its carrion-like smell. This is to attract flies on which it depends for transporting pollen.

The Prickly Pear (*Opuntia ficus-indica*) begins to show its pretty yellow flowers.

The Yellow Wallflower (*Cheiranthus cheiri*) now in flower.

Various species of Rock Rose (*Cistus*) begin to show their pink, white, or yellowish-white flowers.

The Judas Tree (*Carcis siliquastrum*) sometimes begins to bloom towards the end of the month.

Spanish and Thorny Broom (*Spartium junceum* and *Calycotome villosa*) explode into bright yellow on the hillsides.

The Golden Daisy (*Chrysanthemum coronarium*) decks the fields.

MAY

Parties are formed to go picnicking and 'fetch back the May'; the young men of the village make wreaths of flowers to hang them at their sweethearts' doors. But May is unlucky for marriage because, says the proverb, 'In May the donkeys mate.'

Rock Rose, Wallflower, Periwinkle, Prickly Pear, Snake Wort, still in flower.

The pink Night-scented Stock (*Matthiola longipetala ssp. bicornis*), which in some years starts in April, sheds its delicious scent just after sunset. In the hills and mountains of Crete and Karpathos the white Paeony (*Paeonia clusii*) is flowering, while Rhodes has its own white Paeony (*P. rhodia*).

Judas Trees at their best, in great splashes of magenta all over the countryside.

Broom in full swing. Bog Iris still going strong. Orchids ending.

The Climbing Clematis (*Clematis flammula*) shows its white flowers. The peasants call it the swallow flower – *chelidonia* – probably because it appears at about the time when the swallows return.

The wild Thyme (*Thymus capitatus*) begins to flower, to the delight of the bees which produce the 'Hymettus honey'.

White Acacia Trees (*Robinia pseudacacia*) in full flower.

JUNE

In some places called 'The Harvester' because the harvest begins normally in this month. On the 24th falls the Nativity of St John the Baptist which is celebrated by a great feast with crackling bonfires.

The Oleander (*Nerium oleander*), in full bloom. It begins in May, or even in late April, and continues until late September.

Love-in-a-mist, alias Devil-in-a-bush (*Nigella damascena*), nods its delicate pale blue flowers.

The leaves around the flowers of the Ailanthus Tree (*Ailanthus altissima*) turn orange and red.

The Squirting Cucumber (*Ecballium elaterium*) shows its

pale yellow flowers. Within a month it is ready for action, and then mind your eye. Active until September.

Thyme in full swing. Also wild Mint (*Mentha pulegium*) and yellow Three-lobed Sage (*Salvia triloba*).

Swamp Iris and Prickly Pear still in flower.

The Rock Caper (*Capparis rupestris*) flaunts its large white flowers with their long purple stamens on rocks and cliffs by the sea.

The thistle-like *Eryngium creticum* turns from green to a beautiful metallic blue, giving whole areas a bluish colour.

The bright vermillion flowers of the Pomegranate (*Punica granatum*) are seen; flowers also in July.

The Chaste Tree (*Vitex agnus-castus*), really more a large bush than a tree, shows its purple flowers, especially along the coasts. The ancient Greeks (and also the Crusaders) believed that the scent of its leaves and flowers was an 'anti-aphrodisiac', hence the name.

JULY

In some places called 'The Thresher', presumably because the corn is threshed in this month.

On the 30th there is a huge open-air festival at Soroni, Rhodes, to celebrate the arrival of St Saul who was a fellow-passenger of St Paul during the shipwreck at Lindos. (A case of transferred names and attributes – as with ancient gods and goddesses, one wonders?)

The violet Delphinium (*Delphinium peregrinum*) in flower; also in August.

The Golden Thistle (*Scolymus hispanicus*) shows its yellow flowers in all uncultivated places.

The Mullein (*Verbascum undulatum*) also displays its yellow flowers. Some species are used by fishermen to make fish poisons.

The Oleander is seen in masses of pink; occasionally white or cream.

Prickly Pear still in flower.

The Agave or Aloe (*Agave americana*) rockets upwards, after a flying start in May, and produces a tall (up to 10 m) spike of yellow-green flowers; also in September. This plant takes fifteen to twenty years to flower, and then dies in a few weeks.

The Caper is still in flower.

AUGUST

The Magpie is the bird of the month, and August begins (on the 1st) with the Progress of the Precious and Unifying Cross. This feast prepares one for another feast which is the prelude to the Feast of the Repose of the Virgin, on the 14th. On the 23rd the Feast of the Holy Merciful is celebrated; again on the 29th a feast for the Cutting Off of the Precious Head of St John the Precursor heralds more abstinence.

In general, however, August is the great dancing month, and panagyreias are held on the 6th, the 15th and the 23rd in most of the islands, especially at Trianda and Cremasto on Rhodes.

The beautiful white scented flowers of the Sand Lily (*Pancratium maritimum*) appear in the coastal sands. It is rare and regional.

The Caper is still in flower and continues until September.

SEPTEMBER

On the 14th there is a festival dedicated to the Cross at Callithies of Rhodes. Childless women make a weary pilgrimage to the top of the razor-back hill called Tsambika below San Benedetto – and here, in the chapel of Our Lady, they eat a small piece of the wick from one of the lamps which will make them fruitful. If the resulting infant is not named after the Virgin, it dies.

The Sea Squill (*Urginea maritima*) show its tall, erect, unbranched spike of white flowers, mostly in olive woods. The peasants make a rat poison from its huge bulb which can attain a diameter of 15 cm or more.

The grapes begin to be gathered.

OCTOBER

A golden month which belongs to St Demetrius; at his feast on the 26th wine casks are unstopped and the new wine tasted. Many weddings take place in this month, and an eagerly antici-pated spell of fine warm weather which comes around the middle of the month is known as the Little Summer of St Demetrius.

Grape-gathering in full swing.

The crocus-like *Sternbergia lutea* and *Sternbergia sicula* show their bright yellow blossoms after the first autumn rains.

The Autumn Mandrake (*Mandragora autumnalis*) shows its purple flowers at about the same time; rather rare.

The Autumn Cyclamen have just started their lilac flood; *C. hederifolium* and *C. graecum* are the two autumn-flowering species. The spring-flowering species (March–April) include *C. cretica*, white flowered and fragrant from Crete, *C. repandum*, white or pink in colour from Rhodes, and *C. persicum*, fragrant and variably coloured, from Rhodes and other Aegean islands. These spring-flowering species of Cyclamen are less common than the autumn-flowering species and of very local distribution.

NOVEMBER

In many places still called 'The Sower' because seed-time is beginning; St Andrew is the most popular saint of this month and his feast falls on its last day. He is the bringer of the first snow in mountainous areas (popular saying: 'St Andrew has washed his beard white'). On the 18th is the feast of St Plato the Martyr, whom popular ignorance has transformed into St Plane Tree, the names being very similar (*Platonos* and *Platanos*). The weather which prevails on the 18th will last through Advent (The Forty Days). Now the Pleiades begin to rise in the early evening, and the first sea gales drive the long-shore fisherman to his winter quarters. The melancholy of the dying year is hardly cast off by St Andrew's holiday on which everyone eats *loucumades* – a sort of doughnut-shaped waffle.

The Autumn Crocus (*Crocus laevigatus*) appears, white or mauve.

The Saffron Crocus (*C. sativus ssp. cartwrightianus*) and its Cretan form *C. oreocreticus* also appear, purple blossoms. Its stigmas are used to make the dye and condiment 'saffron'.

Cyclamen in full bloom.

The fruit of the Orange and Tangerine begin to turn golden.

The Corfu Snowdrop (*Galanthus corcyrensis*) makes its appearance, but may be delayed until December; it is rare and sporadic. It may, perhaps, occur in some of the other Greek islands as it, or a very similar species, is found on the Greek mainland, including Macedonia and Thrace.

DECEMBER

The saint of the month is St Nicholas (on the 6th), and rightly so; the seafarer needs his patron saint most at the year's end. But there are plenty more on the list of saints.

4 December – St Barbara, the patron saint of artillerymen
5 December – St Savvas
12 December – St Spiridion, the patron saint of Corfu

Christmas Eve Incense is burned before supper, and those flat hot-cross buns called 'Christ's loaves' are baked in the oven. After supper the cloth is not removed from the table because it is believed that Christ will come and eat during the night. A log or an old shoe is left burning on the fire: the smoke will ward off stray 'Kallikanzari' (little mischievous faun-like imps).

Cyclamen end; Anemones begin.
Almond and Japanese Loquat in flower towards the end of the month.
Oranges and Tangerines ripe.

Fauna

Most of the Greek islands, when their small size is considered, have a rich land fauna, though the larger mammals, as in most European countries, are getting scarcer.

In some of the larger islands the Jackal (*Canis aureus*) is still found, even in densely populated Corfu which is one of its most western habitats. The Fox (*Vulpes vulpes*) is common. The Brown Hare is replaced by the Wild Rabbit (*Oryctolagus cuniculus*). The peasants affirm that from Delos northwards there are only hares, while rabbits only are found to the south. Delos itself would appear to be still contested by these two species, which never interbreed. Other wild mammals include the Pine Marten (*Martes martes*), the Weasel (*Mustella nivalis*), the Hedgehog (*Erinaceus Europaeus*) and the Mole (*Talpa caeca*). In his *Faune de la Grèce* (Athens, 1878), Th. de Heldreich mentions the Otter (*Lutra lutra*) as occurring in Corfu; it has probably been exterminated since that time. Squirrels do not seem to be found; but some kind of nocturnal Dormouse (*Glis glis* or, perhaps, *Dryomys nitedula*) is fairly plentiful in the pine-tree areas. The Corfu peasants call it *Petania* (Flyer) on account of its huge leaps from tree to tree.

In the mountains of Crete the long-horned Ibex (*Capra hircus cretensis*) can still be found, but it is now very rare. It is known by the local name of *Agrimi*.

The marine mammals are represented by the Monk Seal (*Monachus monachus*). Until World War II, a small colony of these seals still inhabited the tiny island of Erikousa to the north of Corfu, but none have been seen since the war. The Monk Seal is no longer found in the Aegean either, and it is probably a disappearing species. Although not eaten, it is killed by the fishermen who accuse it of robbing and damaging their nets and lobster-pots. The Common Dolphin (*Delphinius delphis*) and the Common Porpoise (*Phocaena phocaena*) are very plentiful. The Bottle-nosed Dolphin (*Tursiops truncatus*) is rarer; its presence is often betrayed, especially at night, by its harsh and snorty breathing.

All the islands have a varied, though never very abundant, bird population, including most of the more common European species and many migrants. The Golden Eagle and the Griffon Vulture (*Aquila chrysaetos* and *Gyps fulvus*) can sometimes be seen soaring above the mountains. The Eagle Owl (*Bubo bubo*) and the Barn Owl (*Tyto alba*) are rare; but the Scops Owl (*Otus scopa*) and the Little Owl (*Athene nocturna*) are very common. The first is known as *Gionis* and the second as *Koukouvaya* in imitation of their cries. The Little Owl, as its name implies, was sacred to Athene in classical times and its picture appears on many of the Athenian coins. The Magpie (*Pica pica*) is plentiful and so is the Raven (*Corvus corax*); but the other Crows, so common on the mainland, appear to be rarer.

The Kingfisher (*Alcedo atthis*), the Hoopoe (*Upupa epops*) and the Bee-eater (*Merops apiaster*) are among the more striking and rarer birds. The drabber Nightingale (*Luscinia megarhynchos*) is plentiful in gardens and coppices and can sometimes be heard singing in full midday.

Several species of Gulls, including the Mediterranean Gull (*Larus melanocephalus*) and the Black-headed Gull (*L. ridibundus*) fly around the islands. The Pigeons, Doves, Swallows, and Swifts are well represented. Among the smaller birds, the Goldfinch (*Carduelis carduelis*) flies in small flocks, especially in summer when the various thistles are seeding.

The migrant species include the White Pelican (*Pelecanus onocrotalus*), the Bittern (*Botaurus stellaris*), the Great White Egret (*Egretta alba*), the Grey and the Purple Heron (*Ardea cinerea* and *A. purpurea*), the Mallard (*Anas platyrhynchos*), the Moorhen (*Gallinula chloropus*), the Coot (*Fulica atra*), the Woodcock (*Scolopax rusticola*) and the Snipe (*Gallinago gallinago*). These species, with the exception of the Coot, are becoming rarer as their habitats are given over to cultivation and the game-birds are more hunted.

Reptiles and *Amphibians* are plentiful on all the islands except the smallest. The only venomous snake is the Horned Viper (*Vipera ammodytes meridionalis*). The harmless snakes are far more common and include the water-loving Ringed Snake and Tesselated Snake (*Natrix natrix* and *N. tesselata*); also the beautiful Leopard Snake (*Elaphe situla*) with its striking red and black markings. These last three snakes are of a peaceful disposition. But there is another serpent, whose bad temper has earned it the name of the Angry Snake (*Coluber viridi-flavus carbonarius*), which will attack even without provocation and sometimes hang on bulldog-like after biting. Though it is not poisonous, it is much feared by the peasantry who call it *Saïta* or *Saïtià* (Javelin) as it will sometimes dart out at its victim from a bush or tree.

Among the Lizards, the Agama Lizard (*Agamo stellio*) is the most striking as, with its large size – up to 30 cm, black and white coloration, and sharply pointed scales, it puts one in mind of a miniature dinosaur. The Disc-fingered Gecko (*Hemidactylus turcicus*) has adhesive discs on its fingers which allow it to run across smooth walls inside houses which it often enters in pursuit of winged insects. It is quite harmless, but held in superstitious dread by the peasants who call it *Molintiri* (Defiler).

The islands harbour the 'Greek' Land Tortoise (*Testudo hermanni*) and two freshwater terrapins, the European Pond Tortoise (*Emys orbicularis*) and the rarer Caspian Terrapin (*Clemys caspica*). The False Hawksbill Turtle (*Caretta caretta*), which reaches a length of 1 metre, is sometimes seen, especially in the Ionian Sea.

Amphibians are plentiful in the larger well-watered islands. Among these are the Greek Newt (*Trituris vulgaris graeca*), the Common Toad (*Bufo bufo*) and the Green Toad (*B. viridis*); the male of the latter has a long musical croak resembling the trill of a bird. Frogs include the Agile Frog (*Rana dalmatina*), the Greek Frog (*Rana graeca*) and the Marsh Frog (*Rana ridibunda*). The latter is the species celebrated by Aristophanes in his comedy *The Frogs*, and its loud call of 'kek-kek-kek-croax-croax' proves that the ancient playwright was a good observer of Nature. The beautiful little Tree Frog (*Hyla arborea*), with its polished emerald-green back and snow-white belly, is common, especially in gardens and in orchards. It lives during most of the summer among the shiny leaves of Orange and Lemon Trees and climbs easily by means of the adhesive discs on its palms and toes. In autumn it returns to some pond or pool for mating and laying its eggs, which develop into tadpoles as with other frogs.

Owing to the small size of their rivers, the islands are poor in freshwater fish. Minnow, Dace and Roach represented by *Leucaspius stymphalicus*, *Leuciscus peloponensis* and *Rutilus pleurobipunctatus*. Perhaps the commonest fish is the Central American Mosquito-fish (*Gambusia affinis*) which was introduced before and after World War II to help combat malaria by destroying the aquatic Mosquito-larvae. It has spread itself to many of the streams, ponds and marshes. The Common Eel (*Anguilla anguilla*) inhabits some of the larger ponds and streams.

The *Invertebrates*, Insects, Spiders, Crustacea, etc., are those of the south-eastern European region. The most spectacular of the Insects is the Oleander Hawkmoth (*Daphnis nerii*) which has a wing span of 12 cm and a conspicuous green colour marbled with white and pink. Its huge green caterpillar is equally striking and will raise the front end of its body in a menacing manner when startled.

The islands' mountain streamlets contain a freshwater Crab; *Potamon fluviatilis* for the Ionian Islands and *Potamon potamios* for those in the Aegean.

A few words may be said finally about a phenomenon which can be observed in the Greek seas during the summer months, especially August and September. This is a *phosphorescent sea*, which seems to be brightest when a thunderstorm is impending. An evening swim is then an experience that will long be remembered as a stream of green sparks seems to be swirling past one's body. The cause of this display is *Noctiluca miliaris*, a minute unicellular animalcule which is only just visible to the naked eye. Under the microscope this organism is shaped rather like a tiny cherry, the stalk being a short flagellum with which it propels itself through the water.

Index